Dirty Gold

Earth System Governance

Frank Biermann and Oran R. Young, series editors

Oran R. Young, *Institutional Dynamics: Emergent Patterns in International Environmental Governance*

Frank Biermann and Philipp Pattberg, eds., *Global Environmental Governance Reconsidered*

Olav Schram Stokke, *Disaggregating International Regimes: A New Approach to Evaluation and Comparison*

Aarti Gupta and Michael Mason, eds., *Transparency in Global Environmental Governance: Critical Perspectives*

Sikina Jinnah, *Post-Treaty Politics: Secretariat Influence in Global Environmental Governance*

Frank Biermann, *Earth System Governance: World Politics in the Anthropocene*

Walter F. Baber and Robert B. Bartlett, *Consensus in Global Environmental Governance: Deliberative Democracy in Nature's Regime*

Diarmuid Torney, *European Climate Leadership in Question: Policies toward China and India*

David Ciplet, J. Timmons Roberts, and Mizan R. Khan, *Power in a Warming World: The New Global Politics of Climate Change and the Remaking of Environmental Inequality*

Simon Nicholson and Sikina Jinnah, eds., *New Earth Politics: Essays from the Anthropocene*

Norichika Kanie and Frank Biermann, eds., *Governing through Goals: Sustainable Development Goals as Governance Innovation*

Michael John Bloomfield, *Dirty Gold: How Activism Transformed the Jewelry Industry*

Related books from Institutional Dimensions of Global Environmental Change: A Core Research Project of the International Human Dimensions Programme on Global Environmental Change

Oran R. Young, Leslie A. King, and Heike Schroeder, eds., *Institutions and Environmental Change: Principal Findings, Applications, and Research Frontiers*

Frank Biermann and Bernd Siebenhüner, eds., *Managers of Global Change: The Influence of International Environmental Bureaucracies*

Sebastian Oberthür and Olav Schram Stokke, eds., *Managing Institutional Complexity: Regime Interplay and Global Environmental Change*

Dirty Gold

How Activism Transformed the Jewelry Industry

Michael John Bloomfield

The MIT Press
Cambridge, Massachusetts
London, England

This book was set in Sabon LT Std by Toppan Best-set Premedia Limited. Printed on recycled paper and bound in the United States of America.

Library of Congress Cataloging-in-Publication Data

Names: Bloomfield, Michael John, author.
Title: Dirty gold : how activism transformed the jewelry industry /
    Michael John Bloomfield.
Description: Cambridge, MA : MIT Press, [2017] | Series: Earth system governance |
    Includes bibliographical references and index.
Identifiers: LCCN 2016025658 | ISBN 9780262035781 (hardcover : alk. paper)
Subjects: LCSH: Jewelry trade--Moral and ethical aspects. | Jewelry trade--Political
    aspects. | Gold mines and mining--Environmental aspects. | Corporate governance. |
    Social responsibility of business. | Business and politics.
Classification: LCC HD9747.A2 B56 2017 | DDC 382/.456882--dc23 LC record
    available at https://lccn.loc.gov/2016025658

10 9 8 7 6 5 4 3 2 1

Contents

Series Foreword

Humans now influence all biological and physical systems of the planet. Almost no species, land area, or part of the oceans has remained unaffected by the expansion of the human species. Recent scientific findings suggest that the entire earth system now operates outside the normal state exhibited over at least the past 500,000 years. Yet at the same time, it is apparent that the institutions, organizations, and mechanisms by which humans govern their relationship with the natural environment and global biogeochemical systems are utterly insufficient—and poorly understood. More fundamental and applied research is needed.

Such research is no easy undertaking. It must span the entire globe because only integrated global solutions can ensure a sustainable coevolution of biophysical and socioeconomic systems. But it must also draw on local experiences and insights. Research on earth system governance must be about places in all their diversity, yet seek to integrate place-based research within a global understanding of the myriad human interactions with the earth system. Eventually, the task is to develop integrated systems of governance, from the local to the global level, that ensure the sustainable development of the coupled socioecological system that the Earth has become.

The series Earth System Governance is designed to address this research challenge. Books in this series will pursue this challenge from a variety of disciplinary perspectives, at different levels of governance, and with a range of methods. Yet all will further one common aim: analyzing current systems of earth system governance with a view to increased understanding and possible improvements and reform. Books in this series will be of interest to the academic community but will also inform practitioners and at times contribute to policy debates.

This series is related to the long-term international research program "Earth System Governance Project."

Frank Biermann, Copernicus Institute of Sustainable Development, Utrecht University
Oran R. Young, Bren School, University of California, Santa Barbara
Earth System Governance Series Editors

Preface

Picture a continuum. This is a continuum of corporate political activity. Specifically, this continuum shows corporate responses to activism—environmental activism.

At one end, corporations fiercely fight activists. Or simply ignore them altogether. At the other end, corporate actors join the activists. They *convert* (or appear to). The corporations help build environmental governance institutions. Or even lobby for increased public regulation of the industry by government agencies.

Even in the same industry—like the global jewelry industry—corporate responses stretch all the way along this continuum. Companies act very *differently* from each other. Even when they sit in the same national economy, even when they occupy the same position in the supply chain. *Why?* If market logic prescribes corporate behavior, why the divergences?

When I began asking these questions, the answers I was hearing from those working in NGOs, those working in corporations, and consultants working with both were strikingly similar. It often came down to the people within the individual companies, they claimed; if a company diverged from the expected norm, there was always some leader who had championed change from within. For a political economist like myself, this was difficult news to digest. We tend to be better at structural accounts. Structures, after all, help us identify patterns and propose theoretical explanations for them. People—and worse yet, individuals—are hard to model.

For example, when told that a company responds enthusiastically to calls to clean up industry practices because the CEO is an environmentalist, we have trouble explaining this with the analytical tools at our disposal. We struggle to know what to do with this information. We struggle with agency.

Scholars agree business actors have immense power and resources at their disposal. That much is clear. But, collectively, we scholars have managed to deny businesspersons agency in their actions. Instead, we have tended to treat the actors working within the private sector as more or less interchangeable pawns or automatons. They fulfill structural functions, no more. Or at least so it goes when viewed through certain analytical lenses.

In this book, I have set out to construct a framework that recognizes business actor agency. Yet this framework must still explain the patterns we see in corporate action. The patterns that are apparent with close study of the market institutions that channel the individual actions of business agents.

The agency of non-state actors in global environmental governance is a research gap that the Earth System Governance (ESG) project seeks to fill (see, for example, Biermann, 2008; Biermann et al., 2010; Biermann, 2014). By interrogating traditional treatments of business actors, I hope to further our understanding of these agents driving earth system governance. Focusing on the political mobilization of gold jewelers may surprise some readers. I have chosen the story of gold because it allows us to explore: (1) the conditions under which firms mobilize as political agents; (2) the governance institutions firms build and, importantly, (3) these institutions' potential impacts on earth system governance. Business actors are implicated in the environmental problems we all face on this planet. They will inevitably be involved in the solutions. It is paramount we improve our understanding of the actors and institutions channeling the formidable power of business, and evaluate their role in global governance.

The work undertaken by the ESG founders, Frank Biermann and Oran Young, as well as by its growing network of scholars, has greatly influenced my work. This should be evident in the contents of this book. I am extremely grateful for their invitation to join the network and to contribute to this series.

This book began as a doctoral dissertation at the London School of Economics and Political Science (LSE). I owe a great deal to my PhD supervisor, Robert Falkner, who provided critical, constructive, and consistent supervision throughout the process. I would also like to thank the Social Sciences and Humanities Research Council of Canada (SSHRC), as well as the LSE, for their generous financial support.

As with any academic endeavor, there are many intellectual debts to acknowledge. Peter Dauvergne at the University of British Columbia has been a wonderful mentor through the years. Anybody who knows him will know just how generous he is with his time and expertise. At the University of Victoria, Michael C. Webb, Claire Cutler, Kara Shaw, Jeremy Wilson, and Rob Walker deserve recognition for their various roles as supervisors, examiners, and friends. I wrote much of the original manuscript while visiting the Haas School of Business at UC Berkeley. I would like to thank David Vogel for his invitation and guidance during that time. Ben Cashore, Philipp Pattberg, and Michael Mason also need mention for the insightful comments and selfless assistance they have delivered at various stages. And I am grateful to my colleagues at Queen Elizabeth House, University of Oxford, who have been extremely encouraging during the revision process. This includes Corneliu Bjola, Stefano Caria, Imane Chaara, Joerg Friedrichs, John Gledhill, Nandini Gooptu, Tristen Naylor, and Olly Owen, among others. I also want to thank my new colleagues at the University of Bath, for being so supportive during the final stages.

Of course, there are the many people who make up my close cohort of friends and intellectual confidants. Joe Hoover, Paul Kirby, Nivi Manchanda, and Meera Sabaratnam are the people I have turned to most often for both celebration and commiseration. Chris Emery, Kathryn Fisher, Myriam Fotou, Aggie Hirst, Marta Iñiguez de Heredia, Mark Kersten, Diego De Merich, Zahrah Nesbitt-Ahmed, Chris Rossdale, Amin Samman, Philip Schleifer, Elke Schwarz, Nick Srnicek, and Michiel Van Ingen also need special mention. I would also like to single out my good friend, Patrick Loughran, who worked with me on finalizing the manuscript. His editorial insights have been invaluable and I have learned a great deal from the process.

Beth Clevenger, Marcy Ross, and their colleagues at MIT Press have been wonderful throughout, and I thank them sincerely for the opportunity and guidance. I would also like to thank the three anonymous reviewers. The quality of the reviews has been phenomenal, truly a master class in peer reviewing. The comments were critical and constructive, and the manuscript is much improved having been through the process.

Importantly, I would like to thank those who volunteered their valuable time to inform the book, in London, San Francisco, Washington DC, New York City, Bentonville, and beyond. People spoke freely about their experiences and expectations, and the book could not have been written without them. I hope they feel my analysis has done justice to their efforts.

And, finally, I would like to thank my network of friends and family back home, who are too many to name but without whose unwavering love and encouragement this (or any) book would not be possible. This is especially the case when it comes to my mum, my dad, and my sister. The book is for them.

Acronyms and Abbreviations

ARM	Alliance for Responsible Mining
ASM	Artisanal, Small-scale Mining
CI	Conservation International
CIBJO	World Jewellery Confederation
CRB	Commodity Research Bureau
DDI	Diamond Development Initiative
DRC	Democratic Republic of Congo
EDF	Environmental Defense Fund
EITI	Extractive Industries Transparency Initiative
EPA	Environmental Protection Agency
ETF	Exchange Traded Funds
FJA	Fair Jewelry Action
FLO	Fairtrade International (formerly Fair Labour Organisation)
FT/FM	Fairtrade/Fairmined
GRI	Global Reporting Initiative
ICMM	International Council on Mining and Metals
IIAP	Instituto de Investigaciones Ambientales del Pacífico
ILO	International Labour Organisation
IRMA	Initiative for Responsible Mining Assurance
ISEAL	International Social and Environmental Accreditation and Labelling Alliance
KPCS	Kimberley Process Certification Scheme
LBMA	London Bullion Market Association
LSM	Large Scale Mining
NDG	No Dirty Gold campaign

OTC   Over-The-Counter (gold trading in physical bullion)
RAN   Rainforest Action Network
RJC   Responsible Jewellery Council
WDC   World Diamond Council
WGC   World Gold Council
WWF   Worldwide Fund for Nature

1

Introduction: The Responsible Corporation

Two activists walk into a bar in Washington, DC. They pull up a couple of stools and order a tequila shot each. They slam these and order two more. These men work for Earthworks, a small Washington-based NGO working on mining issues. This tiny organization has very few resources, and so has struggled to grab the attention of the giant mining companies whose practices they would like to change. But Steve and Michael have a plan. Steve reaches over the bar and grabs a small white napkin. He pulls a pen from his pocket and breathlessly draws up the strategy he and Michael have been discussing. He writes the name "Tiffany & Co." in the middle, and below that, "Rolex," "Bulgari," and "Cartier." The leading luxury jewelers. Scratching out lines with his black ballpoint pen, he then links these names to metals refiners, and the mining companies themselves. A rough map of the gold supply chain takes shape. And, as with so many ambitious ideas, the "No Dirty Gold" campaign was conceived on the back of a bar napkin.

I stand with Steve in his K Street office in the heart of DC. It is five years since that night, and he is now head of a different organization, his activist days long behind him. But the campaign blueprint survives. We stand admiring the napkin, which is mounted and framed, hung with pride over his desk. It seems slightly out of place in this rather corporate setting; a trophy from adventures past. Pointing at the napkin, he runs me through the plan as it unfolded. They identified high-end jewelers as their target because the jewelers had a vulnerability: their brand value. Steve and Michael knew they could easily begin to test that vulnerability. Boycotts, demonstrations outside stores, briefing journalists at major media outlets—all of this could potentially lead to the jewelers' reputations being tarnished. The activists weren't confident any of this would work. They certainly weren't confident that they could affect the bottom line of these companies in terms of sales or market share. But they had a strong hunch these firms would go to bat for their brands and this would give the activists the leverage they needed. So they really only wanted to raise the threat, to target specific firms without pulling the trigger. Take aim and see who jumped. Steve explains that the idea was to get a core group of high-end jewelers on board. Once they had this core group, they could take this campaign to the lower-end jewelers with some added credibility—showing them it could be done. So these lower-end jewelers— the Walmarts, Targets, and Coscos—would then have to defend them- selves against that: if x can do it, why not y? But while this strategy seems to have been a fairly accurate estimate of the opportunity and leverage available to the activists, it didn't unfold as planned. Before they even had a chance to launch the campaign, Tiffany called them. The company had already been looking into their supply chain and identified gold's social and environmental impacts as a potential problem—a vulnerability both for the company and for mining communities. The company was engag- ing with key people from the NGO sector and with their suppliers. They were way out in front of the industry. They had a sense of the lay of the land and were looking for partners to work with them. In other words, Tiffany had beat them to it. Getting Walmart was even more of a surprise. Although Walmart sells more gold than any other store in the world, the activists had ruled out targeting them. These big box companies were known for being stubborn on similar issues. Steve didn't think anybody really had a strategy to get them to the table from a consumer or public pressure point of view. The company, he thought, was just too big and jewelry really not a key component of their interests. The activists also didn't think they needed Walmart. The goal was to target the high-end jewelers and so the name "Walmart" did not appear on the napkin. Earth- works did send a few letters to the company, and included Walmart on the "laggards list" in some of their public campaign materials. But it came as a shock when the activists received a call from Dee Breazeale, a senior vice president at Walmart.

Steve picked up the phone to be greeted by Dee's southern drawl: "Y'all need to get yourselves down to Bentonville and have a conversa- tion because we need to get off that laggards list." "Yes ma'am. We'll be right down," he replied.

So they went to Walmart headquarters in Bentonville, Arkansas, and began working with the Walmart people, putting ideas out there. They hadn't thought Walmart would engage with these issues. And they certainly hadn't expected Walmart to call *them*. But once Walmart came, the thought among the activists was "We'll take 'em." Similarly, the plan was never to target small jewelers. The activists wanted the big brands. But another funny thing happened once they launched the campaign. So-called ethical jewelers began entering the market. These are jewelers who base their company and product on responsible sourcing methods and an overall commitment to sustainability. And San Francisco-based Brilliant Earth is one of the most successful. The founders, Beth Gerstein and Eric Grossberg, came up with the idea while studying for their MBAs at Stanford Business School. Beth was getting married. She was aware of the issues associated with the mining end of jewelry supply chains and wanted an ethical engagement ring. Searching in vain for a company in the Bay Area gave Beth and Eric the idea that they could fill this gap in the market. Once again, it was a case of business seizing the opportunity to take the lead on this. While each company displays a very different type of political engagement, they all have one thing in common—they are spearheading the corporate response to "dirty gold." When, why and how did these retailers come to play a lead role in global environmental governance? And what impact are they having? Answering these questions is crucial to understanding the role of the corporation in politics, and the link between activism, business power, and environmental governance.

Responsible Corporations?

At first it seems like an oxymoron, almost a gag: the corporation as the responsible citizen of the global village; the saloon villain wearing the sheriff's badge. Countless lawmen of the Wild West started as outlaws, mind you. Times change. So it is in the field of global governance. Everybody knows big business throws its weight around in politics. Yet our explanations for when, how, and why business actors engage in politics are often too simplistic. Rather than developing better theories, there is a tendency to fall back on the tired, existing explanations: profit maximization, shareholder value, monetary self-interest. The simple fact is that these concepts alone fail to explain current developments or forward our understanding of business in politics. If we want to see clearly the changing trends, we need to stop treating business as a monolithic bloc. We have to look at individual firms and the people within them. This is my contribution. I want to see business agency afresh. Business managers and executives must be recognized as political actors. Specifically, I want to explain how corporations respond to activist pressure to curb their industries' negative impacts. My focus is on jewelry retailers and the role they are playing in the governance of gold's global supply chains. Yet my hope is that the analysis will resonate with many industries and across the field of global governance. From the charter companies in the age of Empire to today's biotech giants, business actors often jostle alongside the biggest political players on the world stage. Yet we still know comparatively little about how business decides and acts. This book attempts to redress that. Activists concerned with mining practices are currently trying to link consumer demand for gold jewelry to what has long been an insulated mining industry that has a history of violence. The activist tactics targeting gold jewelry retailers have been used to target other industries before. Threatening a company's reputation is common when trying to get a corporation to change its practices. One of the first such campaigns targeted Nestlé for its aggressive marketing of breast milk substitutes in Africa in the 1980s. But corporate direct-targeting really took off in the 1990s with high profile campaigns against Nike for sourcing products from "sweatshops"; Shell for the planned at-sea disposal of the Brent Spar platform; Home Depot for purchasing tropical forestry products; and DeBeers for its alleged complicity in the "blood diamonds" trade. These campaigns have had mixed results at best. This is largely due to different companies responding differently. Even among similar firms operating in similar markets facing comparable threats, there are a wide variety of reactions. Some respond proactively, while others ignore demands altogether. Even the firms that lead the response in a particular market do so in very different ways—with wildly varying implications for the public interest. When companies respond substantively, it is usually to create or at least participate in a so-called private governance initiative (Falkner 2003). Private governance can be thought of as "governance without government" (Rosenau and Czempiel 1992) and refers to standards and rules developed and enforced by actors who are not part of the state.[1] In practice, this means that some combination of actors from industry and civil society will devise rules and institutions to regulate the behavior of those who sign up for them.[2] While there have been a number of exciting studies on the form and function of private governance, less attention has been paid to its creation and, importantly, the instrumental role business actors play in this.[3] It is at precisely this point that this study enters the fray.

Regardless of the industry, a small number of proactive firms tend to play a lead role in shaping private governance. Over the course of this book I develop a theory of why these firms lead, the different ways they do so, and the impacts of their varied leadership.

This book informs wider debates surrounding corporate involvement in global environmental governance. While many celebrate business leadership on social and ecological issues (see, for example, Esty and Winston 2009; Ruggie 2013), others remain more skeptical (see, for example, Vogel 2005; Dauvergne and Lister 2013). Most agree these contributions are limited to issues that present a "business case" for corporate leadership.

This is because corporate managers and executives must justify their actions based on the interests of the firm and its shareholders. But the "business case" is not always as clear-cut as it appears; it must be interpreted. Tiffany, for example, may not have had any more of a business case for acting than its intransigent competitors. And yet act they did. Why? That is what we must account for. So in this book I argue that the assumed limits to business power and its impact on global governance may not be so limited after all. While the parameters for corporate participation in global governance differ among firms, these parameters may be expanded through a combination of external pressure and internal leadership. My firm-level "opportunities" approach to understanding corporate political mobilization, and its application to the case of gold jewelers, reveals the wheels and cogs behind the continuing expansion of proactive corporate engagement in global governance.[4]

Although the book's main focus is on jewelry retailers, it is still worth spending a short time understanding the gold supply chain in its entirety, and the mining practices that activists are ultimately concerned with.

The Case of "Dirty Gold"

Mined by the ancient Egyptians as early as 2000 BC, gold is without doubt the universal symbol of power and prestige, attaining a deep cultural significance that cuts across human societies (see, for example, Bernstein 2000; CRB 2009). This precious substance is sourced from every continent, save Antarctica (and it's easy to imagine mining on even that continent taking off once necessity and possibility converge).

Demand is predominantly driven by jewelry manufacturing, which accounts for up to 80% of the gold destined for consumer markets. Most of the remaining 20% is bought by the electronics industry with a small percentage used in dentistry. Activists publicize this high percentage of gold demanded by jewelers in an attempt to simplify the gold supply chain from mine to retail, conveying a clear message to their target audience and maximizing their perceived leverage.

But the fact is, consumer markets are not the only markets for gold. Considered a safe asset, gold remains a very popular investment option in global financial markets. It first took on a formal monetary role in 1792 when the US adopted a bimetallic standard (along with silver) and continued to play an enormous role in the global financial system until the US went off the formal gold standard in 1971 (CRB 2009, 103).

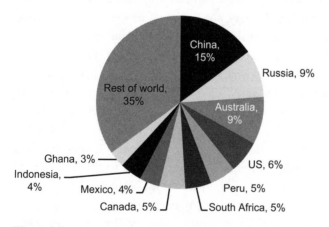

Figure 1.1

Percentage of world production for top ten gold producing countries, 2014 (GFMS 2014; Mittal 2014)

While gold no longer officially underpins the world's major currencies, states and other large institutional traders continue to horde vast sums as a secure store of value. These large investors can significantly impact the gold market. For example, in 2015, Cypress declared its intention to sell off much of its reserves to service its debt. The price of gold immediately plummeted, as investors feared other indebted countries might soon follow suit.

While people still buy physical bars and coins, there are many more options available to the gold investor. This includes "unallocated" bullion now being offered by banks, which is "unallocated" in that there is no physical gold actually allocated to individual investors (unless they take delivery). Instead, the physical gold backing the investment remains a part of the bank's liquid reserves, which allows them to continue to lease, loan, or swap the gold as they see fit. You can also buy and sell gold via Exchange Traded Funds (ETF), futures and options, warrants, gold accounts, Gold Accumulation Plans (GAP), gold certificates, mining stocks, gold oriented funds, and so on. For example, individual and institutional investors from around the world trade gold futures regularly, which are, in turn, sold in major trading centers across the globe (CRB 2009, 103; WGC 2011, 8).

My point is just that the gold commodity chain is anything but simple. Even the gold jewelry supply chain itself can be bewilderingly complex. While mining takes place in a fixed territorial location, the creation of a gold ring is a truly international endeavor. For example, the gold may be mined by a Canadian company in South Africa, where the ore is then shipped to a refiner in Dubai, after which the gold bullion is sold by a bullion bank to a gold dealer through the Shanghai Gold Exchange, who then ships it to a manufacturer in Thailand, where it is converted to 18-karat, made into a ring in accordance with a standing order, and shipped to a gold retailer in the US.[5]

Gold jewelry supply chains are further complicated by the many above ground sources. As a nearly indestructible metal, all the gold that has ever been mined still exists in various forms. This means the gold used in the manufacture of a gold ring could just as easily come from gold mined by the ancient Egyptians as from a currently operating mine (WGC 2011, 6). The *World Gold Council* (WGC) estimates that above ground stocks, the total amount of gold that has been mined over the course of human

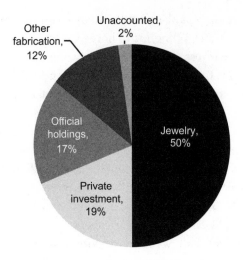

Figure 1.2

Total above ground stocks, 2010 (WGC 2011)

history, are approximately 168,300 tonnes, 50% of which exists as jewelry (WGC 2011, 7).

Supply chain characteristics also change as markets shift. For example, with the recent financial downturn, the gold price reached record highs. While just over four decades ago the US dollar was pegged to gold at 35 US$/oz., in 2011 the price surpassed 1900 US$/oz., before dropping dramatically as the global economy—and the US dollar—began to recover. This has had an effect on the flow of gold through the commodity chain. The high price of gold from growing investment demand, along with the negative impact the economic downturn had on consumer spending, led to a slump in fabrication demand and a surge in the "scrap" supply (GFMS 2010, 7). So while there is always a large scrap supply of gold being fed back into the commodity chain from all stages of production and trade, this scrap supply reached a high of about 42% of the total gold supply in 2010, making the commodity chain anything but linear (Hewitt et al. 2015; Olden 2010).

Of course, these market fluctuations also impact the supply and demand of newly mined gold, with mining companies expanding operations when the price is high and contracting again when it falls. Ultimately, it is the mining company practices that have driven activists to

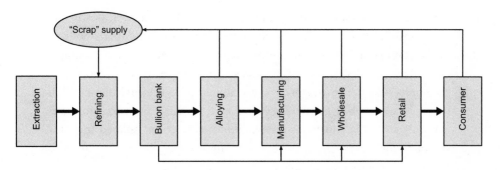

Figure 1.3

Gold jewelry supply chain (Adapted from Olden 2010)

target gold jewelers in the first place. So although this book's main focus is not on gold mining itself, it is still worth spending a short time understanding exactly what the activists are concerned with.

Impacts of Gold Mining

Gold is mined in around 90 countries worldwide. In developed countries like Canada, Australia, and the United States, and in such developing nations as Peru, Ghana, and Mali, the gold mining industry moves vast sums of rock, people, and money on a daily basis. Disagreements abound as to what the net effects of these movements are for the planet and its inhabitants. But the potential impacts range from fueling development and funding social programs to compelling human rights abuses and destroying the environment. These impacts are the driving force behind the demand for regulation.

Environmental concerns include the ways in which natural materials and chemical compounds are used and disposed of, especially when projects are located in ecologically sensitive areas. That gold mining moves a lot of rock and uses massive volumes of water is no point of dispute between miners and activists. The main disagreement comes down to what happens next.

Technological innovations have increased efficiencies such as the recycling of water for further processing, yet gold mining still creates immense amounts of toxic materials that are difficult to dispose of. Small-scale artisanal mines tend to use mercury while large-scale industrial mines usually use cyanide leaching to extract the gold from rock. Both chemicals are extremely toxic. In fact, the US EPA's Toxic Releases Inventory consistently shows metals mining to be the largest industrial polluter in the country (EPA 2015). Although some of the worst polluters simply dump leftover waste directly into the surrounding ecosystem, more conscientious miners can still pose significant risks to the environment. For example, even when the sludge left over from large industrial mines is carefully stored in enormous tailings ponds where it is isolated from the surrounding ecosystem, the threat of tailings dam collapse is an ongoing liability for companies and the environment for generations.

In an industry riddled with scientific uncertainty and variable transparency, claims and counterclaims get batted back and forth at a dizzying pace. Much of this will be specific to the particular project. For our purposes here, though, it is enough to note the potential for the mining industry to have negative and large-scale impacts on the environment, and to stress that the decisive factor behind this impact is the type of practices employed.

This also holds true for the potentially negative social impacts of gold mining. These include the macro-level impacts on economic and social development, such as those associated with the so-called "resource curse," as well as local-level impacts, including a lack of free prior and informed consent from the communities in which the mine is located.

History shows us that violence is the stubborn handmaiden of mineral extraction. Precious commodity mining without the spilling of blood has been all too rare, and the gold commodity chain is among the bloodiest. In 2012, for example, miners at the Marikana platinum and gold mine near Rustenburg, South Africa, staged a wildcat strike for better pay and working conditions. Before the dispute was settled, 44 people were killed and at least 78 injured. Almost all of those killed were miners, shot dead by automatic fire from police and mine security forces. This chilling moment was actually caught on camera by South African television news, and led to global outrage. An inquiry was ordered, a report drafted, and, yet, little seems to have changed. The thinly veiled links between mining, politics, and violence in South Africa remain underexplored. In the Democratic Republic of Congo, tragedy has accompanied gold mining on an even larger scale as the income generated through precious metals mining has helped fund the brutality of a decades-long war (see, for example, Nest 2011). Other examples abound.

From the Rosia Montana project in Romania to the Wassa district in Ghana to the Cajamarca region in Peru, local communities have struggled to stand up against mining companies and the governments that back them. Wherever such unwanted projects take place, forced relocations are possible, mass relocations common, and appropriation of land from its traditional uses almost guaranteed.

Enter the Activists

To challenge inadequate regulation of global mining, activists in the US have recently turned to a now common tactic—the market-based, "shame campaign" (Bloomfield 2014). Shame campaigns operate by targeting the most branded (and, by extension, most vulnerable to negative PR) firms within a commodity chain, attempting to shame them into securing sustainable practices from their suppliers. NGOs have thus discovered a powerful gateway into global commodity chains that allows their influence to ripple outwards from the target, pushing businesses to change their practices throughout the network.[6]

In 2004, Earthworks joined forces with Oxfam America to launch that No Dirty Gold (NDG) campaign, which Steve and Michael conceived on a bar napkin. It aimed at targeting gold jewelry retailers in an attempt to create an incentive for mining companies to deliver a more ethical product. As it turned out, these retailers have been the most responsive actors in the chain.

From an initial deafening silence to proactive cooperation, jewelers' reactions have been mixed—although the number of firms engaging continues to grow. Some have joined activists in publicly calling for mining law reform and boycotting gold from certain mines while others continue to resist involvement. Many firms have joined multi-sector or industry-led groups. Others have opted to go it alone by devising corporate social responsibility (CSR) policies and "green" product categories, developing their own criteria in consultation with more moderate NGOs.

The Private Governance of Gold

Although the leverage that activists can bring to bear is intangible, the reputational threat to jewelers has elicited industry response. A number of emerging non-state institutions along the gold commodity chain seek the legitimacy necessary to alter industry practices. The jewelry industry is awash with competing or complementary private codes and certifications emanating from activists, industry groups, and multi-stakeholder initiatives. Private institutions break down into three types: first-party, second-party, and third-party (Gereffi et al. 2001; Raynolds et al. 2007).[7]

First-party initiatives are commitments made by an organization that, regardless of who developed the codes or standards, have no official monitoring or compliance mechanisms. Second-party initiatives are developed by an industry organization in which the group maintains control over standards development as well as over the results from audits and enforcement mechanisms, regardless of whether these audits were conducted by a contracted third-party or not. So third-party classification is reserved for those initiatives in which the standards were developed through a multi-stakeholder process and are verified by independent, third-party auditors. This preserves the distinction between those initiatives that may offer robust outputs, but lack the input or procedural legitimacy that can only come from a process that is transparent as to what is included and excluded from these standards.[8]

First- and second-party initiatives constitute what is known generically as CSR while third-party initiatives exemplify a more institutionalized form of private governance.[9] While third-party initiatives have enjoyed comparatively widespread support by activists and academics alike, CSR has increasingly come under attack (see, for example, Christian Aid 2004). Many argue that corporations self-regulate to avoid the more cumbersome legal restrictions that could be imposed by the state (Rowe 2005). Ronnie Lipschutz and James Rowe argue that we have seen corporations use this strategy in the past "to stall the regulatory impulse integral to previous liberal societies" and that if these social investments were ever substantial, the legitimacy crises of corporations would not continue to occur (Lipschutz and Rowe 2005, 124).

The counterargument put forward by advocates of CSR is that such initiatives make it far more effective to condemn a company when they are not adhering to their own stated codes of conduct than to hold them to account for failing to follow some externally defined norm (Shaw 1999; Schurman 2004). Furthermore, activists hope these admittedly weaker forms of regulation will eventually lead to binding regulation as information is disseminated and best practices are defined (Smith 2003;

Rowe 2005). John Ruggie contends that while effective government action may be desirable, voluntary initiatives are not merely second best (Ruggie 2002). What he describes as a "learning network approach" to global governance allows for consensus to be formed around environmental and social concepts, such as the precautionary principle or corporate complicity in human rights abuses, which is a necessary precursor to viable codes of conduct and the advent of legally binding rules (Ruggie 2002, 32).

These background debates are highly relevant when considering the current regulatory architecture along the gold supply chain. While the industry-led certification is plowing ahead despite dissenting voices questioning its input legitimacy (only firms may be members; NGOs can merely consult on standards), the multi-stakeholder initiative is facing problems achieving output legitimacy as it struggles to develop standards with both business and activist groups as members. Large-firm CSR policies and labeling are questioned on the basis of both input and output legitimacy; NGOs are often suspicious of criteria formulated in-house, leading them to accuse these companies of "greenwashing." The reality is that the actual impact of these initiatives and how they will eventually interface with one another remains unclear. But here I focus on the political contests shaping their creation. Below, I reveal the emerging governance landscape and the patterns of engagement among jewelers as a prelude to the in-depth cases to follow in chapters 3, 4, and 5.

First-Party Initiatives

First-party initiatives are the most widespread as they generally refer to a firm's internal codes of conduct. It is the weakest form of private governance because it amounts to a firm developing its own rules, or adopting outside rules, and undertaking the monitoring and enforcement itself. For most industries, this will often take the form of CSR commitments in annual reports and on the company's website. To both devise and increase the legitimacy of these CSR commitments, firms will often partner with more mainstream NGOs whose staff can both provide expertise on the issues at hand while, importantly, adding credibility to the commitments.

Each company in the jewelry market has its own sourcing strategies, whether it be only buying gold from certain certified sources or achieving chain-of-custody assurances through vertical integration—for example, Bario Neal only buys recycled gold while Tiffany & Co. only sources gold from the Bingham Canyon Mine (Solomon and Nicholls 2010, 8). Some jewelry traders have established their own label (e.g., Open Source Minerals and the Jeweltree Foundation administer the "Wishes Jewels" label) while retailers are also getting in on the act (e.g., Leber Jeweler Inc. has "Earthwise Jewelry" and Walmart now has its "Love, Earth" line) (Solomon and Nicholls 2010, 9).

Activists from the NDG campaign have drawn up a ready-made set of assurances that companies can sign on to. For all intents and purposes, these constitute an activist-endorsed first-party commitment. The NDG shame tactics directly targeting corporations include the goal of attempting to persuade them to sign on to these so-called Golden Rules, a set of voluntary standards that signatories agree to abide by.

This initiative continues to gain the support, if sometimes grudgingly, of firms within the industry. As the number of signatories continues to increase (there are over 70 corporate signatories at the time of this writing) and each signatory works toward streamlining their practices to match the expectation of the Golden Rules, an increasingly robust regime takes shape. And non-signatories look increasingly isolated and vulnerable to criticism.

Table 1.1
No Dirty Gold Golden Rules (adapted from the NDG website at nodirtygold.org)

The No Dirty Gold Campaign's Golden Rules
• Respect basic human rights as outlined in international conventions and laws;
• Obtain the free, prior and informed consent of impacted communities;
• Respect workers' rights and labor standards, including safety;
• Not operating in areas of armed or militarized conflict;
• Not forcing communities off their lands;
• Not using water bodies or streams for mine waste or tailings;
• Not operating in fragile ecosystems, protected areas, or other places of high conservation or ecological value;
• Not polluting water, soil or air with acid drainage or other toxic chemicals;
• Paying all costs of closure and reclamation of mine sites;
• Allowing independent verification audits.

Second-Party Initiatives

Second-party initiatives are usually invoked by an industry association that develops an industry-wide code of conduct, in consultation with its members, and either monitors or requires reports by member firms. Firms that face the most risk from name-and-shame campaigns are the most likely to devise and implement this type of institution, and accept its costs. While these costs of building the organization and the associated membership fees can be significant, many firms will choose this option because it allows the industry to control the membership, rules, verification, and enforcement. Second-party initiatives have been implemented proactively, in the case of the Responsible Care certification for the chemicals industry, and reactively, in the case of the many national agency/industry certifications that have been devised to challenge the leading third-party certification in forestry (see, for example, Cashore et al. 2004; Humphreys 2006; Bloomfield 2012). Many of these initiatives have improved their perceived legitimacy of late by requiring third-party audits using these industry initiative standards, while maintaining control over the rule-setting, reporting, and enforcement mechanisms.

Based in London, the World Gold Council (WGC) is the market development organization for the gold industry, representing the interests of the large-scale, industrial mining (LSM) sector. It is an industry association boasting the world's foremost gold mining companies as members. The WGC has taken the lead in developing the most comprehensive Conflict-Free Gold Standard to eradicate gold mined by armed groups in the DRC from the mainstream gold supply chain (WGC 2012b). Although they have engaged with actors from all spheres of social activity, inviting feedback from governments, NGOs, business actors along the supply chain, investors, academics, and industry groups, it remains a second-party certification as the standards were not developed through a true multi-stakeholder initiative. However, the standards are quite comprehensive and are a significant advancement toward tracking gold along its supply chain. Nonetheless, the WGC standard only traces the material from the mine source to the refiner's door. This is where individual product certifications take custody of the precious metal.

For gold jewelry, the Responsible Jewellery Council (RJC) certification takes over the tracing from the refiner to retail. The RJC is a not-for-profit organization formed in 2005 by 14 members of the business community representing all stages of the jewelry supply chain. Its raison d'être is to counter the threat posed by increased scrutiny of industry practices and to differentiate its members from the less scrupulous competitors in the industry. The mission statement is: "To be the recognised standards and certification organisation for supply chain integrity and sustainability in the global fine jewellery and watch industry." (RJC 2012). RJC membership requires signatories to abide by the RJC "Code of Practices," a general set of industry best practices covering business ethics, human rights, environmental performance, and management systems. With a membership of 732 and growing, the norms and rules enshrined in the Code of Practices are quickly becoming the industry benchmark (RJC 2016). While the RJC trains and accredits third-party audits to verify their members' compliance, they are still considered a second-party certification here as they set their own rules and maintain control over the results of monitoring and compliance. In other words, they do have third-party audits by both accounting firms and environmental auditing firms, whom they certify themselves, but the results are handled internally and not published (Rio Tinto, personal communication, August 7, 2011). They have recently added a voluntary "Chain of Custody" standard for its members, defining the requirements for systems to trace materials through the firm's supply chain, including systems for sourcing, segregating, and transferring eligible jewelry materials (RJC 2016). Additionally, the RJC is continuously improving its transparency, is incorporating independent (non-industry) directors into its board and, reflecting these changes, has become a recognized standards-setting body by the ISEAL Alliance, a group that certifies certifiers (RJC 2016; ISEAL 2012). So there is a definite evolution taking place as the organization ratchets up its standards in the face of continuous scrutiny from both civil society and, especially, from the ethical jewelers who remain outside the RJC system.

Third-Party Initiatives

Third-party initiatives tend to be the most robust private governance institutions as they require both multi-stakeholder rule-setting and third-party monitoring. There are a very limited number of these initiatives to date. Usually they result from activists successfully pressuring industry to accept these stricter standards and to acquiesce a certain amount of operational autonomy. By offering a multi-stakeholder decision-making process and independent verification through which members are more easily held to their commitments, these initiatives tend to carry more legitimacy. A prominent example of a third-party initiative is the Forest Stewardship Council (FSC) certification scheme in forestry. Other well-known initiatives include the Fairtrade International (FLO)[10] and Fairtrade USA labels, both of which cover multiple industries.

A small number of attempts have been made at creating third-party certifications to govern gold. The Initiative for Responsible Mining Assurance (IRMA) is a true multi-stakeholder initiative spawned from a 2006 Vancouver meeting involving key players from industry and civil society. It produced the "Framework for Responsible Mining," pledging to work toward a third-party certification for mines. The original steering committee included representatives from mining companies, from civil society (including Earthworks), and from jewelry retailers (including Walmart, the RJC, and Tiffany). The mission is: "[t]o develop a multi-stakeholder generated and supported assurance program for environmentally and socially responsible mining that:

- is independently verifiable;
- ensures the fair and equitable distribution of benefits to communities (including First Nations and indigenous people), while respecting and protecting their rights;
- responds effectively to potentially negative impacts to the environment, health, safety, and culture;
- enhances shareholder value"[11]

IRMA is not yet up and running and at times it has seemed that many in the industry had given up on it. However, as a multi-stakeholder initiative seeking wide representation at every stage of development, IRMA is proving to be a complex, sometimes tedious, but hopefully, worthwhile endeavor. From the very beginning, the initiative's architects consulted with the experienced contributors to existing third-party certifications in other industries (e.g., the FSC in forestry); in fact, they were told to expect it to take about ten years before it would be operational (NDG, personal communication, April 24, 2012). They are nearing that mark and seem set to launch. Right on schedule, then.

There are also third-party certified options currently available in the form of Fairtrade (FT) and Fairmined (FM) gold, although the quantities being supplied at this point can only really supply a niche market. Originally developed together through a partnership between the Alliance for Responsible Mining (ARM) and FLO, the labels have since been split, but both continue to ensure high environmental and social standards, benefitting ASM miners by guaranteeing a minimum price and a premium paid to help develop the mining community where the gold originated. The standards relate to the elimination of child labor, respect for women miners' rights, worker safety and environmental practices, formal organization of miners, and living conditions in the community (Fraser 2011). As they apply only to ASM mining, and only those communities that have applied for and been granted the right to use the labels, the supply of FT and FM labeled gold is very small and constitutes probably less than 1% of the gold supplied for jewelry (Industry analyst, personal communication, November 22, 2011). However, they are important and growing initiatives that benefit the local mining community and environment directly, making them first-rate, third-party standards.

While the focus of this book is on the different responses of business actors to civil society pressure and their role in the creation of these institutions, rather than the institutions themselves, arranging firm responses according to which initiatives they support is a good starting point for understanding the patterns of corporate political mobilization in the market.

Patterns of Convergence and Divergence among Jewelers

Table 1.2 shows the major retailers in the US market for gold jewelry and the significant variation in their preferences for non-state initiatives.

While corporate engagement varies widely across the industry as a whole, if we divide up the US jewelry market into categories of firms based on business model, patterns of engagement begin to appear. Table 1.3 shows clear patterns in the types of political mobilization chosen between the different categories of firms under investigation.

The first category is made up of the relatively small number of boutique, *ethical jewelers* that have entered the market in response to growing consumer demand for responsibly sourced jewelry.[12] While the ethical jewelers position themselves as political actors, many less

Table 1.2
Summary of jewelers' preferences for non-state initiatives*

	First-party (NDG)	Second-party (RJC)	Third-party (FT/FM)
Amazon	✗	✗	✗
Argos (UK)	✗	✓	✗
Bario Neal	✓	✗	✗
Ben Bridge	✓	✓	✗
Birks & Mayors (Canada & US)	✓	✗	✗
Blue Nile	✓	✗	✗
Boucheron	✓	✓	✗
Brilliant Earth	✓	✗	✓
Bulgari (IT)	✗	✓	✗
Cartier (FR)	✓	✓	✗
Chopard	✗	✓	✗
Costco	✗	✗	✗
Cred (UK)	✓	✗	✓
Faberge	✗	✓	✗
Fifi Bijoux (UK)	✓	✗	✓
Harry Winston	✗	✓	✗
HSC	✗	✗	✗
JCPenny	✓	✓	✗
Leber	✓	✗	✓
Macy's	✗	✗	✗
Piaget	✓	✓	✗

(US Jewelry Retailers)

Table 1.2 (continued)

	First-party (NDG)	Second-party (RJC)	Third-party (FT/FM)
QVC	✓	✗	✗
Reflective Images	✓	✗	✓
Rolex	✗	✗	✗
Sears (and Kmart)	✓	✗	✗
Signet (UK and US)	✓	✓	✗
Target	✓	✗	✗
Tiffany & Co.	✓	✓	✗
Van Cleef & Arpels	✓	✓	✗
Walmart	✓	✗	✗
Zale	✓	✓	✗

*While this table is not a comprehensive list of every jeweler that sells gold, it includes the key players in the US industry and is indicative of the divisions between types of jewelers and the patterns of political mobilization emerging in the industry.

obviously engaged firms have also mobilized since the market became politicized. This includes those from each side of the greatest division in the jewelry industry: that running between *specialty jewelers* and more *diversified jewelers*. The latter are firms that sell large quantities of gold jewelry along with many other, non-related items. While the household names synonymous with jewelry tend to fall into the specialty category, most of the world's largest sellers of gold jewelry fall into the diversified category. In fact, seven of the nine largest US-based jewelers are diversified retailers while the remaining two are specialty retailers (Hoovers, 2011).[13]

Two types of variation in corporate political mobilization stand out within the US jewelry market. The first type refers to what we might expect *across* different categories of firms: variation in responses to activist pressure across firms that have different business models and market strategies. The second type refers to variation *within* each category of firm: variation across like-firms in their speed and depth of engagement with political issues.

Table 1.3
Summary of jewelers' preferences for non-state initiatives by jeweler type

		First-party (NDG)	Second-party (RJC)	Third-party (FT/FM)
Ethical	Bario Neal	✓	✗	✗
	Brilliant Earth	✓	✗	✓
	Cred (UK)	✓	✗	✓
	Fifi Bijoux (UK)	✓	✗	✓
	Leber	✓	✗	✓
	Reflective Images	✓	✗	✓
Specialized	Ben Bridge	✓	✓	✗
	Birks & Mayors (Canada & US)	✓	✗	✗
	Blue Nile	✓	✗	✗
	Boucheron	✓	✓	✗
	Bulgari (IT)	✗	✓	✗
	Cartier (FR)	✓	✓	✗
	Chopard	✗	✓	✗
	Faberge	✗	✓	✗
	Harry Winston	✗	✓	✗
	Piaget	✓	✓	✗
	Rolex	✗	✗	✗
	Signet (UK and US)	✓	✓	✗
	Tiffany & Co.	✓	✓	✗
	Van Cleef & Arpels	✓	✓	✗
	Zale	✓	✓	✗
Diversified	Argos (UK)	✗	✓	✗
	Amazon	✗	✗	✗
	Costco	✗	✗	✗
	HSC	✗	✗	✗
	JC Penny	✓	✓	✗
	Macy's	✗	✗	✗
	QVC	✓	✗	✗
	Sears (and Kmart)	✓	✗	✗
	Target	✓	✗	✗
	Walmart	✓	✗	✗

We Need a New Perspective

The case of jewelry retailers reveals gaps in our understanding of corporate political mobilization. In order to provide parsimonious and generalizable models, analysis of business political strategy has tended to focus on either economic or sociological factors while emphasizing structural drivers. These approaches have proven instructive, but they cannot account for the variation we observe among gold jewelers. So what is missing?

There are many theories to explain the remarkable homogeneity among like-firms in an industry when it comes to their organization and actions. Neo-classical economic arguments, for example, assume firms with similar structures and facing similar market conditions will make similar strategic choices to optimize their efficiency and general performance (Seth and Thomas 1994; Shapiro, Russell, and Pitt 2007). Equally compelling are approaches originating from sociology and organizational theory. One of the most prominent is the new-institutionalist perspective that stresses isomorphic activity whereby firms imitate lead firms to gain legitimacy or otherwise guide their policies under conditions of uncertainty (Meyer and Rowan 1977; DiMaggio and Powell 1983; Powell and DiMaggio 1991; Deephouse 1996). There are theories that in some ways bridge this gap by claiming that efficient strategies tend to diffuse across organizations through learning networks and the practice of benchmarking. Firms evaluate their management practices by comparing them to industry best practices, leading to emulation and strategic convergence (Porter 1996; Dobbin and Baum 2005; Shapiro et al. 2007). In other words, all these rather convincing explanations predict homogeneity in firm activity. So variation becomes even more puzzling.

Understanding variation in the type, timing, and depth of political engagement requires understanding how lead firms have come to lead. While organizational routines in an industry appear to converge over time, how do we explain those firms at the front of the movement? Why and how have these "lead" firms managed to shed the structural constraints that theories of homogeneity predict?

Similar to explanations of homogeneity, there has been some excellent work on heterogeneity—explaining why different industries and types of companies pursue different political strategies. Past studies have explained how firms from different locations along production chains often respond differently to social and environmental challenges based on their unique sets of interests (Falkner 2005; Andree 2005). Likewise, related studies have shown how firms from different national political environments often respond in divergent ways (Skjaerseth and Skodvin 2001; Levy and Kolk 2002). This has been attributed to the particular modes of organization (Doremus et al. 1999), distinctive lobbying tactics (Coen 2005) and business-civil society relations (Sasser et al. 2006) associated with the political and industrial cultures of their respective home states (see also Newell and Levy 2006). Some important studies focused specifically on why firms choose one private governance initiative over another have used a combination of these explanations to explain patterns in forestry (Cashore et al. 2004) and apparel (Fransen and Burgoon 2012).

As insightful as these contributions are, these explanations still cannot account for the variation we see in the mobilization of gold jewelers. Clearly, corporate political mobilization in response to societal demands not only varies greatly across industries, positions in the supply chain, and national contexts, but also among firms in the same industry, occupying the same position of the supply chain, within the same national market, and even within the same firm over time. Any comprehensive model of corporate political mobilization must account for both the similarities and the differences in how these firms from the same market are engaging in the governance of gold. The model I develop in this book shows how the preferences of key decision-makers from the private sector and their ability to implement these preferences are the outcomes of power relationships mediated by environmental conditions.

My goal is to offer a nuanced and empirically informed account of business power outside the state system. And, specifically, to do so through an explanation of the impacts of industry structures, both economic and institutional, on the responses of business actors to civil society contestation. To fulfill this goal, I explain this variation through a theory of structured agency in which firm responses are a product of the divergent opportunities for and constraints upon corporate political mobilization within the industry. I undertake a firm-level investigation for this purpose, focusing predominantly on lead firms representing the major divisions within the US retail market for gold jewelry and investigating the conditions that enable the development and impact of proactive political mobilization.

Learning from Leaders

In this book, I use a combination of historical process tracing and comparative methods to infer causality, seeking to understand the mechanisms connecting firm-level structures to policy preferences and outcomes. (See Appendix A, "Research Methods and Design," for more detailed information.) To get the best sense of the changes rumbling in the US gold jewelry market, you have to look at the lead firms, those firms that are most actively engaged in the sector's politics. So over the course of the book, we'll look at three in particular: Brilliant Earth, Tiffany & Co., and Walmart. I want to offer just a brief justification for why we should be focusing on lead firms at all, and on these three firms in particular before visiting the theory in the next chapter.

A major reason to focus on lead firms is to control for imitation. Organizational sociology scholars have shown how many firms will imitate the policies of lead firms, especially under conditions of uncertainty (see, for example, DiMaggio and Powell 1983; Powell and DiMaggio 1991). When activists politicize markets they introduce just such an element of uncertainty.

In fact, it is this uncertainty that makes the guidance of corporate culture and leadership so important. In these circumstances, there are no clearly "correct" responses when it comes to political mobilization. While firm-level structures demarcate the field of possibility, it is the policy leaders within their respective categories who find the limits to corporate political mobilization; most of the late-movers simply follow.[14] By focusing on lead firms, I push the followers to the background and concentrate on those institutional entrepreneurs who initiate the creation of private governance.[15]

My focus on the actors who drive lead firms allows for the tracing of agency through the opportunity window that activist pressure has opened. Past studies of direct-targeting campaigns in other industries have tended to treat firms as reactive actors acquiescing to activist demands. Such studies offer a general idea of why some firms comply. But they underplay the role of business leaders in the design and implementation of these initiatives. They also miss out on explaining what limits their role, or even on acknowledging that such limits exist. While campaign pressure can convince most companies to at least recognize the potential link between their business practices and social and environmental issues, I seek to identify both the opportunities and the limits these policy leaders face.

Brilliant Earth, Tiffany, and Walmart are lead firms in each of three basic categories of jewelers within the US jewelry market. So as well as having here the full range of firm types within the industry, looking at the leaders reveals what the institutional entrepreneurs are up to. Ultimately, it is the combination of leadership and the opportunities available that explains the variation we see both across and within the different categories of firms.

Brilliant Earth is a small, private company specializing in ethical jewelry. The company officially launched after the NDG campaign had already established "dirty gold" as a political issue. The NDG campaign created the opportunity window for the private sector to mobilize and the Brilliant Earth founders drove their idea through this opening. Self-proclaimed "ethical" jewelers are the most conspicuous form of corporate political mobilization, and although recently established, are politically significant. In many different industries, these boutique manufacturers and retailers constitute an important response from the private sector to the politicization of their market. As a firm attempting to overturn the political landscape of the jewelry supply chain, Brilliant Earth is an interesting counterbalance to the other two cases; instead of struggling to reform their supply chain to bring it in line with the requirements of responsible gold sourcing, the company designed its supply chain to exceed these standards from its inception, which allows us to contrast this form of corporate political mobilization with those of its larger rivals and to investigate the potential and limits of such an approach. While certainly constituting a niche market, a number of similarly small, private jewelers have emerged to fill the "ethical" gap in the market.

The specialty jeweler category includes those household names we normally associate with fine jewelry and fashion.[16] These jewelers have been generally proactive through the creation of an industry group and "responsible" labeling to counter activist claims. Tiffany is a very interesting case as the company has taken onboard the suggestions of the campaigners and gone even further than expected. By actually lobbying for increased regulation they have arguably reached the pinnacle of CSR; by pushing to make standards legally binding they have acted counter to the expectations of those who argue that corporations embrace CSR and other forms of non-state regulation to avoid hard regulation by the state. The company was certainly a first-mover within its category so it will be important to ask not only why specialty jewelers have been active in their political mobilization but, also, why Tiffany seems to have led the pack and what this can tell us about the sources and limits of this engagement.

Diversified jewelers show slightly more varied responses as a group, but the general trajectory seems to be toward a weaker, more individualized political mobilization. Walmart initially ignored campaign pressure, but has since become one of the most actively engaged diversified retailers. Many lessons can be learned from studying the company's response, as we attempt to identify the tipping point and reasons it got involved in the politics of gold. The company has signed on to the NDG campaign's general standards, the Golden Rules, but opted for in-house, private labeling. Walmart makes an excellent case for a couple of reasons. First, they are one of the largest companies of any industry in the world and the largest gold jewelry retailer in the US market by sales (GFMS 2010). Therefore, their political mobilization within any market is significant. Second, they represent a diversified retailer that many analysts (and activists!) did not expect to become engaged in the politics of gold and so present a chance to investigate how and why this unexpected involvement occurred. We can also look at what such a large and diversified retailer can contribute to the regulatory architecture of the gold commodity chain.

Outline of the Book

In chapter 2, I establish a political economy approach to conceptualizing business actors as political agents. From this vantage point, I discuss the dimensions of business power—structural and instrumental as well as economic and institutional. Mobilizing a framework from the study of social movements and adapting it for the study of business actors, I build a model of embedded agency that considers both economic and institutional dimensions of the operational environment that channel the responses of business actors to societal demands.[17] Specifically, the model focuses on how *exposure to risk, cost of compliance, corporate culture,* and *leadership structure* create conditions that shape managerial choices regarding firm responses to activism and their selection of private governance mechanisms.

Chapters 3, 4, and 5 are the case studies. In these chapters, I focus on lead firms from the ethical, specialist, and diversified categories, namely, Brilliant Earth, Tiffany, and Walmart, respectively. Each case chapter traces the key phases of the private institution-building process from the perspective of the firm, following the same basic model to aid in comparison. I show that while institutional entrepreneurs demonstrate cautious deference toward the economic dimensions of their business model, corporate culture and leadership play influential roles in the responses of each company.

Chapter 6 brings the three cases together for a more structured comparison, tracing the emergence, development, and impact of each firm's political mobilization. I analyze the processes through which these firms came to lead industry engagement with these issues, as well as the mechanisms through which their engagement is expanding the opportunity window for future engagement across issue areas. I explore the different ways in which they lead, detailing the differences between the forms of political leadership mobilized among the cases. I end the chapter by evaluating how each type of firm is contributing to global environmental governance, from the initial politicization of the market to the institutionalization of their evolving preferences.

Chapter 7 concludes the book by reflecting on the empirical findings and the analytical model itself. In it, I explain the ways in which civil society contestation and corporate political mobilization have combined to drive the process of non-state institution-building in the US jewelry industry. Yet my conclusions reach beyond this particular industry. This book shows how activism can create market opportunities that allow for proactive corporate engagement in politics. Activist pressure creates political space both within and outside of firms, and creative corporate executives can use this space to launch new sustainability initiatives and positively influence global environmental governance. So this book not only explains why we are seeing an expansion of proactive corporate engagement in global governance, but also suggests that there may be more to come.

2

Opportunities Model for Corporate Political Mobilization

Activists rarely force business to do their bidding. Business is simply too powerful a political force. Activists can, however, change the calculations of business actors. And in doing so, they change the political possibilities within the market. This is obviously important, as the ways in which firms respond to activist pressure will shape the governance initiatives that emerge. Business actors may not always exercise complete control over the process, but they certainly impact the results.

To understand when, why, and how retailers have responded to activists requires understanding the sources of business power and preference in global environmental politics. I set this up by discussing the multidimensional character of business power. This gives us the entire range of possibilities for how business actors might respond to activists. Then we need to understand the ways in which corporate executives form their preferences given these possibilities, and the constraints these executives face once these preferences are formed. This is where the "opportunities" model comes in.

While the theoretical grounding is drawn mostly from political economy and economic sociology, the model itself is built predominantly from organizational and social movement studies. The model was originally developed to understand the opportunities for political leverage available to social movements in national political institutions. Here I adapt the model and apply it to business actors. The opportunities for political leverage now reside at the firm level, and the political actors are the people working within the firm.

Perspectives on Business Power

Most existing studies of business power have focused on the political power of business vis-à-vis national governments (Dahl 1961, 2005; Dahl and Lindblom 1976; Lindblom 1977, 1982; Vogel 1983, 1990, 1996; Hacker and Pierson 2002) with some recent studies focusing on business power in international environmental governance (Pulver 2002, 2007; Levy and Newell 2005a; Falkner 2008, 2010a; Clapp and Fuchs 2009a, 2009b; Meckling 2011a, 2011b, 2015). For the most part, the focus has been on the ability of firms and interest groups to influence the policies of states and intergovernmental organizations. Clearly, the ability of business actors to influence the creation of private governance institutions is a different matter.

However, there are many common goals shared between these intellectual endeavors. Pluralists and their critics have focused on the relationship between the power of business and the structure of national political systems (Lindblom 1977) or the power of business and changing economic climates (Vogel 1990); so too, this study focuses on the relationship between the power of business actors and the industrial structures that constitute the political field upon which private governance is negotiated. While I shift the focus from state-led regulation to non-state regulation, the question of what makes business actors more or less powerful when devising policy remains the same.

Studies of business power are vast and varied in their approaches and focus, yet the most prominent divide can be said to run between pluralists and Marxists. Pluralists maintain that business operates as an interest group like any other in domestic politics and, as such, competes for political influence on a level playing field with other interest groups (see, for example, Lipset 1959; Dahl 1961). Marxists have tended to view business elites as representing an international capitalist class imposing its interests on society through the capitalist state, which is obviously a far cry from being simply another interest group (see, for example, Mills 1956; Miliband 1969; Jessop 1982).

In the mid-to-late 1970s, some scholars working within the pluralist and Marxist traditions separately sought models of business power that would better match observed reality. They needed to explain the variety of business interests, variable government policies in relation to these interests, a lack of evidence of consistent penetration of governments by business-friendly elites, and yet policies that seemed to systematically favor business interests.[1] From the Marxist camp, Fred Block (1977) argued convincingly of a structural power enjoyed by business where policymakers were inclined to pass favorable policies for business interests to maintain "business confidence," which encouraged investment, led to full employment, and secured their government jobs. From the pluralist camp, Charles Lindblom (1977) was making similar arguments—albeit using different language—about the structural power of business that ensured a "privileged position" for business interests within policymaking circles.

While there are clear normative differences between theorists from either tradition, and the terminology they use differs, there are similarities to these approaches, and these combine to offer us a nuanced perspective on business power. Both perspectives hinge on identifying the presence of structural forces that offer business a privileged position within state institutions—that is, by inducing policymakers to maintain a regulatory environment conducive to business interests. Business does directly influence state institutions as well, but there is little need under these analyses for recourse to conscious or direct forms of power (nor to class consciousness for that matter) to understand business's privileged position. This is because, according to theorists of structural power from both intellectual traditions, policy decisions tend to be made to attract investment. The incentive for this is the maintenance of full employment and continued economic growth. For individual policymakers, the incentives could be instrumental, such as reelection or personal job security, but could also simply be selfless acts by those charged with the responsibility of public office. Either way, the results are the same. The key point is that private investment decisions are made based in part on how policies affect the aggregate of individual investor interests. These individual investment decisions are not made based on the short- or long-term interests of a monolithic business community or capitalist class. They are made based on individual investor interests. And there are powerful incentives for policymakers to maximize the aggregate value of these individual investment decisions. This explains how business enjoys a privileged position within policymaking circles. Policy decisions will not always favor business interests, and most policies will favor some firms or industries to the detriment of others. But, overall, the privileged position of business in market democracies is maintained through the structural power afforded it by the aggregate effect of individual investment decisions.

Dimensions of Business Power

Power can be a difficult concept to grasp, and one that is hotly contested among scholars. It is also a core component to my analysis, so I must lay out my case with care. Any comprehensive framework for understanding business power must account for both the instrumental power that business actors mobilize to create and shape private governance institutions and, importantly, the structural dimensions that encourage or discourage the use of this power. There have been numerous productive debates on the dimensions of power and these have led to a proliferation of typologies. While there has been significant agreement among scholars that a multidimensional approach is appropriate, and there is substantial overlap between the typologies produced, the dimensions remain in dispute.[2] I offer a simple matrix containing four dimensions of power, based on differentiating between economic and institutional forms of both instrumental and structural power. It should be noted, though, that different dimensions of power are not competing but, rather, there are connections running between them (see also Barnett and Duvall 2005a, 2005b on this point). The separation between instrumental and structural power serves simply to draw attention not only to the ways in which power is wielded, but also to the conditions under which agents form identities and interests, and the structures that channel their actions.[3] Likewise, the distinction between economic and institutional dimensions ensures that analysts go beyond simply measuring financial resources (an all too common practice in studies of business power), and so also consider discursive and organizational forms of business power.

Instrumental Power

Instrumental power is a function of an actor's resources and capabilities. Often this power is exercised vis-à-vis other actors in the system as in Dahl's (1957, 203) classic definition: "A has power over B to the extent that he can get B to do something that B wouldn't otherwise do."

However, it can also be used to build institutions as well as define and operationalize ways in which to do things, indirectly influencing others.[4] It is a function of the underlying resources, economic and institutional, of an identifiable actor or group of actors. Therefore, the key difference between structural power and instrumental power is that structural power is not controlled by specific actors. In order to avoid conflating the dimensions of power, a rule of thumb is that if it is wielded by an actor, it is instrumental power. One of the key features of instrumental power from the social scientist's perspective, and the core reason why it has been the privileged dimension of power throughout mainstream analyses, is that it can be more easily observed and measured than its structural counterpart. Instrumental power itself can be unpacked into economic and institutional variants.[5]

Economic Dimensions of Instrumental Power   Business actors exert their instrumental power by way of their economic resources in multifaceted ways. Firms are able to leverage their financial power into political power within the state through activities such as lobbying governments for favorable policies, funding political parties sympathetic to their regulatory needs, and making strategic investments in jurisdictions governed by favored or fortunate policymakers.

In markets, firms mobilize the economic dimensions of instrumental power when they leverage their buying power to influence suppliers upstream, and when they leverage their control over production to manipulate consumers downstream. Firms also wield their power when they implement official, public policy by translating regulations into actionable practices (Scholte 2000; Falkner 2008). While policymakers may define the rules of the game in many cases, it is firms that ultimately mobilize their informational and financial resources to innovate and implement the technological and managerial fixes necessary to meet the demands of these rules (see also Lindblom 1977).

Particularly important for the present study, firms also exert their instrumental power by directly engaging in private institution-building through negotiation and funding, as well as supporting their preferred initiatives indirectly, through purchasing priorities, or directly, through their membership fees.

Institutional Dimensions of Instrumental Power The institutional dimension of instrumental power parallels what Doris Fuchs (2005a, 2005b, 2007) and others have referred to as "discursive power."[6] Business actors seek influence through public and private advocacy, using coercion and incentive—for example, when company executives threaten to move their operations abroad if government passes a particularly unfavorable regulation. But they also attempt to influence policymakers and groups directly engaged in an issue area, and sometimes the wider public, by "framing" issues in ways that redefine those actors' interpretations of their interests (see, for example, McAdam, McCarthy, and Zald 1996; Klandermans 1997; Keck and Sikkink 1998; Khagram, Riker, and Sikkink 2002). For example, business groups might make claims about market-based solutions being more efficient than government legislation and taxation, or offer statements like "what's good for General Motors is good for America."[7] When focusing on firm–NGO interaction, framing and meaning construction are mobilized by both sides in a contest to define the issues and outline a framework for appropriate action in response to these issues.

This power is readily apparent in the creation and development of private governance initiatives. Executives negotiate with their peers and activist groups as to the appropriate structure and function of these institutions, including the rules and norms set within them. Sometimes they will vocally advocate for or against different initiatives. Other times they will simply act as role models, setting the standard for best practice and demonstrating ways business might engage with the issues at hand.

This serves as a reminder that despite the automatic and impersonal nature of structural forces operating in markets, it is important not to naturalize the institutions that entrench them. Markets contain myriad institutions, both formal and informal, which establish the rules of the game and act as instruments through which structural forces shape incentives. Often business actors use instrumental power to shape these institutions in their favor.[8] At other times, they will merely adapt to existing structures by building institutions at the firm level to fit those of the market. Markets are never more political than when actors wield power to shift the ways in which structural forces channel expectations. Once institutions are in place, unless acted upon with sufficient force, they favor certain actors and actions while suppressing others.

Structural Power

Structural power is different from instrumental power in that it is almost automatic and apolitical in nature (Lindblom 1982; Hacker and Pierson 2002). It is deep seated and widespread in any given system, but the key to the definition offered here is that it functions automatically and appears apolitical in the sense that there is no distinct and identifiable actor or group of actors that wield this power. Instead it is created and maintained by the aggregate of innumerable individual decisions or, what we can refer to as, structural forces. So while structural forces often benefit, or privilege, some agents, groups, or beliefs to the detriment of others, these actors do not control them.[9]

Economic Dimensions of Structural Power   The structural power enjoyed by business within state institutions is sometimes difficult to discern. It is generated through the central role business plays in the economy by way of the multitude of individual firm investment decisions. Generally speaking, policymakers recognize the immense contribution to society that the private sector makes. This contribution is nowhere more apparent than in the business community's creation of and control over employment. The aggregate effect of private sector decision-making is a structural force that fosters business-friendly decision-making in policy circles across the globe, most obviously in market-oriented economies. While structural forces are generally conservative in nature (i.e., they serve to conserve the status quo), they are not insurmountable. They channel interests but, as we have seen, agents can also shape these structures by exercising their instrumental power. These structures will shift with changing conditions and expectations.

Market-based structural forces, as they exist relative to state agencies, drive the expectation that policymakers will be disciplined by their supervisors or by voters if they create a business climate unfavorable to investors. Structural forces in markets operate in much the same way, as markets punish actors who create conditions unfavorable to investors. So the mechanisms by which structural forces function in markets, as opposed to the state sphere, similarly favor some policies over others; however, in a market environment, the policymakers are often the business actors themselves.

Institutional Dimensions of Structural Power There is certainly an overlap between the discursive power already discussed and the more sociological elements of structure, such as institutional logic and institutionalized language. The difference can be captured using the concept of framing versus frame. As a verb, "framing" describes strategy, while as a noun "frame" labels a structure. When discursive power is wielded, it is instrumental, and when it becomes accepted and institutionalized, it is structural. Naturally, these concepts are intimately related; for example, if there is a fit between the dominant logic operating in a system and the goals and interests of a particular group, this would increase that group's latent discursive power.[10]

To be clear, structural power, as defined in this book, is the latent or passive power enjoyed by agents, either individuals or organizations, by virtue of the alignment of their interests with the forces emanating from a system's structures. In other words, structural forces produce structural power for certain actors in a given system. The forces work for those actors whose interests and goals are aligned with these forces, and against those whose interests and goals are not aligned. Conventional understanding within International Relations (IR) and International Political Economy (IPE) about the effect of the structural power of business in state institutions is that the market, through the aggregate effect of often uncoordinated investment decisions, will discipline policymakers who do not promote business interests by maintaining business confidence.

Table 2.1
Dimensions of business power in non-state institution-building

	Economic	Institutional
Instrumental	• Donations • Strategic investments • Buying power and preferential procurement • Translating regulations into actionable practices • Paying membership fees	• Lobbying, advocacy, and issue framing • Creation and maintenance of institutions internal and external to the firm • Acting as a role model for others to benchmark
Structural	• Aggregate effect of investment decisions	• Deep-seated notions of efficiency, growth, fiduciary responsibility, and profit-maximization • Taken for granted practices and routines

Perspectives on Business Preference and Mobilization

The most coherent way of understanding how firms conceive of and operationalize their interests in any given situation is an analysis that considers both economic and institutional influences.

Economic factors are usually favored by scholars working from a rationalist perspective. This perspective takes interests as given and deduces preferences from cost–benefit analyses based on the competitive position of industries, firms, and managers. Agents within firms will conduct these analyses based on strategic factors such as transaction costs and risk mitigation. IR/IPE scholars have mobilized such models to great effect, with the competitive position of firms within domestic and world markets often portrayed as the major determinant of corporate political strategy (see, for example, Rogowski 1987; Frieden 1988; Milner 1988a, 1988b). Differences in preferences among firms materialize based on their competitiveness in world markets, their ability to adapt technologically, and their flexibility relative to buyers and suppliers along their supply chain (Falkner 2008). This is the approach traditionally favored by the majority of economists as it deduces outcomes from a simplified model based on the firm as a rational, unitary actor working to maximize profits and operating with full information.

The more sociological, institutionalist perspective on firm preference formation emphasizes that firms are themselves social institutions that are embedded within complex layers of social institutions through which their economic interests are defined. In other words, their interests are not defined a priori and, even once defined, the path that leads toward achieving them is not always clear and often in dispute. Markets are political fields of contestation and compromise. Firms do not react mindlessly or perfectly to price signals and so a model that conceives of economic incentives as the driving force for change is incomplete at best. As the institutionalist perspective on market organization suggests, markets are social constructions, rife with systems of power that stem from public agencies as well as private actors (Campbell 2007). Powerful actors may change the rules of the game and, therefore, social interaction plays an important role in the evolution of markets. As Neil Fligstein (1990, 302) argues, managers are neither omnipotent nor irrelevant, as economists at times seem to suggest with their theories.

Naturally, economists recognize that many of the assumptions they make obscure some nuance of a complex reality; they simply argue that their models offer the best option for making predictions about firm actions and market change. So economists take economic forces as their starting point while sociologists begin with social interaction. The reality is, and probably the majority of analysts across disciplines would agree, that a mix of economic forces and social interaction drives change. Any comprehensive evaluation must consider both dynamics when deciphering firm responses to societal demands. Economic reality is not a given, but instead must be interpreted through the frames provided by social and institutional contexts. Even in markets, where business actors have a strong desire and incentive to maximize profits, any approach that fails "to consider the ways in which everyone's interests are multiple, conflicting, and of different kinds" will miss important drivers of social action (Lukes 2005b, 13). So while economic analysis is central to firm decision-making, Simone Pulver (2007, 47) explains that firms may form different preferences and mobilize conflicting strategies based on "divergent understandings prevalent in the particular economic, political, and socioideological networks in which individual firm managers are embedded." However, this by no way means that economic forces are insignificant. As Robert Falkner (2008, 37) has succinctly put it, "Economic incentives and pressures are major drivers of business responses to emerging global political issues, but the social, organizational and political environment in which firms operate define how they perceive of their interest and define strategies."

Of course, every political economist recognizes the inherent interplay between political and economic forces. But even in this field there remains a deep divide between those who apply models of social interaction borrowed from economics and those who take a more sociological approach, making ideas, interests, and institutions the core of their study. The former prefer to assume rational actors with fixed interests, providing simple but often effective explanatory models while the latter sacrifice parsimony at the altar of complex causality, accepting the risk that their models may sometimes rival the messiness of the social phenomena they seek to understand. Here I take the latter approach, but aim for simplicity. As such, the model considers both economic and institutional forces that channel the agency of business actors embedded in markets.

To understand when, how, and why business actors mobilize corporate resources in pursuit of these preferences we must study business actor agency within the economic and institutional structures that shape and constrain this agency. Because I want to account for the responses of lead firms, this becomes a bit tricky. Lead firms are the ones that break free from the existing patterns in the industry. Accordingly, this book tackles one of the central problems of institutional theory, which is how to incorporate a theory of action and explanations for change into an approach built to explain continuity (Powell and DiMaggio 1991; Fligstein 1997, 1999, 2001). Institutional theory is a powerful approach, but one that has been rightly criticized for emphasizing structure over agency and, in so doing, struggles to explain change. As Levy and Egan (2003, 811) have put it, "How institutional entrepreneurs escape the rules, routines, and norms of institutional fields is unclear."

An opportunities model offers a two-part explanation for our purposes: activists create enabling conditions by creating a business case for engaging in non-state institution-building; while institutional entrepreneurs, armed with this rationale, champion the process using the firm's resources. Therefore, this book rejects the exclusivity of explanatory power that has been created in institutional theory between exogenous and endogenous drivers of change. While earlier theories emphasized exogenous shocks or crises as the key to institutional change (Selznick 1949, 1957), latter theories sought to explain change through endogenous agents, or "institutional entrepreneurs" (DiMaggio 1988; Fligstein 1997, 1999, 2001, 2002; Beckert 1999, 2003; Leca, Battilana, and Boxenbaum 2006, 2008).[11] There is little reason to think these forces need be mutually exclusive. In fact, it is the confluence of exogenous and endogenous factors that explains corporate political mobilization.

So we need to consider both here. Exogenous agents (activists) create the political space, while endogenous agents (business actors) fill this space. In fact, the exogenous agents in civil society may do more than simply expand the parameters for endogenous agents from the private sector. Through collaboration and contestation, they are capable of creating the conditions for endogenous action, including the encouragement for internal agents to transcend preexisting institutional barriers by providing the seeds of change when conditions are ripe (Larana, Johnston, and Gusfield 1994; Levy and Egan 2003, 811).

Explaining Variation

Now, how to put this all together in a way that explains the emergence of different types of corporate political mobilization? An "opportunities model" accounts for variation in firm strategies and influence through the channeling effects of industry structures, deepening our understanding of the ways in which firms mobilize politically and the political leverage they can achieve.

To recap, corporate political mobilization is the act of mobilizing firm resources for political purposes. Different firms possess different combinations of these resources. Business actors within firms have different opportunities to mobilize these resources in response to activist contestation. These opportunities are a function of the economic and institutional structures of the firm and its environment, within which these business actors are embedded. Activists operating outside the firm play an enabling role by freeing up these resources for political mobilization. But it is the task of institutional entrepreneurs within the private sector to actually implement the strategies and mobilize the instrumental power of their firms for the task.

There are four key forces that channel business power and preferences. First, governments, as representatives exercising their sovereign rule within states, often regulate to limit the power of individual firms and industries when they deem this to be in the greater public interest, the structural power of business notwithstanding. Naturally, this will be less of a concern for the cases to follow as the focus of the study is the political power of business actors in non-state institution-building, which has controlled for the immediate national regulatory system by focusing on the US market for gold jewelry.

Second, divisions within the business community—whether these are due to divergent market positions, competitiveness, location in the supply chain, or business models—prevent corporations from forming a collective front to counter forces that limit their power.[12] Sharing similarities with studies operationalizing a "business conflict model" (Skidmore-Hess 1996) or a "corporate conflict approach" (Mügge 2008), one of the key insights offered by the neo-pluralist camp is that particular market structures will offer political space for policy interventions by political activists as firms are unable to mount a cohesive counter-strategy and some may even break ranks and form coalitions with civil society groups (Falkner 2008, 2010a). Different market structures will also offer political space for policy interventions by business actors; that is, political opportunities for business influence will vary with the structural characteristics of the industry and firm.

Third, the structural forces within markets themselves can constrain the political power of business actors. If firm managers are not maximizing profits or, for publicly traded companies, not maximizing shareholder value, they can expect to be punished by the market. Investors may deny them access to capital and threaten the job security of managers. Overcompliance and the concomitant use of firm resources could lead to a competitive disadvantage in the market as these costs become reflected in price. Unless the firm can differentiate itself to the extent that it can charge a price premium, it will almost certainly lose market share as consumers substitute their purchases for competitor products with lower prices. Simply the expectation of this, and the expected reaction of investors, is usually enough to dissuade managers from implementing such policies, and this is how the structural forces within markets constrain and channel the political power and policies of business actors. If the operations of a firm are a fit with the structural forces residing in the institutions, mechanisms, and logic of their market, then these forces will protect the firm. If there is a mismatch, these same structural forces will discipline the firm, and eventually, the managers themselves.[13]

So, latent institutional entrepreneurs working within the private sector are also constrained by the structural forces operating within markets that, real or perceived, act to sanction those that do not maintain this business confidence or otherwise promote the maintenance of a business-friendly environment. Structural forces, therefore, create the economic and institutional constraints on the actions of agents working within a given system, and are reflected and reinforced by the system's institutions.

Fourth, and finally, civil society has been well accounted for as a force limiting business power in global governance (Wapner 1995; Keck and Sikkink 1998; Tarrow 2005). NGOs and social movements increase the societal expectations for business's social responsibility; lobby governments for increased regulatory standards; monitor and scrutinize the actions of firms; and directly target culpable firms with shaming tactics designed to negatively affect the firm's economic interests. However, by focusing on the structural forces operating in markets and the requirements of business actors' industrial environments, civil society actors can be understood as not only constraining business power, but also creating the conditions under which latent institutional entrepreneurs within the industry may mobilize their firm's resources for political purposes. When civil society activists shift these structural forces, they create room for institutional entrepreneurs working within firms to leverage the resources of their organization to build institutions that will align or realign the interests and goals of the firm with the structural forces of the market. To put it differently, civil society actors may also increase the public policymaking power of business actors.

In a somewhat counterintuitive proposition then, the political influence of business actors on non-state policymaking may be positively correlated with the amount of pressure countervailing forces can bring to bear on their firm's business interests. When the firm's economic interests and organizational routine are threatened, latent institutional entrepreneurs receive an expanded mandate from the market to mobilize politically to influence its internal and external environments. This perspective is consistent with the neo-pluralist conception of limits to business power (see Falkner 2008; Meckling 2011); it simply emphasizes the additional effect of the structural constraints imposed by market forces on the political power of business actors in a non-state context.

To summarize, *business interests* occupy a privileged position when creating non-state institutions in a market context. Structural forces in markets constrain and channel the efforts of private sector institutional entrepreneurs by systematically reinforcing and rewarding conformity to the perceived business interests of the firm. As the perception of these business interests varies, so too do the opportunities to mobilize the firm's resources. So the ability for institutional entrepreneurs to shape or create institutions, inside and outside the firm, is a function of both the firm's resources and their ability to leverage them. The different political strategies are a reflection of the ways the instrumental power of the firm can be mobilized to build non-state institutions within the parameters defined by the structural constraints of the market and the opportunities created through civil society contestation. In other words, institutional entrepreneurs, empowered by civil society contestation, mobilize the instrumental power of the firm to "impose the institutional change they promote" (Leca et al. 2008, 11). In order to understand the precise nature of the opportunity structures faced by private sector actors, I now turn to the work of social movements scholars.

Political Opportunity Structures for Activists

One of the core approaches within the social movement literature stems from the concept of "political opportunity structures" (POSs) and their effects on the traction and results that activists are able to achieve.[14] POSs are those dimensions of the political environment that provide incentives for or place constraints upon actors undertaking collective action (Tarrow 1998). Campbell (2005, 44) offers one of the clearest definitions of a POS approach, which envisions "a set of formal and informal political conditions that encourage, discourage, channel, and otherwise affect movement activity." The POS model has been most often used to show how conditions external to the movement itself can provide activists with resources for leverage and spaces for access within formal political institutions (Khagram, Riker, and Sikkink 2002).

While the concept originated in studies focused on national political institutions and the opportunities these institutional structures offered domestic social movements (see, for example, Kitschelt 1986), it has since been usefully transferred to the international realm by scholars interested in explaining transnational activism operating in international forums (Tarrow 1994; Keck and Sikkink 1998; Khagram, Riker, and Sikkink 2002). The concept has been further extended to studies taking markets as their political field of analysis and, more specifically, to disaggregate industrial supply chains to reveal industry opportunities for activist leverage in what have been termed "industry opportunity structures" (Schurman 2004).

The insights from such an approach include: which stage in production is generally targeted by market-based activist campaigns; which types of industries are likely to be targeted successfully; and what the results of such campaigns might look like (Bartley 2003; Sasser 2003; Schurman 2004). These studies can be said to fall within a narrower category of "corporate campaign" literature, the main assertion of which is that the capacity of activist movements to affect outcomes depends on the relevant industry's structure.

The essential insight of an opportunities perspective is that the context in which political mobilization emerges influences its development and potential impact—to paraphrase David Meyer (2004, 125). This is because political actors face different opportunities and constraints for political action based on the operating environment they are embedded within. So in the case of corporate political mobilization spurred forward by internal institutional entrepreneurs, their political strategies and potential leverage will vary with the type of firm and industry they are embedded in. And this, I argue, explains why different firms at the same position of the supply chain implement different political strategies and impact these non-state political processes in different ways.

In the literature on social movements, the concept of POSs came from recognition among scholars that the political leverage of social movements is affected by "a shifting constellation of factors exogenous to the movement itself" (Meyer and Staggenborg 1996, 1633). While applications of the POS approach have varied in practice, conventional understandings perceive it as standing in contrast to the resource mobilization perspective (see, for example, McCarthy and Zald 1977a, 1977b). This latter approach draws its explanatory power from agents, their strategies, and resources internal to the organizations themselves (see also Gamson 1975).

When explaining variation in firm mobilization and impact, factors internal to the firm clearly remain important. But an opportunities approach also considers firm-level structures. Both the structures of the firm and the agents within it play integral parts in the analysis. The key point is that this is an embedded agency. Approaches that favor agency, without emphasizing its embedded nature, would miss how structural forces channel managerial actions and, therefore, be hard-pressed to explain the patterned variation and impacts of corporate political mobilization.

While some critics have accused such approaches of being structural to the point of being deterministic (see, for example, Goodwin and Jasper 1999), others have countered that the approach does not preclude agency, but rather qualifies approaches that use agency as their primary explanatory variable.

> The idea of political opportunity structure involves not more (and not less) than the claim that not all of the variation in levels and forms of collective

action is due to the strategic wit, courage, imagination, or plain luck (or the lack of those) of the different actors involved in conflict situations, but that an important part of it is shaped by the structural characteristics of the political context in which social movements, willingly or unwillingly, have to act. The relative extent to which structure and agency contribute to the explanation of such variation will undoubtedly vary from case to case and is, again, a matter for empirical investigation. (Koopmans 1999, 100)

Critics of the POS model either misunderstand how it is operational- ized or, perhaps more likely, take issue with the term and the connotation that "it overemphasizes the structural aspects of political opportunities while ignoring agency" (Sell and Prakash 2004, 147). In practice, the emphasis on structure is core to the model, but it most certainly does not ignore agency. Rather, it recognizes that patterns visible in social phenom- ena are indicative of the channeling potential of the structural context.

Studies have shown that these structures, by definition, condition the development and effectiveness of social movements (Shadlen 2007). However, it is important to note that these structures are not only taken advantage of by social movements, but are also often created by activists themselves (Khagram, Riker, and Sikkink 2002). In other words, individual and collective actors are capable of becoming active agents in shaping their opportunities and creating their own openings for political intervention.

Complementary findings have been reported from the field of organi- zational sociology, which tells us that we can view organizational elites as "constrained entrepreneurs" (see, for example, Brint and Karabel 1991, 346). They are constrained in that they must act within the structures of power and the spaces of opportunity provided by their industry and firm. This leaves room for semiautonomous activity by organizational leaders. Not all elites will make the same assessment of interest in any given situ- ation (Scott 1991). But one can determine organizational interests with a high degree of probability from the power structures and opportunity field faced by decision-makers (Brint and Karabel 1991, 346).[15] The ana- lyst's task is to illuminate the organizational field within which a focused, empirical investigation can take place and the roles of economic and insti- tutional variables can be evaluated.

To summarize, in contrast to purely structural or purely agency-driven theories, this study offers a neo-pluralist reading of "structured agency" (Falkner 2010b; Cerny 2010). Industry characteristics shape the power and channel the preferences of non-state actors en route to the creation of private governance. The literature utilizing the concept of political opportunities contains a diverse range of approaches, and so, while uniformity is not the goal, it is important to be explicit about the type of model one is using (Meyer and Minkoff 2004). The opportunity structures envisioned in this study are at the firm level, shaping and channeling the efforts of institutional entrepreneurs. While there is always a danger of "conceptual stretching" when building new models from existing concepts or attempting to include both structural and non-structural factors in an analytical model (Goodwin and Jasper 1999), it is equally important to design models of inquiry with the conceptual space to recognize the interplay between these explanatory elements.

Adapting the Model for Business Actors

Organizational scholars have demonstrated how firms sometimes behave as social movements (Davis and Zald 2005; Soule 2012), noting that both firms and social movements often face external opportunities and constraints when acting politically (Davis and Thompson 1994; Jenkins and Eckert 2000; Walker and Rea 2014). With this in mind, the POS toolkit has been usefully extended to explain opportunities for corporate political action in environmental politics at the international level. Jonas Meckling (2011a, 2011b) has recently argued that the existence of policy crises and state allies impact the political opportunities for business coalitions to influence international climate politics. Building from these important studies, I apply the POS model to the business actors themselves in an attempt to offer a nuanced account of the political strategies they choose and the political leverage they can achieve in non-state institution-building.

Because there are patterns within each type of retailer, but not across different types, I have argued that little can be gained from treating firms as unitary actors under these circumstances. There are clearly firm-level forces impacting upon their engagement. Others have previously "unpacked the firm" to explain the uptake of individual corporate environmental policies (Prakash 2000a) and corporate social responsibility more generally (Dashwood 2014). Aseem Prakash achieved wonderful results by focusing on how managers within firms come to champion "beyond compliance" policies and how they convince or coerce their more skeptical colleagues into accepting their implementation within the firm. More recently, Hevina Dashwood has undertaken a comprehensive study of the rise in corporate social responsibility among mining companies and, through extensive interviews with mining company managers, convincingly argues that learning and leadership were key variables in pushing these policies through.

While Prakash and Dashwood's studies differ from this one in that they focus on the detailed internal politics of the individual firms and the company-specific initiatives they produce, they offer a nice starting point for thinking about variation in corporate decision-making at the level of the firm. Both of these fine books recognize that rational, profit-maximizing motives play a role in executive decision-making, but reject any possibility that we can explain firm behavior through this lens alone. So when thinking about corporate responses to activist campaigns and the institutions they build inside and outside the firm from an opportunities perspective, we should be looking for the actions of executives within firms to be channeled by both economic and institutional structures at the firm level.

This fits with the findings of past studies that have adapted the POS model to study the development and efficacy of activist campaigns that target industries directly. These scholars have identified economic, organizational, and cultural variables—along with characteristics of the commodity itself—as affecting the campaign outcomes (Schurman 2004). In this investigation, the characteristics of the commodity are held constant. This leaves three classes of variables—economic, organizational, and cultural—from which to build the opportunities model for corporate political mobilization.

The model can be further simplified as the organizational class of variables is subsumed by the economic and cultural or—using the slightly more expansive concept—institutional ones. This is because the organizational dimension really channels political mobilization in two ways, one economic and one institutional. Through an economic lens, organizational factors will be seen to affect the speed and cost of compliance as elements like the firm's sourcing strategy and its business model will facilitate or inhibit its mobilization. Through an institutional lens, organizational factors will also be seen to affect the ways in which the firm mobilizes politically as CSR departments, strategies, and expertise have the capacity to change the company culture while the amount of discretion the organization offers managers will stifle or amplify the effects of leadership. Therefore, the opportunities model applied to the political mobilization of firm resources is constructed from two classes of variables, economic and institutional, both of which contain organizational dimensions.

The major economic opportunity for mobilization is clearly how the activist campaigns expose companies to risk. Campaigns have not necessarily affected the sales of the firms they target; what they have done is create risk. Exposure to risk may be punished by markets; firms attempting to reduce their economic exposure hence drive the process forward. However, just as different firms face different levels of exposure, they also face different costs of compliance based on their organizational model. Therefore, their economic interests are a function of both their exposure to risk and the cost of compliance.

Likewise, institutional structures at the firm level refer to both the firm's culture and the opportunities for political leadership within the firm, both of which are intimately related. Corporate culture shapes leadership and vice versa. The capacity for agents within the firm to act as political leaders also depends on the firm's organizational model. Therefore, the institutional character of the firm is a function of both the corporate culture and organizational capacity for leadership.

Economic elements create opportunities and constraints for corporate political mobilization while institutional elements dictate the ways in which firms respond to the opportunities within these constraints. The specific form the political mobilization takes is, therefore, a function of both. While useful as guidelines, these classes of variables do not yet hold enough precision from which to build a robust explanatory model to guide the process tracing and aid in the later comparison. This is our next task.

Table 2.1
Economic and cultural dimensions of the opportunities model for corporate political mobilization

Economic dimensions	Institutional dimensions
Exposure to risk	Corporate culture
Cost of compliance	Leadership structure

Economic Dimensions   The central argument is that the structural forces emanating from the existing equilibrium in markets curtails the public policy-making power of would-be institutional entrepreneurs in the private sector. Activist campaigns targeting firms create opportunity windows for these latent leaders. Then, the window open, they may expend organizational resources to pursue political goals without being disciplined by the market. Direct-targeting campaigns create this window by threatening the firm's reputation.[16] This is accomplished by connecting the firm's brand to the product it sells, which, in turn, is connected to the practices the activists oppose. This exposes the firm to risk, and markets punish risk through decisions by investors, who tend to be risk averse. Managers will be expected to leverage the firm's resources to enact policies to reduce its exposure. The exposure of the firm will depend on various elements, including its investment in the brand and its reliance on the product itself. Thus, an opportunity window for political mobilization opens.

The response of a firm to social and environmental demands will be influenced by the cost of not complying with these demands which, when we are dealing with non-state pressure, depends in large part on the firm's market strategy. Even within the same industry firms will have different market strategies (e.g., customer base and line of products and services). These will be affected differently by non-state, political pressure. As the cost of noncompliance increases, more resources may be allocated to cover the costs of cooperation, expanding the opportunity window. The cost of compliance will be based largely on the cost of eradicating the offensive products out of its supply chain, and the ability to either absorb these costs or pass them on to the consumer.

The suggestion here, then, is that variation in firm responses to societal demands within the same industry is influenced by two major factors: the extent to which the core market interests of the firm are threatened and the relative cost at which compliance can be achieved. In other words, it is a cost–benefit analysis in which the cost of compliance is measured against the benefits of risk mitigation. Ways in which to measure the level of threat a firm faces from activist campaigns include its reliance on reputation and the diversification of its business interests. Meanwhile, the cost of compliance will be a function of the complexity and flexibility of its supply chain and the price sensitivity of its core customer base.[17] We will look at these indicators in slightly more detail before moving on to the institutional dimensions of the opportunities model.

One way that firms mitigate rivalry and the threat of new entrants is through product differentiation. Brand name and exclusive rights to designs are two of the main avenues to differentiating products and creating brand loyalty. Naturally, firms differ in the extent to which they rely on branding. While we understand branded nodes of the supply chain are more susceptible to NGO pressure, we can also differentiate between the level and type of branding within a sector. Individual firm branding has two potential impacts on variation in firm responses—namely, heavily branded firms should be more susceptible to NGO pressure, and should be more likely to respond individually rather than collectively.[18] The first expectation is rather obvious, while the second is related to the industry level of analysis in that more strongly branded firms have a larger cumulative investment in their *individual* reputation and are thus more likely to respond proactively regardless of the response of others in the industry (Sasser 2003). Therefore, the more a firm relies on its brand image as part of its marketing strategy, the more likely they are to respond proactively to non-state political pressure.

The extent to which a firm relies on a particular product will decrease as the diversification of its products and services increases. Larger companies operating at scale also reduce the threat of rivalry through the sheer diversity of their retail products. They are less invested in any single product type and may walk away from deals that are not perceived to be in their favor. This drastically reduces the power of suppliers upstream and buyers downstream, making the companies much more immune to leverage exerted through supply chains, including that by would-be regulators. The less dependent the firm will be on any particular product or supply chain, the more easily it should be able to shift its interests away from contentious areas of business (see also Schurman 2004, 249). In addition, the more diversified a firm's business interests, the more diverse its internal interests across departments. Shaffer and Hillman (2000) have argued that the greater the diversification within a firm, the greater the likelihood of intra-firm conflict and the greater the costs of coordinating political strategy. Taken together, the more diversified the firm is, the less likely it is to engage proactively in response to civil society contestation.

The cost of eradicating the offensive product from the firm's supply chain depends on its sourcing strategy. Some firms opt for a fully integrated supply chain to maintain control of the quality and price of its supply, while also reaping the financial benefits of any value-adding activities upstream. Others will opt to source via arm's-length, short-term contracts from varied suppliers, giving them the freedom to source the best products available at the best price. Much of this depends on the industry, but much also depends on an individual firm's market strategy as well. Clearly the vertically integrated firm will have an easier time maintaining standards, tracing products, and controlling processes along the supply chain. However, arm's-length sourcing could potentially offer the advantage of flexibility in switching suppliers or, in some cases, passing the cost of compliance on to suppliers if the buyer holds sufficient market power.[19] Therefore, the sourcing strategy of individual firms is an important factor as the complexity and flexibility of their supply chain will influence their ability to respond to political risk in a timely fashion. However, explaining precisely how the elements of complexity and flexibility influence a firm's political mobilization is a task for empirical investigation.

The ability to absorb the cost of compliance or to pass these costs on to the consumer will depend on the margins at which the firm operates and the price sensitivity of its customers. Large retail companies, especially the discount superstores, compete largely on price. They leverage suppliers and squeeze margins by utilizing their scale economies. Rivalry and the threat of new entrants are diminished, as smaller retailers will find it difficult to compete based on price. Additionally, the price sensitivity of a firm's clientele will also affect its ability to mobilize politically. Absorbing the initial costs of compliance is difficult for many firms, especially those with low profit margins. The ability to pass a portion of these costs on to the consumer is dictated by how price sensitive these consumers are. The smaller the margins and the greater the price sensitivity of the firm's clientele, the less opportunity there will be for business actors to mobilize the resources of the firm for political purposes.

Institutional Dimensions While economic elements shape the opportunity window available for business actors to mobilize their firms politically, this window only represents an opening for political activity. Whether and in which ways a firm takes advantage of this opening is less an economic issue and more an institutional one.

The corporate culture of the firm will affect how firms respond to activist pressure as managers interpret issues (such as the concept of "dirty gold") through the institutional lens of the firm and initiate a response based on this interpretation. Not only will managers systematize solutions as they push possibilities through the filter of their organization's culture, but their ability to spearhead policy innovations will be affected by the management structure of the firm and the position of would-be institutional entrepreneurs within it. Some insights from organizational sociology will assist us in expanding on these ideas.

Firms constitute a specific form of organization, but otherwise demonstrate many of the characteristics common to all forms of social organization. Powell and DiMaggio (1991, 27–28) note that "organizational environments are composed of cultural elements, that is, taken for granted beliefs and widely promulgated rules that serve as templates for organizing." In the case of a corporation, this culture is referred to as the corporate culture of the firm. This corporate culture is sometimes formal, such as the official values and goals stated in company documents and referenced or amended in stakeholder meetings. But it also includes informal cultural elements that develop and evolve over time and through repetition of the firm's operations. Whether formal or informal, elements of corporate culture will be closely aligned with the business model and marketing strategy of the firm as these characteristics will develop simultaneously.

Edgar Schein has written arguably the most influential works on the subject of organizational culture and leadership from a management perspective (see, for example, Schein 2010). He explains that leadership and culture are intertwined (Schein 2010). Leaders are the main architects of culture and founders of a firm often act as norm entrepreneurs in establishing the firm's culture. Once culture is established it guides and constrains behavior, to the point of influencing what kind of leadership is even possible. Cultures evolve and as they mature they become increasingly stable. They develop from shared learning experiences that lead to shared, taken-for-granted basic assumptions held by the members of the group or organization (Schein 2010, 21).

However, there are mechanisms to change elements of a culture within an organization. If elements become dysfunctional, it is up to leaders to speed up cultural evolution by intervening with managed culture programs (Schein 2010, 3). Cultures become dysfunctional when they no longer lead to appropriate actions in any given situation and will usually be dislodged and reformed when a firm faces a "crisis" situation that threatens their core operations, which are intertwined with the firm's culture. So leaders ultimately create, embed, and manipulate corporate culture to meet the firm's operational necessities. In the words of Schein (2010, 3), "These dynamic processes of culture creation and management are the essence of leadership and make you realize that leadership and culture are two sides of the same coin."

So how does corporate culture influence corporate political mobilization? Executives draw upon corporate culture, explicitly or implicitly, when interpreting alternative courses of action the firm may take under any given circumstance and, more often than not, make decisions that will orient the firm accordingly. Rules of conduct and standard operating procedures will be aligned to these cultural elements. Even if they are not specified, these cultural elements act as a simplifying model, or guide, for organizing firm activities. As Ann Swidler explains, "culture represents a tool kit from which people select both institutionalized ends and the strategies for their pursuit" (1986, 28).[20] The main point is that managers regularly rely on the cultural structures to help them orient their actions. It is also worth remembering that one can expect the level of impact of corporate culture on decision-making to be greatest when uncertainty is high and there are multiple possibilities for action and reaction (DiMaggio and Powell 1983; Powell and DiMaggio 1991).

Schein (2010) has provided a succinct framework to understand and analyze the interdependent roles of culture and leadership in shaping firm decision-making. According to Schein, organizational culture can be understood as existing on three levels: as artifacts, espoused beliefs and values, and basic underlying assumptions (Schein 2010). The first two levels are utilized in the framework as they lend themselves to empirical analysis while the third level, basic underlying assumptions, can only really be deduced from gathering evidence at the other levels.[21]

Artifacts are those elements of culture that are the most visible to the observer and are demonstrated by actions and processes. They constitute observed behavior, which is easily viewed but not always so easy to decipher. The role of the researcher is to interpret what agents of the firm do and hypothesize reasons for it, which can be accomplished by looking at how they do things in other areas and drawing parallels with their actions in the area under investigation. In this case, it consists of looking for similarities between how the firm is approaching and operationalizing its response to "dirty gold" with its responses to issues it faced in the past or issues it faces in other areas.

Espoused beliefs and values refer to the firm's ideals, values, goals, and aspirations. Corporations will often have a set of written goals and ideologies that form the foundation of the rationalizations agents will give for various actions when asked. It is important to note that these stated goals and ideologies may or may not be congruent with actual behavior and other artifacts. In the case of "dirty gold," these espoused beliefs and values are available in the form of CSR strategic goals in company documents as well as verbal rationalizations given in media interviews and when talking to me.

Additionally, the management structure of a firm will affect the ability of internal champions of policy innovations to drive initiatives forward. The main factors affecting the ability for latent institutional entrepreneurs to mobilize the firm will be its ownership structure and the position within the firm of those tasked with responding to the issue at hand. Whether a firm is publicly traded or privately owned should affect the ability for managers to mobilize company resources for political activities. Owner-operators will naturally have more leeway in that they are not accountable to shareholders in financial markets or the board of directors overseeing company management. Policy decisions and firm expenditures can affect share values, and managers must gain approval for significant policy shifts and use of company resources from the board. These accountability mechanisms are conservative structures that rein in institutional entrepreneurs and temper the effects of agency on the political mobilization of the firm.

Similarly, the position institutional entrepreneurs hold within the company will affect their ability to mobilize firm resources in response to an issue. Thus, who is in charge of spearheading the initiative and what type of power they have within the firm matters. Are CSR initiatives handled by a marketing and public relations department, or is there an established political arm developing and implementing policy? Do CSR representatives have power in the boardroom, or are they employed to attend workshops while decisions are made without their input? These are difficult questions to answer for the researcher dealing with a large, and by its nature, secretive corporation. But investigating who is tasked with driving corporate responses to the issues at hand and the decision-making process through the phases of corporate political mobilization is clearly of critical importance. Once again, a historical process-tracing approach is appropriate, especially as past crises will almost certainly affect both the power of CSR departments and the embeddedness of CSR norms within the industry and firm.

Conclusion

Corporate political mobilization is the act of mobilizing firm resources for political purposes. Different firms possess different combinations of these resources. Business actors within firms have different opportunities to mobilize these resources in response to activist contestation. These opportunities are a function of the economic and institutional structures of the firm and its environment, within which these business actors are embedded. Activists operating outside the firm play an enabling role by freeing up these resources for political mobilization. But it is up to entrepreneurial executives within the private sector to actually implement the strategies and mobilize the instrumental power of their firms for the task.

Table 2.3
Economic and cultural dimensions of the opportunities model for corporate political mobilization—extended version with indicators

Economic dimensions	Institutional dimensions
Exposure to risk	**Corporate culture**
• Level of branding	• Artifacts
• Reliance on product	• Espoused beliefs
Cost of compliance	**Leadership structure**
• Sourcing strategy	• Ownership structure
• Price sensitivity of consumers	• Position of institutional entrepreneurs

Industry opportunity structures for corporate political mobilization are defined as, to adapt Sidney Tarrow's (1994, 18) now classic definition of POSs, dimensions of the industry environment, which either encourage or discourage business actors from using the resources of the firm for political action. There are four dimensions: the level of risk that activists expose the company to; the relative cost of complying with activist demands; the normative fit with the existing corporate culture; and the position of institutional entrepreneurs within the leadership structure of the organization.[22] This opportunities model offers a number of fairly intuitive propositions to carry forward into the case studies that will guide the investigation into the impact of firm-level structures upon the political mobilization of firms, as well as help us evaluate the model itself through the empirical findings:

1. As the exposure to risk *increases*, the level of firm engagement with the issues and the strength of the commitments they make are likely to *increase*.

    a. The *higher* level of product branding, the *higher* the exposure to risk

    b. The *higher* the reliance on the targeted product category, the *higher* the exposure to risk

2. As the relative cost of compliance with activist demands *increases*, the level of firm engagement with the issues and the strength of the commitments they make are likely to *decrease*.

    a. The *higher* the level of complexity in the supply chain, the *higher* the cost of compliance.

    b. The *higher* the price sensitivity of the customer base, the *higher* the cost of compliance.

3. As the embeddedness of social responsibility in corporate culture *increases*, the level of firm engagement with the issues and the strength of the commitments they make are likely to *increase*.

    a. The *higher* the prominence of social responsibility concerns in company materials, the more receptive the corporate culture.

    b. The *higher* the prominence of social responsibility concerns in company actions, the more receptive the corporate culture.

4. As the autonomy and decision-making power of institutional entrepreneurs *increases*, the level of firm engagement with the issues and the strength of the commitments they make are likely to *increase*.

    a. The *higher* the proportion of external investors, the *lower* the autonomy and decision-making power of institutional entrepreneurs.

    b. The *higher* the position within the company of internal champions for the issues, the *higher* the autonomy and decision-making power of institutional entrepreneurs.

Note that there is no claim being made that presence or absence of these opportunities causes or negates this political mobilization. But the likelihood—as well as the timing and intensity—of political mobilization increases when these opportunities are present.[23] The approach switches the focus from *drivers* of firm preference formation to the *opportunities* available for institutional entrepreneurs to mobilize firm resources for political purposes. It proposes that leadership is likely to be a key element in all of the lead firms investigated, and one seemingly missing from those that have yet to respond. Without this leadership, the opportunities are more likely to remain dormant.

The next three chapters trace the political mobilization of each type of firm from the initial politicization of the market through to the creation of non-state, or private, institutions.

3

Brilliant Earth and the Ethical Jewelers

It's mid-October and the sun is shining in the San Francisco Bay Area. At Brilliant Earth's downtown store in Union Square, co-founder Eric Grossberg greets me enthusiastically, explaining they are running full throttle, already filling orders for the Christmas rush. Though busy, he's excited to talk about my project.

The Bay Area—known for hippies, student movements, and activism— is hardly an unexpected place for an ethical jewelry brand to pop up. The demand for ethically responsible lifestyles has long been here. The money, too.

After all, Silicon Valley is right around the corner. In 2010, while I was a visiting scholar at the Haas School of Business at Berkeley, it seemed every second person I met was involved in a start-up. Or at least had an idea for one. The Bay Area is one of the innovation and entrepreneurship capitals of the world.

Stanford Business School supplies many of Silicon Valley's future staff. It also produced the founders of Brilliant Earth, a company filling a gap in the market and taking on the politics of gold while they're at it.

Their case has peculiar differences from those to follow. Self-proclaimed ethical jewelers stand out because their business models were actually built to become political entities operating within markets. Although some existed before the rise in activist pressure and others were created afterwards, they can all be seen as market actors colonizing the space created by activism. This means the opportunities and constraints faced by executives working within ethical jewelers are significantly different from those working within specialist and diversified retailers, who were operating conventional company models in the pre-politicized market. But in the later chapters, I will show that there is also significant variation among the more conventional jeweler responses to activists too. So as I attempt to explain the causes and consequences of this variation, what better way to start than with the category of politically active firms along the gold commodity chain who hold themselves to the highest standards—the ethical jewelers.

Opportunities Profile and Expectations for Ethical Jewelers

Almost by definition, we should expect the ethical jewelers to opt for the highest standards available, which are generally third-party initiatives. While this would hardly be surprising, the ethical jewelry case offers a great example of proactive political action originating in the private sector. Exposure to risk works a little differently for ethical jewelers. The risk for these jewelers really emanates from the possibility that mainstream jewelers would implement the same standards and erode their product differentiation. But that's an event most of the ethical jewelers would probably welcome. Overall, in this category we should expect to see active engagement with the issues surrounding "dirty gold" and cooperation with civil society actors in advocacy and institution building.

Expectation: High Level of Engagement and Very Strong Commitments

While just a small number of firms, the ethical jewelers unsurprisingly meet our expectations of adhering to the most robust private regulatory initiatives. The only outlier in this group was Philadelphia's Bario Neal, but only to the extent that they used 100% recycled metals and have only

Table 3.1
Opportunities profile for ethical jewelers

Economic dimensions	Institutional dimensions
Exposure to risk	**Corporate culture**
• Level of branding—High	• CSR artifacts—Strong
• Reliance on product—High	• CSR espoused beliefs—Strong
Cost of compliance	**Leadership structure**
• Complexity of supply—Low	• Ownership—Private
• Price sensitivity of consumers—Low	• Position of institutional entrepreneurs—Owners

Table 3.2

Profile of non-state initiatives for ethical jewelers

	No Dirty Gold (NDG)	Second-party (RJC)	Third-party (FT/FM)
Bario Neal	✓	✗	✓
Brilliant Earth	✓	✗	✓
Cred (UK)	✓	✗	✓
Fifi Bijoux (UK)	✓	✗	✓
Leber	✓	✗	✓
Reflective Images	✓	✗	✓

recently incorporated the very new, third-party sources.[1] Perhaps not surprisingly, none of the ethical jewelers have opted for the industry-led RJC certification. This is because, from those I have spoken with, they either feel it is too weak or because they would like to maintain their product differentiation, or both.[2] Instead of signing onto the RJC certification, ethical jewelers claim their place atop the ethical jewelry pyramid through sourcing only recycled or, increasingly, FT/FM-certified ASM gold. They uphold the seemingly highest standards for sourcing. Indeed, one could argue this market demands there be "less-ethical" jewelers in existence in order for the "ethical" business model to set up an effective differentiation. I want to now investigate the details by taking an in-depth look at one of the largest US-based ethical firms, Brilliant Earth.

Company Profile—Brilliant Earth

Brilliant Earth is a specialty jeweler focused on providing ethical jewelry and operating primarily in the US market. The company is a "for-profit, social enterprise" in that it was founded with a social mission, donates a percentage of its resources and proceeds to fund this mission, but is otherwise run as a profit-making entity (Yee 2007). Its San Francisco showroom is open to the public though much of its jewelry is sold online through its website. This comes complete with virtual appointments via a live chat function for geographically distant customers. In addition to gold, the company's offerings include colored gemstones, diamond, sapphire, and pearl jewelry in engagement rings, earrings, pendants, and custom designs.

Company History

Beth Gerstein and Eric Grossberg founded the company in 2005, while students at the Stanford Graduate School of Business—an institution with a strong tradition in social entrepreneurship. Eric became part of this tradition when he began researching the potential for ethically sourced jewelry to help lessen the devastating impacts of so-called conflict diamonds, which were linked to the brutal conflicts raging in Angola and Sierra Leone. Beth, one of Eric's classmates, was about to get married. She was also well aware of the issues surrounding "conflict diamonds." So when her fiancé, Alex, was looking for an engagement ring, he searched for a more ethical option. When such a ring proved elusive, Beth and Eric decided to fill this gap in the market. Brilliant Earth was thus founded on a social mission: to supply responsibly sourced jewelry and use the business as a vehicle to drive change within the industry.

How Jewelry Fits into Their Business Model

Beth Gerstein talks about the difficulties they faced in entering the jewelry market as one of the first ethical jewelers in the US market. "[Fine jewelry] is a trust-driven business," she says. "There are lots of family businesses with relationships going back a very long time. You would think that if you want to retail their products, companies would be happy to work with you" (Gerstein 2008). However, seeing Brilliant Earth as an overtly political company, many in this long-established industry were skeptical. "We were asking questions that they weren't used to. We have certain specs and parameters we want our suppliers to meet. We only want manufacturers that use recycled platinum and gold" (Gerstein 2008). Since then, the company has expanded its sourcing criteria to include certified gold originating from specific sites of ASM extraction, but the difficulty in finding and maintaining sources of gold within these strict parameters remains challenging. Their recycled gold obviously comes from secondary sources such as jewelry items and industrial products. Their fair trade gold comes from mining cooperatives in the Chocó region of Colombia.

Brilliant Earth also depends on the availability of "ethical" diamonds, most of which come from the Ekati and Diavik mines in the Northwest Territories of Canada. They have diversified their suppliers to now include mines in Namibia and, most recently, Botswana. As far as their diamond supply goes, the company sources these stones from mines that supply local cutting and polishing, increasing the value-adding opportunities in these mining communities (Brilliant Earth, personal communication, October 10, 2011).[3] They employ their own gemologists and designers, with manufacturing taking place in the United States where labor standards can be easily monitored, and the company's production facilities utilize the highest environmental technologies to keep the impact of manufacturing low (Brilliant Earth 2012b).

History of Interaction with Civil Society—Filling the Gap

Conflict-Free Diamonds

The company was launched to provide jewelry to consumers who wanted products harvested using best practices. They did so by originally offering only Canadian diamonds in settings made from recycled metals, including gold (Brilliant Earth, personal communication, October 10, 2011). This reminds us that not only are there political issues surrounding gold, but there have also been high profile battles waged to eradicate conflict diamonds from jewelry supply chains. The issue of diamonds was the first that politicized the jewelry market, and it taught hard lessons for many jewelers later involved in gold politics. So understanding the history of conflict diamonds is vital background information for any thorough investigation into gold.

In the late 1990s, the issue of conflict diamonds was hitting the headlines. "Conflict diamonds" (or "blood diamonds") was the name attributed to diamonds taken from alluvial deposits in African conflict zones, notably Angola and Sierra Leone.[4] They were labeled as such due to the role these diamonds played in funding the brutal campaigns against local populations by armed military groups, with kidnappings and forced labor in the mines commonplace.

In 1999, human rights groups, such as Amnesty International and Global Witness, began a movement to eradicate conflict diamonds from the global supply chain. These groups took the lead in garnering the necessary publicity to force an industry response. Initially caught off guard by the crisis, in July 2000, the industry formed the World Diamond Council (WDC) with the goal of eliminating conflict diamonds from the global supply chain (WDC, n.d.). Governments became involved through the United Nations, with a resolution to establish an official certification scheme for diamonds to track them through their supply chain from retail outlets back to the mine. The activist pressure drove the process forward and, by 2002, a joint government-industry program was in place to control the cross-border trade in diamonds. The now well-established Kimberley Process Certification Scheme (KPCS) compels diamond traders to track their supplies via "certificates of origin" that must accompany the diamonds through the supply chain. Participants are subject to audits and monitoring, and legislation was introduced to tackle noncompliance. The KPCS remains a work in progress and certainly has its share of critics—including sharp words from one of its key architects, Ian Smillie from Partnership Africa Canada, who recently cast a vote of "no confidence" and quit the scheme in protest (Hildebrandt 2009). Despite the salient criticisms of the KPCS, the campaign to spark the movement has, until recently, been generally hailed as a success.[5] Most importantly for our analysis, it served as a lesson to industry leaders, with many swearing that they would not be caught out again.

Why Canadian Diamonds?
Canadian diamonds were the obvious answer for a company looking to avoid the egregious conditions under which some diamonds were being mined around the world. When these issues were coming to light, large supplies of Canadian diamonds were not yet available. From the late 1990s, large diamond projects in the northern region of Canada began producing high quality and "conflict free" diamonds—a situation the Canadian diamond industry was happy to publicly endorse. The mines are operated through partnerships that include three of the largest mining companies in the world: Rio Tinto, BHP Billiton, and DeBeers. They utilize best practices on the ground, with Canadian social and environmental laws being some of the strictest in the world.[6] Interestingly, Brilliant Earth only sources from two of the three major diamond mines in the Northwest Territories, avoiding the one operated by DeBeers, making it clear this is due to the company's practices, past and present (Brilliant Earth 2012a).

Incorporating Diamonds from Namibia and Botswana

The major downside of sourcing diamonds exclusively from Canada is that it denies many poor communities in Africa a vital source of income. One of the major, albeit unintentional, effects of the conflict diamonds campaign was that companies became nervous about doing business in Africa, lest they become tainted by activist targeting. Public opinion often acts as a blunt force and, even for many diamond mining regions of Africa that had no involvement with conflict diamonds, reputations were quickly tarnished. The result was that some companies began switching their sourcing from the continent altogether, resulting in a transfer of resource opportunity from developing to developed countries.

Once Brilliant Earth identified responsible practices on the ground in Africa, namely, in Namibia and Botswana, it incorporated diamonds sourced from these regions into its supply chain. The company boasts that the diamonds originating in Namibia are sourced in a socially and ecologically responsible manner, and contribute to the development of the local community by adding value through cutting and polishing activities that allow the immediate region surrounding the mines to capture a larger share of the diamond wealth (Grossberg 2010). Additionally, the company maintains funding programs, such as its Diamonds for Africa initiative, which aim to reduce child labor in the DRC and to create local diamond processing facilities in Madagascar (Grossberg 2010).

Brilliant Earth, a Response to "Dirty Gold"

So there seem to be two main factors that lead to a company taking significant steps toward changing policies to meet demands for social and ecological governance. The first is a crisis moment—something that shakes the status quo and changes how the company perceives the market landscape. This leads to a response based on pragmatism, where new market forces push changes in strategy and policy. The second factor is leadership—there is a person or people involved, willing, and able to become the champion for change. While individual agency is certainly a factor, there are structural factors that will facilitate or inhibit latent leaders from becoming institutional entrepreneurs, namely, their interpretation of the issue and their ability to push change through the organization. Evaluating the causal links between these factors and changing policies is

difficult in practice, but both market-driven pragmatism and institution-
ally driven leadership are clearly visible in all three cases and is therefore
the focal point of the case chapters.

Crises in markets, created by activists, are the external shocks necessary to dislodge the status quo. This is consistent with one of the core
insights of organizational sociology: organizational structures tend not
to change unless acted upon by innovation, corporate challengers, or
external shocks that force responses from managers of lead firms who
otherwise would have little incentive to veer from the status quo (Fligstein 1990). Such external shocks create not only an incentive, but also
an opportunity for business actors to mobilize the resources of their firm
for political purposes. In other words, even if managers wanted to implement social and environmental policies pre-campaign, the structural
forces in markets dissuade them from spending the resources necessary
to do so. And, in the case of ethical jewelers, the market for their products barely existed in the US before the jewelry market was politicized,
and even still only accounts for approximately 1% of the market (GFMS
2010).

Brilliant Earth was not operating at the time the NDG campaign was
launched. At the time there was very limited consumer demand for ethical
jewelry and there were already a couple of companies catering to this
demand, for example, Reflective Images in the US and CRED in the UK.
While information about the social and environmental issues associated
with the jewelry supply chain were being circulated through some media
sources, the founders of Brilliant Earth felt there was not only a gap in the
market, but also an opportunity to increase demand through education
and awareness campaigns.

Therefore, the company knew of the NDG campaign before they had
even launched, and have continued to interact with the activists in various
forums (Brilliant Earth, personal communication, October 10, 2011).
Much of the information provided on the Brilliant Earth website links
directly to reports conducted by the environmental groups themselves.
The much more visible bone of contention seems to be between the company and industry groups, evidenced by the recently heated exchange
between the WDC and Brilliant Earth over their divergent public positions on what constitutes a "conflict diamond."[7] While Brilliant Earth has
taken issue with the diamond industry's claim that less than 1% of

diamonds are conflict diamonds—the company argues that this is simply due to an overly narrow definition—the WDC has responded by defending the 1% claim and attacking the position of the company. The WDC points out that this definition has been endorsed by the UN as recently as January 2011, namely, that conflict diamonds are "rough diamonds which are used by rebel movements to finance their military activities, including attempts to undermine or overthrow legitimate governments." They go on to accuse Brilliant Earth of depriving African countries of revenues and people of employment by only sourcing diamonds from Canada, which is not actually the company's current policy but rather the policy at one point.

Recycled and Fair Trade Gold
Only offering recycled metals for their jewelry allowed the company to be strong critics of gold mining practices, while offering an alternative for consumers. Gold is a material that, when melted down and recast, is indistinguishable from newly mined varieties, provided the purity and alloy content remain the same. The major downside in only dealing in recycled gold is that gold mining, like diamond mining, provides valuable jobs and income to some of the poorest communities in the poorest regions of the world. Simply boycotting newly mined gold regardless of the practices employed has the potential to delegitimize a livelihood strategy undertaken by millions of miners worldwide. With this in mind, the company has diversified its sourcing now that a viable option has become available in the form of FT/FM gold.

Brilliant Earth avoids most of the problems associated with large-scale mining by sourcing gold from one of the first-ever, independently certified, FT/FM cooperatives producing gold—Oro Verde. The ASM operations certified under the label supply safe working conditions and fair wages while restricting chemical usage and restoring the surrounding landscape. This provides even more jobs in the local community and ensures that soil fertility and biodiversity remain intact for agriculture and other uses. All of this is undertaken in a transparent and inclusive manner with the direct involvement of local community councils (see Oro Verde, n.d.).

At the time of writing, demand was currently outstripping supply by quite a large margin. Other ethical jewelers, such as CRED (UK), FiFi

Bijoux (UK), and Noen (Germany) also source from Oro Verde, while Noen and Garavelli (Italy), with their GLOBO collection, source from the EcoAndina cooperative in Peru. However, note that these companies are all based in the UK or EU markets, where Fairtrade and similarly ethical product labels are much more established than in the US. While the Fairtrade Foundation hopes that certified gold will account for 5% of the gold jewelry market over the next fifteen years (Industry analyst, personal communication, November 22, 2011), there remains a long road ahead. Market research in 2014 suggested only about 3% of jewelry consumers even knew the option existed (Hudson 2015). Even if this could come in at an acceptable price point for mainstream jewelers, the supply is still a long way off from meeting their demand. It will continue to be a niche market for the foreseeable future.

Opportunities Model Applied to the Ethical Firm—Brilliant Earth

Now to apply the model and gauge the extent to which it can account for how the firm mobilized politically, and the extent to which the firm has been able to impact the process of private institution building. We should expect differences between firm opportunity structures to lead to variation in political mobilization across different types of firms. The puzzle is not so much whether a firm will engage with a given issue, as all firms will respond in one way or another, but *how* institutional entrepreneurs working within different types of firms operationalize their engagement in accordance with their organizational environment.

We need to temporarily suspend the historical narrative in order to apply the opportunities model to ethical jewelers. The model consists of first investigating the relevant economic dimensions of the firm, tracing the parameters of the opportunity window through the firm's exposure to risk and cost of compliance. It then considers the institutional dimensions that shape how business actors might fill that window, including the company's corporate culture and the position of internal champions within the organizational hierarchy.

Economic Dimensions
Exposure to Risk Brilliant Earth was founded with a social mission, and this is the concept behind their brand. Generally speaking, branding

is a way for companies to differentiate their product from competing products. The company is highly branded as they operate in a niche market for ethical products where the ethical brand differentiates their jewelry, letting the company escape competition with conventional jewelry retailers.

Business actors have to take careful consideration over branding, especially in relation to decisions over how to engage with political issues, as more branded firms tend to face more risk. However, Brilliant Earth is not engaging in these issues to mitigate risk, although it does face risk of a different variety. Certainly any deviation by the company from its ethical values espoused in its mission statements would pose a huge risk for the brand and so branding is simply another factor that compels the company to continue to operate using best practices.

Brilliant Earth is clearly the most specialized of the cases under investigation, as the company specializes not only in jewelry, but ethical jewelry. Diversification is an important variable in that it suggests there is more risk faced by a firm specializing in a politically contentious product than a firm that is more diversified and, therefore, less invested in this product category. If the issues surrounding the product posed a serious risk to the wider business interests of a diversified company, they could simply drop the product from inventories. Again, Brilliant Earth is different from the other cases in that it is not engaging in the politics of gold as a risk mitigation strategy, but it is instead filling a perceived gap in the market for ethical jewelry. In fact, the depoliticization of the market could reduce demand while the colonization of the ethical market by conventional jewelers could increase competition. Additionally, one could argue that small, ethical jewelers are actually taking a risk by innovating in the realm of ethical sourcing and demonstrating the possibility to both consumers and those in the industry (Ethical jeweler, personal communication, August 1, 2011). Taken together, ethical jewelers have every incentive to keep the market politicized while continuing to innovate and utilize best practices.

Cost of Compliance   The structure of each firm's supply chain will differ within an industry, which will affect its willingness and ability to engage in different forms of political mobilization. The complexity and flexibility of the chain will determine the firm's speed and ability in getting its house in order and making commitments with confidence. Pure retailers specializing in diversified products tend to have enormously complex supply chains for a very wide range of goods. Specialized firms should have relatively simple supply chains as they will usually be more vertically integrated and rely on a smaller number of suppliers. This will give them a stronger sense of their position in terms of environmental and social issues, allowing for stronger commitments from the beginning.

Brilliant Earth's supply chain is the least complex of those we'll examine. Starting out as an ethical jeweler meant the company did not have to investigate the upstream processes in existing supply chains. They began only selling recycled gold in order to eliminate any demand for newly mined gold from the company, which is simply a matter of finding a metals refiner or trader who can offer verifiable assurances about their product's provenance. This isn't always easy, but with the small volumes demanded by ethical jewelers, it's certainly easier than tracing and verifying already existing supplier networks. Additionally, the company has recently begun selling FT/FM gold now that this certification has been created, but this certified gold is already traced by definition. Therefore, Brilliant Earth's chain of custody for newly mined gold has proven to be straightforward for the company: the tracing and certification is conducted by third parties. However, the company did contribute to the process in the form of consulting with the certification developers during the draft stages (Brilliant Earth, personal communication, October 10, 2011). The company founders readily admit that due to the size of their operations, they are able to source using the highest standards criteria; the bigger companies have a much more difficult time with this as they have significantly more complex supply chains and simply need much more gold to meet their much larger sales volumes (Brilliant Earth, personal communication, October 10, 2011).

The price sensitivity of customers is inseparable from a firm's business model. As will be presented in the coming chapters, Tiffany and Walmart are not direct competitors, even though they each account for two of the largest chunks of US market share in jewelry sales. They sell to different customers in quite different markets; Walmart competes largely on price; Tiffany enjoys significant mark-ups based on its promise of quality, design and image.[8] Likewise, Brilliant Earth could be said to occupy a third market within the larger US market.

As customers seeking a specialty item in a niche market, consumers of ethical jewelry are willing to pay a price premium for the product. But its ultimate impact depends in part on how large this market becomes. This, in turn, depends on the awareness raised among consumers and the extent to which these best practices will be replicated throughout the industry. Some ethical jewelers feel that, in the UK at least, certified gold will eventually become the industry norm and so any price premium relative to competitors' products should dissipate (Ethical jeweler, personal communication, August 1, 2011). This would, somewhat ironically, raise the competitive pressures for ethical companies and their product differentiation would be reduced. However, not only would most ethical jewelers welcome this outcome despite the increased competitive pressures, most also feel their jewelry design and quality could compete even without the ethical label (Ethical jeweler, personal communication, August 10, 2012). But, as it stands, the more they politicize the market by disseminating information and advocating for change, the more they grow their brand.

The extent to which ethical jewelers pass the cost of their higher standards onto their customers is contested. Interestingly, Brilliant Earth does not necessarily charge a price premium for its jewelry and, in fact, the company claims to offer its high quality jewelry at a discount (Yee 2007). The company is able to do this by keeping overheads low; instead of running a chain of cost-intensive retail outlets, it relies on Internet sales to complement those done directly through its three showroom locations. However, with jewelry prices ranging from US$400–30,000 (Williamson 2006), they are clearly not catering to the discount market.

Institutional Dimensions

Corporate Culture The corporate culture of a firm plays a large role in how it responds to the environmental and social issues brought before it. This culture is in large part a reflection of its customer base and marketing strategy. While managers often act strategically based on the firm's material market interests, often there remains a significant amount of uncertainty and, therefore, discretion in how the costs and benefits are interpreted. The corporate culture will often guide, consciously or not, the response of firm managers to external pressure. The response to the issues by the firm's leadership group will differ in interpretation and individual autonomy. As we will see, Tiffany caters to upper-income, urban consumers, while Walmart prides itself in being for the "working man." Brilliant Earth, on the other hand, is a very small firm with a very clear corporate culture that arose in response to the concerns raised by civil society activists. This means its corporate culture, and that of most ethical jewelers, should be very well-suited for a strong environmental and social ethos.

As these firms are fairly new and quite small, the culture will bear a strong resemblance to its founders and will facilitate a robust position on political issues. James Collins and Jerry Porras (1994) document how many companies have contributed to their success by building their firms around values, visions, and goals other than profit maximization; while David Vogel (2005, 41) notes that only in a few instances do these values have anything to do with social responsibility. However, self-identified ethical firms may be one such instance.

Brilliant Earth's entire business is based on producing high-quality ethical jewelry for those who desire it and increasing demand for ethical consumption of jewelry through their public awareness programs; the corporate culture reflects this as the founders embedded these norms and values in the company from the beginning. As the company has grown, it has added associates who are themselves committed to the social mission of the firm. These new members include the designers, sales associates, and gemologists, all of whom were hired with the goals and values of the company in mind (Brilliant Earth 2012b).

Brilliant Earth's corporate culture is based entirely upon delivering on their assurances of ethical jewelry. Unsurprisingly, their corporate culture is a perfect fit on all levels with the task of keeping irresponsibly mined gold out of the supply chain.

Their goals and values are clearly stated on company documents, namely, providing quality jewelry sourced from socially responsible practices, fostering change by providing education about the challenges of and solutions to the social and environmental problems facing the jewelry industry, and supporting mining communities that have suffered from irresponsible mining practices by donating a share of their profits to organizations working within these communities (Brilliant Earth 2012b). Similarly, their espoused values reflect their basic underlying belief that the jewelry industry can thrive without great human or environmental cost and that aware consumers can drive change through their purchases (Brilliant Earth, personal communication, October 10, 2011). The company runs a blog with regular posts that leave little doubt as to where the company leadership stands on the most important issues facing the industry.[8]

Leadership Structure   As discussed in chapter 2, while Scott (1991, 164) rightly points out that institutional constraints always leave space for the autonomous play of interests and improvisation, Brint and Karabel (1991, 346) recognize that it is probably best to think of organizational elites as constrained entrepreneurs. While not all elites will necessarily make the same assessment of where their interests lie in a given situation, analysts can read organizational interests with a high degree of probability out of the power structures and organizational field the actors must operate within.

An important factor in a firm's response will still be internal leadership from agents within the company. One consultant for some of the world's largest corporations—including Walmart—confirmed that there always seems to be one person who takes the issue personally, who does not wish to be a laggard, and who champions the cause for change from within the company (Conservation International, personal communication, September 18, 2010).

It is difficult to disagree with these assessments. Nor is it easy to dismiss Brint and Karabel's (1991, 346) claim that the socially conditioned mental sets of leaders during decisive periods of decision-making play a role in organizational responses. However, it is always dangerous to guess at the underlying beliefs, intentions, and preferences of individuals—especially when a study is not set up to make rigorous assessments of this nature. The present study is designed to look for instances of structured agency at play, where leadership matters, but is channeled through the structures of the firm. Such a model allows for an investigation into the role of constrained leadership as decisions are channeled through the constraints of corporate culture and the leadership, or management, structure of the firm.

Brilliant Earth, for example, is a private company and so it is not subject to some of the structural constraints of larger public companies that many analysts feel lock these firms into a particular model making them much more resistant to change and innovation. Some in the industry feel ownership structure is an often overlooked variable; the corporate structure of publically offered firms limits their ability to be innovative and to spend the money necessary to be ethical (Ethical jeweler, personal communication, August 1, 2011). It is true, to a certain extent, that public companies are driven by the need for capital. They then need to deliver profit and are subject to the free market dogma that permeates the industry. To be ethical costs money—there is no denying or getting around that—and they are locked into a corporate structure that makes this difficult until proven profitable (Ethical jeweler, personal communication, August 1, 2011). However, it must be noted, and the latter cases demonstrate, that Michael Kowalski from Tiffany claims that shareholders have not questioned the company's expenditures on social responsibility (Kowalski 2004a), and Andrew Ruben from Walmart states that their sustainability initiatives create value as opposed to costing the company (Ruben 2006).

So while the tolerance of investors may vary, the general consensus of those in the industry, backed up by the requisites of fiduciary responsibility, and the findings of the studies cited in chapter 2, suggest that ownership structure and the perceived expectations of investors is likely to impact upon managerial decision-making when it comes to mobilizing firm resources for political purposes. For Brilliant Earth, while the company has investors, it is not publicly traded; and this private ownership structure means that, while certainly subject to the necessities of market survival, it does not need to report its expenditures, quarterly earnings, or related business decisions to a board of directors or release them publicly. This offers the company's leadership much more freedom than publicly traded companies have. It is also the owners who are the internal champions of the ethical initiatives and so they also have no need to answer to internal management.

Business Power and Private Governance

Recall the ways in which business actors might mobilize the firm's resources for political purposes when the opportunity arises. Internally, business actors mobilize the firm's instrumental power to build institutions aligning the interests and practices of the firm with market forces.

Table 3.3
Corporate political mobilization—Brilliant Earth

	Economic	Institutional
Internal	✓ Translating regulations into actionable practices	✓ Creation and maintenance of institutions internal to the firm
External	✓ Donations ✓ Strategic investments ✓ Buying power and preferential procurement ✗ Paying membership fees	✓ Lobbying and advocacy ✓ Issue framing ✓ Creation and maintenance of institutions external to the firm ✓ Acting as a role model for others to benchmark

Externally, business actors mobilize their instrumental power to channel market forces in ways that align with the interests and practices of the firm. Thus, it is a strategy of both influencing the new order as well as re-entrenching the firm's favorable position within this order. Brilliant Earth has used a multifaceted approach to political action and the results of these actions alter the opportunity structures moving forward.

Internal

Creation and Maintenance of Institutions Internal to the Firm   Ethical jewelers—as relatively smaller, younger, and more focused firms—have an advantage over conventional jewelers when it comes to mainstreaming environmental and social criteria. This is fairly obvious, but it is worth noting these firms are designed to be political entities, and maintaining rigorous and consistent internal criteria for business practices is a must. These firms tend to have a fairly small management team and so maintaining institutional memory, that is, continuous learning and knowledge retention regarding the various political issues concerning the company, becomes much easier.

Brilliant Earth uses robust, internally defined criteria to evaluate the sources for diamonds and gold used in their jewelry. They define "conflict free" diamonds as stones that were harvested "free from forced labor, child labor, torture, rape and other affronts to human dignity ... and mined with respect for the environment and by workers earning fair wages in safe working conditions" (Grossberg 2010). These criteria go beyond what the KPCS has defined as "conflict free" for diamonds. The

KPCS defines conflict diamonds as "rough diamonds used by rebel movements or their allies to finance conflict aimed at undermining legitimate governments," which is a very narrow definition reserved for rebel movements, saying nothing about violence that may be perpetrated by governments and funded by diamond sales. Therefore, they label their diamonds as "of ethical origin" to avoid confusing definitions of "conflict free" and to indicate that their products are produced using high social and environmental standards and not just meeting the minimum standards as defined by the KPCS (Grossberg 2010).

Brilliant Earth evaluates the mining operations based on how they impact the local community, its workforce, and the environment. In accordance with the company's criteria, all of the diamond mines they source from not only use high standards and technology to minimize environmental harm, but add value to the communities in which they operate through local hiring priorities, local procurement, and local cutting and polishing facilities (Grossberg 2010). In the case of Canada, the mines are independently monitored and certified as ISO 14001 compliant (Grossberg 2010).

The company also offers laboratory-fabricated diamonds to bypass diamond mining altogether. The process is still in its early development and so there is a limited supply of these. Recycled gold and platinum also limit new mine development and the majority of the company's jewelry is produced from recycled gold. It is somewhat unclear at the moment how the average consumer feels about including recycled content—jewelry, and adornment in general, is an intensely emotive market. Additionally, those who feel very strongly about environmental issues do not necessarily buy high-end jewelry in the first place (Ethical jeweler, personal communication, September 10, 2012). While Brilliant Earth is an ethical firm that appears to go after the mainstream market, many others seem content with staying small (Ethical jeweler, personal communication, September 10, 2012). It remains to be seen how much this market will grow, but the ethical jewelers have clearly found a sizeable niche.

External

Lobbying and Advocacy   Brilliant Earth is a vocal critic of the KPCS and calls for its reform or replacement. They view the definition of conflict as too narrow, the system too vulnerable to smuggling. They berate the organization for keeping Zimbabwe as a member, despite the human rights abuses being perpetrated in that country's diamond mining region. In their words, "It is clear to us that [the KPCS] has failed to live up to even its own limited objectives. The organization does not address severe human rights abuses, does not regulate cutting and polishing centers, and is easily circumvented through smuggling" (Grossberg 2010).

The company worries that dysfunctional organizations like the KPCS simply breed complacency instead of getting to the root of problems. As one industry expert and former diamond buyer put it, one would have to be "fucking naïve" to think conflict diamonds were not finding their way into a supply chain that often operates as a "cash-in-hand" business (Industry expert, personal communication, July 29, 2011). Because it tends to push the issue of unethical diamond production down the international agenda, having the KPCS is in some ways arguably worse than having no certification at all (Brilliant Earth, personal communication, October 10, 2011). The founders of Brilliant Earth believe that, along with eliminating the worst abuses in the industry, it is important to create sources of fair trade diamonds to make diamond mining a positive force for economic development (Grossberg 2010).

Brilliant Earth has similar concerns regarding the RJC (Brilliant Earth, personal communication, October 10, 2011). As we have seen in the previous chapter, not one of the major ethical jewelers is a member of the RJC. Ethical jewelers have been among the most outspoken critics of the initiative, providing added incentive for the initiative to continue to ratchet up its standards.

While the founders of Brilliant Earth say they applaud any initiative that is working to improve practices and assurances throughout the gold supply chain, they feel the RJC contains some fundamental inadequacies (Ethical jeweler, personal communication, October 10, 2011). They add their concerns to those being voiced by other ethical jewelers and the NDG campaigners about the input and output legitimacy of the RJC label. The RJC's input legitimacy has been undermined because: NGOs and labor groups were relegated to unofficial consultative roles during the standards development process; RJC members are strictly industry actors; and many feel there is not sufficient transparency in the monitoring and evaluation processes.

Brilliant Earth is not alone in its criticism of the RJC. Marc Choyt and Greg Valerio, founders of the ethical jewelers Reflective Images and CRED Jewelry, respectively, co-founded the website Fair Jewelry Action, which is dedicated to publishing research and commentary on ethical jewelry practices. Choyt and Valerio are probably the most outspoken critics of the RJC, and they summarize ethical jewelers' most salient concerns. Most ethical jewelers have suspicions the RJC is simply a "greenwashing" exercise. It gives the impression it is a third-party certification initiative for gold and diamonds, when it is not. Fair Jewelry Action feels the rules favor large companies to the detriment of small jewelers who are worried about the cost of membership. There have been accusations that the RJC bullies companies to join as members are moving toward only dealing with RJC suppliers and buyers—what Marc Choyt has called a "quasi-cartel" and Greg Valerio has called a "big boys club" (Choyt 2009). Without traceability, or even requiring members to know the details of their sourcing, the RJC is not performing the function that most stakeholders agree is necessary to eradicate irresponsible mining practices (Ethical jeweler, personal communication, August 7, 2011; Grossberg 2010). Additionally, critics claim the RJC allows mining companies to operate in conflict zones and protected areas, dump waste into some water bodies, emit toxic substances, and operate without community consent (Earthworks 2009).

Despite a name that could easily be mistaken for the FSC and MSC, the RJC is, unlike them, not a multi-stakeholder and independent, third-party initiative—nor does it claim to be. In an interview conducted by Greg Valerio, Michael Rae, the CEO of the RJC, says the RJC differs in fundamental ways from certification initiatives that have emerged to regulate commodity chains for other materials. The RJC is a "multi-*sector* organization" whose membership is comprised of industry actors. "A product stewardship group," says Rae, "is how we view ourselves. It has much more in common with a trade association than with any other entity. Its membership is made up of companies and individuals who are participants in the gold and diamond jewelry supply chain, and our governance is by those members … [t]he methodology that we have used is in essence a trade association with a product stewardship focus" (Rae 2009).

This refers to a number of aspects of the RJC that make it decidedly dissimilar to institutions like the FSC and MSC. Standards were developed in-house, though they were loosely based on existing standards in other industries. Why didn't the RJC go for a more inclusive, multi-stakeholder approach? "They decided to get this thing done and deliver a product to market," says Rae of the RJC's founding members, "and they decided that the best governance model was a product stewardship model that was structured as a trade association" (Rae 2009).

RJC membership was not initially created to certify the supply chain. It does not trace or make any claims about the provenance of the materials in member supply chains. In Rae's words, "What we are doing is certifying the performance of the links in the supply chain. We are not certifying the stuff that is moving through the chain" (Rae 2009). This makes it much more analogous to the chemical industry's Responsible Care program than the FSC, MSC, or FT/FM products.[10] So while the RJC is filling a gap by certifying jewelry manufacturers' practices, it does not say anything about where, how, or by whom the gold and diamonds have been sourced.

However, in the time since this interview took place, the RJC has in fact developed a Chain of Custody option, voluntary for RJC members, containing requirements for those members who wish to make claims about the provenance of their materials. It also audits their systems for tracing these materials through the supply chain. It appears that the RJC has begun to ratchet up their standards, slowly meeting their critics' demands. Formed by a small group of industry actors to mitigate the risk associated with the social and environmental issues being linked to their industry, the initiative has seemingly increased its strength and mandate. The persistent monitoring and critique by the ethical jewelers has almost certainly helped stimulate this process.

Donations and Strategic Investments   Brilliant Earth manages to leverage its modest resources through the direct funding of projects. The company donates 5% of profits to charities and community organizations in Africa through its non-profit fund. One example is the direct financial support it offers to the Diamond Development Initiative (DDI), which funds education for children in mining communities in the DRC and removes them from work in diamond mines. The company also funds similar on-the-ground initiatives in Madagascar and Sierra Leone, including initiatives designed to promote cutting and polishing industries to increase the value-added of diamond mining for these communities and further develop the supply chains for ethical jewelry (Grossberg 2010).

Issue Framing   The company founders meet regularly with activists, representatives from communities in which mining takes place, and their suppliers. People within and around the jewelry industry who are engaged with these issues are a fairly small group and so they tend to know one another. Brilliant Earth was another company that participated in the Madison Dialogue and was present in Vancouver when the IRMA initiative was launched (Brilliant Earth, personal communication, October 10, 2011).

Creation and Maintenance of Institutions External to the Firm   Brilliant Earth works with other groups and institutions to further develop fair trade diamonds and gold, including Transfair USA and the FLO in Europe. The company has provided Transfair USA with guidance and feedback while also working through the DDI and the Madison Dialogue on the logistics of tracing diamonds from mine to retail as well as developing appropriate criteria that is both achievable and robust (Brilliant Earth, personal communication, October 10, 2011; Grossberg 2010). Its commitment to working with these groups and also sourcing from these labels once they are formally launched provides small but tangible economic incentives to develop them.

The company originally worked only with recycled gold. Once Oro Verde became the first independently certified source of FT/FM gold, Brilliant Earth began carrying newly mined gold. The company works with other mining cooperatives as well. For example, it sources sapphires from cooperatives in Sri Lanka (Brilliant Earth 2012c). It advocated for including mining cooperatives, such as Oro Verde, in the fair trade model, as they are examples of how mining can provide fair wages for small-scale miners worldwide while avoiding large-scale environmental degradation and the often traumatic upheaval of local cultures and livelihoods (Brilliant Earth, personal communication, October 10, 2011). Gold from these cooperatives has been certified as socially and environmentally responsible by the independent Instituto de Investigaciones Ambientales del Pacífico (IIAP), and is also being certified as part of a pilot program by Transfair USA (Brilliant Earth 2012b).

Acting as a Role Model for Others to Benchmark   Brilliant Earth does not have great market power, and so cannot spur the industry to change their practices by their direct demand for ethical goods. What it can do is to help create a small market for ethically sourced jewelry by offering small producers a committed buyer for their products while helping to increase consumer awareness of and, therefore, demand for jewelry produced from ethically sourced metals and gems.

The important role for small, ethical jewelers to play is as a role model and standard-setter. Brilliant Earth has laid out some simple standards that they feel should be followed by any company trading in ethical jewelry:

- They should be able to trace the gemstones and metals back to the specific mine in which they were harvested.
- They should know the conditions under which the jewelry item was produced with regard to labor and environmental rights.
- They should have a written policy on sourcing standards and be able to provide a written guarantee that the item was produced without contributing to violence, human rights abuses, or environmental destruction (see Grossberg 2010).

While the company takes a strong stance on raising standards of existing certifications, they still see an important role for large jewelers in creating a demand for socially and environmentally sustainable jewelry. They applaud the work of both Walmart and Tiffany and recognize it can be much more difficult for larger companies to bring their operations around in line with strong standards (Brilliant Earth, personal communication, October 10, 2011). This is where small companies specialized in ethical goods can really make a difference. They can act as role models for the bigger, risk-averse firms and show them what is possible.

Big jewelry companies have an important role to play as they not only wield the market power in the industry and are able to use this market power to incentivize change, but they also have the political clout in industry groups to push for reforms of institutions like the RJC and the KPCS. It is to these companies we turn in the following two case chapters.

Conclusion

Ethical jewelers have opted for the highest, third-party certification where available and have helped create a niche market for the products. The arrival of ethical jewelers can be interpreted as the market colonizing the political space that activists opened with "conflict diamonds" and "dirty gold." From a market-based perspective, they fill a gap in supply of a product that activists have helped create the demand for. From a more political perspective, they fill the need for industry role models, showing other jewelers what is possible while helping to create a market for "responsible" suppliers.

It makes sense that the ethical jewelers would not want to advocate for or join the industry-led RJC as their products are subject to much higher ethical standards and this is their way of differentiating themselves in the market. If all jewelers were "responsible," their product differentiation—which allows them to escape competition—would dissipate. They are able to keep these standards high because their turnover is small enough and they are able to trace their supplies back to their handpicked sources. However, this market-oriented narrative does not explain everything. Brilliant Earth's corporate culture—as espoused in the company goals, values, and ongoing narrative—is not just to maintain acceptable standards but, rather, the highest standards. The founders of the company created this culture and the fact that the firm is private ensures they can maintain these standards without the potential constraining force of investor demands.

In reality, the main market limitations facing ethical jewelry firms are the costs of political activity relative to the revenues they can generate. The main challenge is building both supply and demand for their products. The exposure and politicization of the jewelry market that activists and ethical jewelers create channels market forces in ways aligned with the firms' business interests and expands the opportunity window for future political mobilization.

4

Tiffany and the Specialty Jewelers

Taking out a full-page ad in the *Washington Post*, in late March 2004, Tiffany & Co. sent a very public message that big jewelry just wasn't supposed to send.

The ad took the form of an open letter to Dale Bosworth, chief of the US Forest Service, and was signed by Michael Kowalski, Tiffany chairman and CEO. The letter opposed the Rock Creek Mine project near Libby, Montana—a copper and silver mining project that had recently been approved by the Forest Service. At first glance, it made no sense. Here was one of the major players in the US jewelry market opposing the opening of a new mine in its own back yard. Why would they do a thing like that? Wasn't mining essential to their business?

The response of onlookers was certainly confused. The activists appeared satisfied; industry, shocked; and government, angry. "Given the impact of mining for gold, silver and platinum," explains Steve D'Esposito, president of Earthworks, "they are a company who cared about how they were viewed and what their customers think."[1]

Laura Skaer, head of the Northwest Mining Association in Spokane, had a different take: "I was stunned that a person of Mr. Kowalski's stature and obvious business acumen would write a letter like that."[2]

Mark Rey, undersecretary of the Department of Agriculture, which oversees the Forest Service, seemed downright angry: "The ad is as uninformed on the status of the mine project as it is of the address of the Forest Service."[3]

Many corporate executives shy away from talking to journalists and researchers. They tend to be worried about being called out publicly on their company's practices. Or they believe being in the spotlight might lead to unwanted attention from activists and the media. For Tiffany &

Co., it is the potential for backlash from industry itself. In the words of Mike Kowalski: "Certainly all of our fellow retailers, and almost everyone in the mining industry, consider our degree of engagement suspect, stupid, or insane—pick your poison" (Kowalski 2004a).

So how and why has the company become so involved in the governance of gold? And what are the implications of their deep engagement? Let's begin by looking at specialty jewelers in general before zooming in on Tiffany.

Opportunities Profile and Expectations for Specialty Jewelers

Because specialty jewelers have high exposure to reputational risk and high reliance on gold jewelry, we should expect them to engage in the politics of gold. They are generally larger than the ethical jewelers and so the complexity of their supply chain should also be greater as they may need to source from multiple sites and suppliers to meet their demand. However, their supply chains should remain less complex than the large, diversified jewelers who are pure retailers and source multiple brands. Therefore, specialty jewelers should maintain more direct control over their supply chains than the diversified jewelers. Their customers, especially for the luxury brands that represent the largest of the specialty companies, are already prepared to pay a price premium, reducing the median price sensitivity of the customer base for this category. Therefore, we should expect the business actors within them to act both individually and collectively to mitigate the firm's exposure, as well as the exposure of the entire industry, to reputational damage.

Table 4.1
Opportunities profile for specialty jewelers

Economic dimensions	Institutional dimensions
Exposure to risk	**Corporate culture**
• Level of branding—High	• CSR artifacts—Mixed
• Reliance on product—High	• CSR spoused beliefs—Mixed
Cost of compliance	**Leadership structure**
• Complexity of supply—Medium	• Ownership structure—Mixed
• Price sensitivity of consumers—Low	• Position of institutional entrepreneurs—Mixed

Expectation: High Level of Engagement and Strong Commitments

Almost every specialty jeweler of note in the US market has signed on to the industry-led, second-party RJC certification. Most have signed the Golden Rules while none have yet sourced from the third-party initiative. There are two very interesting cases here. By far the most engaged of any mainstream jeweler in the politics of gold has been Tiffany & Co. They were immediately and deeply involved in shifting their supply chain, liaising with activists and industry, advocating for change in the jewelry industry and, ultimately, in mining practices. The other interesting case is Rolex, but for the opposite reasons. They have so far resisted attempts by activists to sign the Golden Rules and are not part of the RJC. They appear to share the same general economic opportunities for mobilization

Table 4.2
Profile of non-state initiatives for specialty jewelers

	No Dirty Gold (NDG)	Second-party (RJC)	Third-party (FT/FM)
Ben Bridge	✓	✓	✗
Birks & Mayors (Canada & US)	✓	(✓ March 2012 – not yet certified)	✗
Blue Nile	✓	✗	✗
Boucheron	✓	✓	✗
Bulgari (IT)	✗	✓	✗
Cartier (FR)	✓	✓	✗
Chopard	✗	✓	✗
Faberge	✗	✓	✗
Harry Winston	✗	✓	✗
Piaget	✓	✓	✗
Rolex	✗	✗	✗
Signet (UK and US)	✓	✓	✗
Tiffany & Co.	✓	✓	✗
Van Cleef & Arpels	✓	✓	✗
Zale	✓	✓	✗

as their peers, so it suggests the main difference can be found in the corporate culture and leadership categories. These are the categories that appear to also separate Tiffany from the pack in the speed and depth of their political engagement.

Almost every major specialty jeweler in the US market and beyond has signed on to both the NDG's Golden Rules and, importantly, the RJC. In contrast, the ethical and diversified jewelers have almost unanimously avoided this latter certification. This indicates that specialty jewelers face somewhat unique circumstances. Their opportunity window for political action was open wide as the specialty firms found themselves significantly exposed to reputational risk by nature of their brands and their reliance on gold products. Additionally, the sector was already highly politicized, having learned important lessons from previous controversies. Therefore, the response of specialty jewelers was based predominantly on risk mitigation. So this explains the general pattern we see across specialty jewelers. But what about Tiffany? Why were they so far ahead of their peers?

Company Profile—Tiffany

Famous for its "Blue Book" catalogue and its little blue boxes, Tiffany is one of the most recognizable specialty jewelers in the world. Engaged in the design, manufacturing and retailing of fine jewelry and other luxury items, they operate primarily in the US and Japan, but also have significant interests across East Asia, Mexico, Canada, and Brazil (Bloomberg 2012). Composed of three operating divisions—US retail, international retail, and direct marketing[4]—Tiffany operates 71 outlets in the US and 114 outside the US, with its flagship store located on Fifth Avenue in New York City (Datamonitor 2009a, 5–6). Tiffany brand jewelry spans a wide price range from the more affordable silver product lines to diamond-based items obtainable by only the very wealthy. While jewelry is their principle product category, the company also sells timepieces, sterling silver goods other than jewelry, china, crystal, stationary, fragrances, and personal accessories.[5] While the company has significant international interests and a certain level of diversification in products, it remains specialized in jewelry and continues to rely heavily on the US market.

Company History

Tiffany & Co. has always been associated with innovation in the industry. In 1837, Charles Lewis Tiffany and John Young founded Tiffany & Young in New York City. They sold all manner of luxury goods, including jewelry. In 1841, J. L. Ellis joined the ownership group and the retailer changed its name to Tiffany, Young and Ellis. In 1845, they came through with their first innovation: selling their goods via direct marketing through their now famous mail-order catalog, the "Blue Book." Another forward-thinking move for the company was adhering to the English standard of silver purity (0.925) when other US manufacturers were cutting costs. In fact, Charles Tiffany apparently personally lobbied Congress members to enact the legislation that made 0.925 the national standard of purity. Tiffany bought out his partners in 1853 and changed the name to Tiffany & Co. As the sole owner, Charles Tiffany forged a close relationship with many of his suppliers, including the silver company started by John Moore, which Tiffany bought and incorporated into the company in 1868. The company continued to innovate. George Frederick Kunz, Tiffany's gemologist and eventual vice president of the company, was instrumental in establishing the "carat" as the international unit for precious gems. Other innovations include the well-known "Tiffany setting," the now classic six-pronged setting for engagement rings and, more recently, the name the company has made for itself in glass and lamps. The point is that the company has a long history of leadership in both design and industry standards, so perhaps it is little surprise to see them leading the industry response to contemporary social and ecological issues.

Tiffany continued to grow throughout the 20th century, adding stores in the US, signing exclusive contracts with prominent designers, and establishing its retail foothold internationally. The 1980s saw the company bought (1979), resold (1984), enter the European market via the opening of London's Old Bond Street store (1986), and become listed on the New York Stock Exchange (1987). Tiffany continued its expansion through the 1990s by adding major manufacturing facilities in Japan (1996) and the US (1997, 2001), while launching its online business in 1999. As of 2016, there are over 300 Tiffany stores worldwide.[6]

Where Jewelry Fits into the Business Model

Although Tiffany has gradually expanded its interests to include a number of luxury items in its retail locations, the company remains first and foremost a jeweler. It is a vertically integrated company continuing to deepen control over its supply chain. Not simply a jewelry retailer, Tiffany has moved beyond retail and design to include jewelry manufacturing and even the cutting and polishing of diamonds.[7] This increasing integration has been undertaken primarily for security reasons—the company felt exposed by its reliance on diamonds, with around 40% of the company's materials incorporating the gem (Kosich 2004). The company recognized that the combination of its dependence on diamonds and the number of intermediaries in the supply chain represented a strategic risk and a fundamental security problem (Kosich 2004). "Vertical integration or chain of custody was a strategic objective of ours for the last 20 years," says Michael Kowalski, Tiffany CEO and Chairman of the Board. "We have been slowly moving in that direction" (Kosich 2004).

History of Interaction with Civil Society—from Crisis to Response

Crisis—Conflict Diamonds

As with ethical jewelers, the conflict diamonds issue was a watershed moment in the political education of specialty jewelers. It marked the first genuine politicization of the market. Unlike many of the ethical jewelers, however, most of the key players in the specialty jewelry market were already in operation when the conflict diamonds controversy erupted, and were caught unawares. They were forced to learn on the fly. In the late 1990s, when the campaign against conflict diamonds was gaining prominence, the industry formed the World Diamond Council (WDC) to tackle the issue and Tiffany was one of the founding, and most outspoken, members. The industry group joined with activists from civil society, governments, and the UN to construct the KPCS with the goal of eradicating conflict diamonds from members' supply chains.

Yet, we have already noted that Tiffany had previously developed its own rationale for shifting its supply chain and expanding its chain of custody for diamonds: the company wanted to achieve security of supply, and access the profits that could be realized by taking on these additional activities. Change was not—at least initially—driven by any desire to ensure social and environmental accountability. In other words, by the time the conflict diamonds issue surfaced, Tiffany had already spent significant resources on integrating its supply chain, thereby expanding its chain of custody.

The opportunity arose in 1996–97 when Aber Diamond Corporation—a Toronto-based diamond mining company (now Harry Winston Corporation)—approached Tiffany with an investment opportunity in the Northwest Territories of Canada (Kosich 2004). In 1999, Tiffany bought a 13.9% stake in Aber for US$71 million, which the company used to develop Diavik diamond mine in Canada, allowing Tiffany to buy diamonds at a discount (Newman 2006). In late 2004, Tiffany sold its interests in the company for US$268 million and went on to provide US$35 million in financing credit to Tehera Diamond Corporation to allow the company to develop the Jericho diamond project, also in Canada, in exchange for similar purchasing rights (Newman 2006). Tiffany now sources the vast majority of its diamonds from Rio Tinto and Harry Winston's Diavik mine, BHP Billiton's Ekati mine, and Tahera's Jericho mine (although operations are currently on hold pending sale)—all of which are located in the Canadian Arctic.

In addition to these sourcing deals, Tiffany took on cutting and polishing activities as well as manufacturing (Kosich 2004; Newman 2006).

According to Kowalski (2004b):

> We began all these activities primarily driven by security of supply and we wanted to control our destiny. As we became more involved, we realized that there were significant incremental earnings to be derived from vertical integration. Our interest became far more intense ... because we believed that there were profit opportunities. At the turn of the century, it became more important for issues of social and environmental accountability. That was actually the very last consideration in terms of time sequence.

So, the risk to the Tiffany brand posed by conflict diamonds was serious, but only reinforced a process of consolidating control of the company's supply chain that was already underway. However, the process was not complete by the time campaigns to eradicate conflict diamonds came into force and Tiffany stores were targeted along with other jewelers. Unlike many in the industry, Tiffany responded to the "conflict diamond" controversy in a very proactive way.

In addition to continuing their movement toward establishing a clear chain of custody for their diamonds, the company also took on an advocacy role and began leading the movement to eradicate the controversial diamonds from the industry as a whole. Toward this end, Tiffany took out another full-page ad in the *Washington Post* in 2001 encouraging the Bush Administration and Congress to pass the Clean Diamonds Trade Act, which enacted US participation in the KPCS. Soon after the conflict diamonds crescendo, the issue of "dirty gold" arose. Tiffany was determined to not get caught unawares again.

Response of Tiffany to "Dirty Gold"

Tiffany was one of the prime targets of the NDG campaign from the very beginning. Its name features prominently on the bar napkin, now framed and hanging in the office of the organization for which Steve D'Esposito, the former president of Earthworks and one of the NDG masterminds, currently works in Washington, DC.

The activists quickly realized that, in terms of engagement with the issues, Tiffany was in its own category (NDG, personal communication, September 20, 2010). Identifying high-end jewelers as principal targets because of their brand value, activists wanted to raise the threat of damage to this brand value. What better way to garner the leverage necessary to influence mining practices? The activists were confident the brands would respond and, armed with a core of high-end jewelers, they would then take this added credibility to the lower-end jewelers, also presenting them with a model of how companies had adapted and a "gold standard" by which to judge all within the industry.

This was an approach that had already proven effective in other industries, notably the forestry sector when Rainforest Action Network (RAN) and others targeted large DIY retailers to force them to shift their sourcing strategies away from old growth timber (see, for example, Bartley 2003; Sasser 2003).[8]

Contrary to the tactics used in the forestry case, however, the NDG campaign leaders decided to directly approach some of the companies first. Not everybody in the NGO community supported this approach. It went against the then-current logic among activists, which was to hit the companies with demonstrations, boycotts, and other forms of negative publicity with the hope of forcing them to acquiesce to the campaign demands. Approaching the companies beforehand to negotiate, and possibly cooperate, was anathema to activists.

Here was the thing though. The campaign leaders for NDG didn't know if demonstrations outside storefronts and other planned actions would actually work. What if they went ahead with them and there was no noticeable decline in sales? Nobody knew what would happen. The threat of a shame campaign was only a certainty while it was still just that: a threat. The campaign leaders decided that leveraging the risk of a shame campaign was worth more than actually pulling the trigger. If they went through with protests, they ran the risk of losing their leverage. So they decided the uncertainty and risk itself might in fact be their most powerful and safest asset (NDG, personal communication, September 20, 2010). That threat was what they would take to the companies. And Tiffany was first on their list to pay a visit to.

Once the decision to contact the companies directly was made, the campaign leaders then put their minds to figuring out how to go about doing this. While gathering information on target companies, which included Tiffany, Cartier, Bulgari, and Rolex, they received a call from Tiffany. Tiffany got to the activists before they could get to Tiffany.

Tiffany explained that it had heard about the campaign and that the company was doing many of the same things—assessing the landscape and trying to make sense of it all (NDG, personal communication, September 20, 2010). Having faced the issues over conflict diamonds, Tiffany was examining its supply chain for other vulnerabilities—and what came up was gold.

The company's gold supply chain constituted a considerable latent problem and environmental concerns that could potentially pose an even greater threat than conflict diamonds. At least conflict diamonds were relatively containable. Gold was far bigger. So Tiffany was looking to have a conversation with the other side—a move that would have certainly been as appalling to many in the jewelry industry as the campaigners' cooperation with companies was to other activists at the time.

Once other jewelers saw the conflict diamonds issue moving along the KPCS track, they went back to doing what they did best—selling jewelry. Having already begun carving out a greater role in governing the industry, Tiffany management saw something deeper and knew they had to go further. They began engaging with key people from the NGO sector as well as with their suppliers, including some of the major mining companies. So by the time the NDG campaign launched, Tiffany had already done its analysis and had a sense of the lay of the land, which enabled the company to formulate a position and a strategy moving forward. Tiffany's perceived interest was changing, and the company would now do things that matched this new interest. They were the ones who had already thought this all through. And after the conflict diamonds situation, they were not going to be surprised again (NDG, personal communication, September 19, 2010).

Lobbying and Advocacy—Regulatory Reform and Opposition to Projects

Tiffany has shown itself to be a leader right from the beginning. One of the first major jewelers to sign on to the NDG campaign's Golden Rules, Tiffany has gone beyond campaign expectations and has actually pushed for increased regulation in a number of areas affecting its operations.

That open letter in the *Washington Post* on March 24, 2004 about the Rock Creek mine in Montana was one such example. Many in the industry were very upset by Tiffany's stance—and were equally very public in showing it. Industry groups attacked the company, accusing Kowalski of being the environmental movement's lapdog and claiming the advertisement was factually inaccurate, that the company had failed to consult with those working on the project, and had wasted an estimated US$50,000 of shareholder money on the personal agenda of the CEO (Northwest Mining Association, 2004, 6). However, it is worth noting that much of this inflammatory language originated from the same source—a regional industry group catering to mining interests—and in the same document referred to the NDG campaign as an "anti-mining crusade" (Northwest Mining Association 2004, 2).

Despite these negative reactions from industry, Tiffany continued its robust corporate advocacy. In a talk centered on Tiffany's CSR policies and delivered at his alma mater, the Wharton Business School at the University of Pennsylvania, Kowalski opened up about the impetus for and backlash against some of Tiffany's actions.

During the talk, Kowalski admitted that Tiffany had not expected the industry backlash to be so strong. Kowlaski himself considered

Tiffany's stance to be "a-political," as "unlike other environmental issues today, mining issues traditionally cut across party lines." However, his perception began to change once newspaper headlines began declaring the likes of "Tiffany Battles Administration over Mining Reform." "It was something that we certainly didn't anticipate," he admitted (Kowalski 2004a).

> Many of the mining communities in this country absolutely believe that we act as a front for the NGO community, that I am a radical environmentalist who is out of control, that we have been corrupted by the NGOs—none of which is true. In terms of brand leadership on this issue, we are at a turning point right now. To some degree, we could walk away from this today and say ... We have done more than any jeweler in the past by basically putting mining reform back on the national political agenda through our open letter ad in *The Washington Post* (Kowalski 2004a).

But Tiffany has not walked away. In 2009, Tiffany ran an ad in an industry magazine, *National Jeweler*, aimed at jewelers urging its peers to boycott gold from Pebble gold mine in Bristol Bay, Alaska, run by the "Pebble Partnership" of Anglo American and Northern Dynasty. Tiffany says it objects to the proposal "to build an enormous gold and copper mine in the very heart of Alaska's Bristol Bay Watershed, home of the world's most productive salmon fishery." The ad continues with the statement that "there are certain places where mining cannot be done without forever destroying landscapes, wildlife and communities. Bristol Bay is one such place." Tiffany has followed up this advertisement with a similar one in *National Geographic* in December 2010.[9]

In an email to Mine Web, an online industry hub and newspaper, Michael Kowalski said, "We have been opposing the Pebble mine in every public forum we have spoken at—the FT and Fortune Green Conferences, the EMA Awards in Hollywood." Kowalski said Tiffany has discussed its objection to the Pebble Lake Mine project with Anglo American, the company behind the proposal (Kosich 2009).

In a separate interview, Kowalski has stated that he thinks it is "a matter of risk assessment" and, after visiting the proposed site for a fly fishing expedition, has even put together a documentary film that helped convince the Tiffany board of directors to back the campaign (Novellino 2009). Along with risk assessment, there are other business explanations for this type of corporate activism.

One of the interesting aspects of the *National Jeweler* ad in particular is that it is directed at industry actors and is, therefore, less public than the *Washington Post* challenge. This suggests two things. First, Tiffany did not wish a repeat of the backlash on the same scale created by the *Washington Post* advertisement. Second, that Tiffany is not simply attempting to create publicity through its activism (Luxury jeweler, personal communication, September 16, 2010).

From the examples outlined thus far, one could easily get the impression that Tiffany's response to the issue of "dirty gold" was simply taking out inflammatory advertisements in newspapers. However, the company has also been active in the creation of industry groups set up to deal with these issues. It was one of the founding members of both the WDC, which works toward the elimination of conflict diamonds from the diamond supply chain, and the RJC (formerly the Council for Responsible Jewellery Practices), created in response to the issue of "dirty gold." The company has played a central role in gathering industry support for collective action as well as reaching out beyond it.

Opportunities Model Applied to the Specialty Firm—Tiffany

So the response of Tiffany has conformed to our expectations for actors in the specialty jewelry category. Due to the structural opportunities available to institutional entrepreneurs within the firm, once activists raised the issue of "dirty gold," these business actors were able to move quickly and decisively. Bringing in the opportunities model offers a more focused explanation of the company's deep engagement, paying particular attention to the unique features of the opportunity structure that business actors within the firm were able to take advantage of to drive this very proactive response. This will also offer a chance to evaluate the framework itself, judging the extent to which the company's response can be accounted for through the channeling effects of the economic and institutional dimensions of the model.

Economic Dimensions
Exposure to Risk   The immediate competition that firms face has a lot to do with their business model. Tiffany enjoys significant mark-ups based on its promise of quality, design, and image. It competes with other luxury

brands and spends large quantities of its expenditures on marketing, for example, in its almost daily advertisements in the *New York Times*. An enormous proportion of the company's value is intangible, and the Tiffany brand has risen to the top of the industry by leveraging its reputation. It is not a needs-based industry and so customers must be convinced that the product is worth its significant price premium. Much of this can be said about the jewelry sector as a whole, but it is especially so in the case of the luxury brands.

The Tiffany brand is arguably of greater value to the company than those of our other cases. Tiffany's brand image accounts for a relatively greater share of the company's value and constitutes a vital part of its business strategy. The company is ranked 76th in *Businessweek*'s "Top 100 Global Brands" annual report (Bloomberg 2010a) with a brand value of US$4.000 billion. Cartier is ranked just slightly behind in the 77th position with a brand value of US$3.968 billion. Noticeably absent is Walmart, which is especially significant when we consider that the company is by far the largest retailer in the world. Clearly, not all firms in the branded node of the supply chain have equal value invested in their individual brand and so the levels of threat and opportunity will also vary.

Tiffany designs and manufactures its own jewelry, emblazoning each piece with the added value of the Tiffany & Co. name. Tiffany maintains exclusive contracts with prominent designers, making its product—for all intents and purposes—a designer brand. It does not compete on price so much as product differentiation and this makes the brand image of Tiffany vital to its business interests, while also allowing for a market strategy based on smaller volumes and double-digit profit margins.[10]

Tiffany's lack of diversification can go a long way toward explaining the company's political activities. Michael Kowalski has stated that prior to NGOs and others raising public concern over the social and environmental effects of the jewelry industry's demand for minerals, this lack of diversification posed a fundamental security of supply predicament (Kowalski 2004a). It left the company at the mercy of its suppliers. This was especially the case with diamonds, because roughly 40% of Tiffany's products required their use. So even before diamonds were in the global media spotlight as fueling armed groups that were adding to the miseries of many in poverty-stricken and war-torn supplier countries, Tiffany was working to integrate manufacturing and supply processes into its market strategy. The conflict diamonds campaign only added a new security issue to Tiffany's strategic supply chain agenda and added extra impetus to the movement underway.

Cost of Compliance   The structure of each firm's supply chain differs within an industry, affecting the firm's cost of compliance and, therefore, the opportunity window available for business actors. Tiffany has a relatively simple supply chain since it sources the vast majority of its gold from a single mine with onsite refining capacity, and controls the design and manufacturing processes.

Tiffany was already in the process of shifting its supply chain toward a more vertically integrated model when the first cries of "conflict diamonds" were heard in the late 1990s. This lowered the marginal cost for participating in the shift away from these damaging sources of minerals.

Tiffany's experience with conflict diamonds certainly prepared the company for what lay ahead when the issue of "dirty gold" arose. However, unlike the diamond experience, Tiffany had not expanded its control over its gold supply chain and so could not immediately respond with chain of custody verification as to how and where its gold was sourced. Michael Kowalski recounts that when he was initially asked where Tiffany gold came from, he realized that he had no idea. "If one were to ask us about the ultimate mine origin of any of our precious metals we couldn't begin to answer that question," he recalls (Kowalski 2004b). So the company put the question to its suppliers—its manufacturers, fabricators, and even bullion banks—but to no avail. "The trail simply goes cold" (Kowalski 2004b).

Since then, Tiffany has shifted its supply chain so that it sources most of its new gold from the Bingham Canyon Mine in Utah, a modern mine where the company can ensure full control of procedures (Friedman 2008; Copping 2009). Like the Diavik diamond mine in the Northwest Territories, Bingham is operated by Rio Tinto, through its subsidiary, Kennecott Utah Copper. Tiffany continued to consolidate its chain by melting and molding jewelry in its own facilities in New York and Rhode Island while continuing to cut and polish rough diamonds in Belgium, South Africa, and Canada (Newman 2006).

So even before the NDG campaign hit its stride, Tiffany already had a very strong sense of its position in terms of the potential environmental and social issues that were beginning to come up. While the rest of the industry moved on from the diamond controversy, Tiffany realized it was still exposed on many fronts and began the process of investigating the provenance of other materials and expanding its chain of custody to reduce this exposure.

Additionally, the consumer base for specialty jewelers should be less sensitive to changes in price than those of diversified jewelers. While the latter compete largely on price, Tiffany emphasizes its name as representing tradition and quality—a major reason why Tiffany's profit margins are triple those of its larger, discount superstore competitors.[11]

Recently, Tiffany has expanded its market into less expensive jewelry for a target market that should be more price sensitive than for its luxury goods customer base. This jewelry tends to use silver as its base metal and so is not directly targeted by the campaigns against diamonds and gold. However, the company has used the diamond experience to inform its response to concerns about gold, and it seems only natural to expect silver to be next in line.

Perhaps more significant is the fact that Tiffany's movement into less expensive jewelry and Walmart's movement into more expensive jewelry means these two very different companies are bringing to market a range of products that has many more similarities to the other company's range than before. However, there are still some major differences between them. Even though the products seem comparable, they may in fact fall into different categories: Tiffany specializes in aspirational goods while Walmart specializes in attainable ones. It all goes back to branding. Tiffany is selling an image. The company does a wonderful job at balancing this with accessibility, but Tiffany is luxury goods company—competing not on price, but on image.

In fact, although Tiffany and Walmart are two of the largest retailers of gold jewelry in the US, industry analysts do not even list them as competitors. For example, Datamonitor, an industry database, lists Tiffany's top six competitors as LVMH Moet Hennessy Louis Vuitton, Zale Corporation, Bulgari Societa per Azioni, Blue Nile Inc., Signet Groups plc (Kay and Jared), and Richemont (Cartier)—despite Walmart accounting for the highest gold jewelry sales in the US market (Datamonitor 2009a, 21).

This reflects the major division in the jewelry sector between specialty jewelry retail chains and department stores with jewelry operations (Datamonitor 2009a, 20). There is, of course, a third category, represented by Brilliant Earth. Taken together, the three types of businesses account for the typology used in this book.

The significance for the analysis here is twofold. First, Tiffany relies far more on its image, making the company much more susceptible to threats against its reputation. Second, Tiffany should be more able to incorporate the cost of mitigating these risks into the price of its product. Both of these factors expand opportunities for institutional entrepreneurship.

Institutional Dimensions
Corporate Culture   Tiffany is associated with classic American luxury. Its elegant Manhattan flagship store emphasizes that. Its market is in aspirational goods. While Tiffany prides itself on being accessible, its main customers are upper-income, urban consumers. All of these factors contribute to the organizational identity of the company, which will be reflected in the artifacts (past actions) and espoused beliefs (written and verbal policies and goals) of the company.

Naturally, this identity leads to different strategies than our other cases when implementing environmental and social directives. Tiffany's customers want the Tiffany brand and everything it represents, and they are willing to pay a premium to attain it. This makes Tiffany more vulnerable to the risks of being associated with irresponsible mining practices, but also more inclined to use its voice against such practices. This can be seen in the public stand the company has taken in all of those full-page advertisements. Tiffany's customers are likely to care about these issues and applaud Tiffany's position on them as it is a cognitive fit with its global brand image.

In fact, the campaigners were counting on this from the beginning. There was a strong business case based on risk mitigation. With so much intangible value invested in its brand, the company would go to great lengths to protect that image. An intimately related factor was that Tiffany customers, wealthy urbanites who have shown themselves to be willing to pay premium prices for this well-groomed *Tiffany* brand, may actually find "dirty gold" to be an issue relevant to them, one they're in touch with—more so than consumers shopping for price. However, at the end of the day, those working closely with the company feel that it came down to culture. "It was less a business case than a given—Tiffany & Co. does not equal protesters outside of stores" (NDG, personal communication, September 20, 2010).

Leadership Structure   As explained in the conceptual framework, the structure of a firm's leadership will influence the autonomy of managerial decision-making; therefore, leadership structure will shape the extent to which individual characteristics of the firm's leadership matter. The leadership structure of the firm will influence the willingness and the ability for internal institutional entrepreneurs to respond proactively to external pressure.

While the vast majority of the major specialty jewelers have signed on to the NDG's Golden Rules and the RJC, there are exceptions. Rolex, the luxury watchmaker, has declined engagement with activists and the wider politics of the market. This is somewhat surprising given that most of the economic opportunities that facilitate Tiffany's proactive stance are also present for Rolex. The difference, it seems, is that the institutional character of Rolex does not favor this type of political activity. Its website does not (at the time of this writing) have a prominent CSR section, and, according to activist accounts, the company leadership simply does not appear interested in participating (NDG, personal communication, April 24, 2012). It suggests that they have not built the systems or the culture that would facilitate proactive political engagement.

For Tiffany it is the CEO and chair, Michael Kowalski, who is driving change because he has the vision to bring a strong CSR analysis to the firm and the capacity in his position to see it through. Campaign leaders note that there are others with a similar vison, but they are not in a position to drive these issues past the board of directors (NDG, personal communication, September 20, 2010). They may not have the board or their senior leadership on their side. They really need that combination to drive ambitious programs forward. The fact that Mike Kowalski is both CEO and chair of the board of directors helps.

Campaigners know the value of private sector leadership:

> Leadership is key—it is at least as important as the brand value. Harry Winston didn't move; Cartier came more slowly—all the other brands needed to

figure out what was going on. There was no leadership; nobody was in a position to really drive it forward. With Tiffany it was the perfect mix. (NDG, personal communication, September 20, 2010)

So while many companies will possess latent leadership potential, any prospective champions must be in a position to expend company resources while creating the cognitive and organizational space for change.

Michael Kowalski holds many of the top positions at Tiffany. In addition to being CEO and chairman of the board, he sits on the Management Board, the Dividend Committee, and the Corporate Social Responsibility Committee (Bloomberg 2012b). While Tiffany's business model and corporate culture do lend themselves to proactive leadership on these issues, Kowalski's position as chairman of the board expands his opportunity window when advocating a very strong position on CSR. With the amount of autonomy these positions afford him, it seems appropriate to expand briefly on the character of Tiffany's leader.

A self-proclaimed "corporate activist," Kowalski is an environmentalist and seems to take the industry's environmental challenges personally. While moving up the Tiffany corporate ladder, Kowalski became involved in various environmental causes, including as Trustee of the Wildlife Conservation Society and the Nature Conservancy (Bloomberg 2012c).

This not only points to a personal commitment to environmentalism, but also hints at an underlying conservationist worldview, as opposed to a more instrumentalist perspective on the core of concepts like "sustainable development" (see, for example, Bernstein 2001). When explaining the logic behind Tiffany's campaign against the proposed mine in Alaska to a reporter for *National Jeweler Magazine*, Kowalski states that "a mine, by definition, is a wasted resource … it will be gone, it will be depleted and likely be abandoned" (Novellino 2009).

What makes this statement interesting—and controversial—is not its sentiment, but rather, the source and context. It is coming from the business community and, moreover, from an industry player with a stake in this sector. It is not empty rhetoric nor is it representative of flexible, market-based instruments. It advocates for strict limits to market activity—prescribing "no-go" zones for extractive industries. It demonstrates a logic that is fundamentally at odds with that of the market-driven environmentalism that permeates the contemporary business community. Michael Kowalski may have been correct when he stated in a Reuters interview that appeared on Forbes.com immediately following the *Washington Post* ad: "For Tiffany, responsible mining is absolutely a part of our brand contract and, if you haven't guessed it already, I'm close to being a radical environmentalist" (cited in Northwest Mining Association 2004). Kowalski was probably having a little fun with the statement, but it has been picked up by some in the industry and treated as a confession of guilt (see, for example, Northwest Mining Association 2004).

It is worth repeating that it is a combination of the company's business model as well as cognitive factors that allow those within the company the "wiggle room" to take this stance. If Michael Kowalski did not hold such powerful positions within the company, Tiffany's depth of engagement would almost certainly have been shallower. Tiffany's value is its brand. In a company where the vast majority of value is intangible, one of the CEO's main tasks must be reputation management. Tiffany's corporate culture is open to strong leadership on both reputation management and issues like the environment. This should be viewed as a positive cycle of sorts: the corporate culture enables strong leadership on these issues, but that corporate culture itself will reflect this strong leadership. The bottom line is, without these favorable opportunity structures, Kowalski's leadership would have likely laid dormant.

Kowalski swears he does not have a problem selling the company's proactive position to shareholders. During the Wharton talk, one student asked Kowalski directly if investors ever criticize him, in his role as CEO, for spending so much time promoting environmental and social responsibility issues, taking his focus off other daily and strategic initiatives. He responded:

> That's a fair question, but investors have not asked. When the subject comes up and when we outline our programs, those investors who are concerned are predisposed to be supportive of what we are doing. And I would say that my role is not to focus on daily operations. My role is to focus on issues of strategic importance. I would place this near the top of our list. It really is about our social license to continue to do business. That is about as fundamental a CEO-like responsibility I can imagine. (Kowalski 2004a)

Business Power and Private Governance

This chapter has thus far offered an explanation for Tiffany's response to activist contestation based on the actions of internal institutional entrepreneurs who drive change through the opportunity structures available. But what are the potential consequences of this corporate political mobilization? In the final section, I bring instrumental dimensions of business power back to the analysis, examining the ways Tiffany has impacted the political landscape, contributed to the creation of private institutions, and expanded the opportunities for future political action. Such an approach helps explain how specialty jewelers might mobilize the firm's resources both to take advantage of and to expand the opportunity window for corporate political mobilization.

Internal

Buying Power and Preferential Procurement   Tiffany is uniquely set to monitor its sourcing. It maintains one of the most vertically integrated supply chains among jewelers. As we've seen, even before the "conflict diamonds" controversy, the company began purchasing interests upstream in mining and processing activities. This has allowed Tiffany to follow its diamond supply from the source and monitor practices along the chain.

Tiffany has advantageously positioned itself when sourcing gold too. In purchasing gold almost exclusively from Kennecott's Bingham Canyon copper mine in Utah, the company is working with an established mining community that uses the highest technology to extract the ore without the use of cyanide and, importantly, has an onsite refinery, which allows the gold to remain segregated from that mined from other sites. This last point is vitally important as it is the refining stage at

Table 4.3

Corporate political mobilization—Tiffany & Co.

	Economic	Institutional
Internal	✓ Translating regulations into actionable practices	✓ Creation and maintenance of institutions internal to the firm
External	✓ Donations ✓ Strategic investments ✓ Buying power and preferential procurement ✓ Paying membership fees	✓ Lobbying and advocacy ✓ Issue framing ✓ Creation and maintenance of institutions external to the firm ✓ Acting as a role model for others to benchmark

which sources often get mixed, posing difficulties for tracing the substance back to its original source (Industry expert, personal communication, July 29, 2011). It also allows the company to have a policy of only sourcing gold when it is mined as a by-product, since the mine predominantly produces copper.[12]

Creation and Maintenance of Institutions Internal to the Firm   Tiffany's mainstreaming of sustainability throughout their business really took off with the "conflict diamonds" controversy and has continued since, growing into a strong CSR program. Tiffany monitors its compliance with its evolving standards through its involvement with certification initiatives, as well as through the Corporate Social Responsibility Committee (CSR Committee), established by the board of directors in 2009. Those tasked by the company with CSR initiatives interact often with operations management in Tiffany's New York offices.

While Kowalski has admitted that Tiffany expends a fair amount of resources working on mining reform issues (Kowalski 2004a), the company manages to do a lot with relatively little and the cost of implementing CSR strategies has never been an issue with investors (Luxury jeweler, personal communication, September 16, 2010). One of its main CSR divisions—the Tiffany Foundation—consists of only two employees, including the president, Anisa Costa, and the CSR Committee oversees CSR efforts.

In line with the CSR Committee Charter (Tiffany, n.d.), the committee includes at least two independent directors and one employee director. The charter defines "social responsibility" as the way in which the business, including its sourcing, affects the communities it operates in. Its mandate is expansive, considering everything from environmental impacts to employment practices to political engagement. The committee monitors and evaluates all management decisions with regard to their social and environmental impacts and offers recommendations directly to the board of directors for improvements. The focus is on any issue that may impact the company's business operations, brand image, and reputation while updating priorities based on evolving industry best practices and community concerns. The committee also reviews the company's engagement with various groups and oversees the reporting on their initiatives to the wider stakeholder community, while maintaining the authority to engage or terminate engagement with any third-party auditors or consultants.

Through its internal policy mechanisms, the company adheres to numerous self-imposed bans on dealing in certain materials and materials of certain provenance. For example, in 2002, Tiffany stopped selling coral and, in 2003, the company stopped trading in gems from Myanmar in line with the US government's Burmese Freedom and Democracy Act, continuing to adhere to the ban even when legal loopholes were being used by other jewelers to sell these items (Tiffany 2012). As previously noted, in 2004, the company pledged to not source silver or gold from the Pebble Lake Mine in Bristol Bay and, in 2010, added diamonds from the Marange region of Zimbabwe to the list of materials banned from company products and stores (Tiffany 2012). In 2002, the company pulled tanzanite from its shelves at a time when the mineral was being linked to terrorist groups; when these rumors proved false, the company began selling tanzanite once more (Newman 2006). The internal policies are meant to protect the company from the reputational risk of being associated with environmental degradation and human rights abuses, as well as to deny a source of financing to those involved in these unethical activities. Tiffany's leadership on these issues also serves as a model for other jewelers and applies both political and market pressure to those who would seek to profit from wrongs.

External
Through its annual sales of over US$3 billion, Tiffany exhibits moderate market power in the fairly fragmented jewelry market. Tiffany's approach to integrating and, therefore, securing its supply chain has further limited its ability to use its market power to change industry practices beyond its immediate partnership with Kennecott's Bingham Canyon Mine. By sourcing exclusively from a single mine, the company is rewarding good practices locally, but limiting its ability to incentivize others to change their own practices. Bingham was already using best practices and so, in contrast to Walmart's approach of bringing suppliers along by working with them to improve their processes, Tiffany's approach has the rather ironic effect of reducing their ability to affect change. Where Tiffany exhibits a much greater capacity to govern is through its institution-building, vocal leadership, and acting as a role model for others in the industry.

Donations and Strategic Investment Tiffany's leadership extends the company's political influence while strengthening its social license to operate through its philanthropic arm, the Tiffany Foundation. Established in 2000, the foundation currently supports a wide variety of projects—including programs to restore areas surrounding abandoned mines, efforts to design programs that maximize the benefits of artisanal mining in Sierra Leone, and programs to combat HIV/AIDS in Botswana (Tiffany 2012).

We see evidence of the company's conservationist approach to environmentalism in Tiffany's philanthropic activities outside of mining as well. For example, the Tiffany Foundation donated US$1 million to purchase the land next to the famous Hollywood sign to spare the woodlands from development. In Tiffany's statement, Kowalski states that "the Hollywood Sign ... cannot be separated from its untrammeled setting of hiking trails and wildlife corridors. Preserving both means that future generations may gaze on this parkland and know the California frontier before freeways and urbanization" (*USA Today* 2010). This conservationist agenda, espoused and funded by Tiffany, parallels many of the statements directly confronting environmental issues in mining and is indicative of the company's basic underlying assumptions about what constitutes effective environmental policy.

Lobbying, Advocacy, and Issue Framing Tiffany has established itself as a vocal proponent of responsible sourcing for jewelers. Through both the Tiffany Foundation and its CEO, the company advocates for industry change in mainstream media.

The *Washington Post* ad calling for the reform of US mining regulations is a political strategy usually reserved for environmental and social rights groups. In this open letter to the US Forest Service, Kowalski argued that "opponents' fears are justified," referring to the opposition of numerous environmental organizations, dozens of local businesses, and a handful of local politicians to the proposed Rock Creek silver and copper mine in Montana. It was the first time that a jeweler of Tiffany's size and stature had taken a public stance calling for reforms to mining regulation, and this did not go unnoticed by civil society or industry groups. The battle between the Rock Creek mine developers and opponents is ongoing, but the Tiffany ad certainly helped place the fight front and center in policy conversations.

Along with the company's activism targeting policy reform, Tiffany took a strong stance aimed at other jewelers as commercial consumers of gold when it called for a boycott of gold and silver from the proposed Pebble Lake Mine. But the company's vocal position on responsible mining goes beyond gold boycotts and newspaper advertisements. Through public appearances, interviews, and information on its website, Tiffany advocates for "no-go" zones for mining operations, which are essentially places that are too environmentally or culturally sensitive to host mine development regardless of the scale or practices employed (Tiffany 2012). The company has advocated for policy reform regarding the reclamation of abandoned mines, reform of the KPCS to close existing loopholes, respect for human rights through boycotts against gems from Myanmar and diamonds from Zimbabwe, and a moratorium on trading in coral to protect the world's coral reefs (Tiffany 2012).

Creation and Maintenance of Institutions External to the Firm   Tiffany is directly and actively involved in institution-building through its involvement in conferences, workshops, certification institutions, and various other collaborations.

Tiffany helped convene a 2003 multi-stakeholder conference leading to the publication of the 2005 *Framework for Responsible Mining: A Guide to Evolving Standards*, which seeks to establish dialogue between government, civil society, and industry that will eventually evolve into actionable criteria for responsible mining practices moving forward (Miranda, Chambers, and Coumans 2005).[13] Additionally, Tiffany set an important precedent for other jewelers to follow by being the first to sign the Golden Rules.

Tiffany was one of the 14 founding members of the RJC and has been an active and instrumental member of the organization since its inception in 2005. This organization encourages ethical business throughout the industry by certifying members within the jewelry supply chain against its internally developed criteria. As a member of the RJC, Tiffany is monitored for compliance against its Principles and Code of Practices.

The company also supports IRMA, whose membership includes many of the RJC's members, but goes beyond industry players to include NGOs, labor groups, and communities impacted by mining. IRMA's wider representation—and, therefore, increased input legitimacy—should allow the organization to define best practices in the mining industry, and its goals include certifying individual mines. However, this wider representation has meant that the initiative remains in the planning stages and is not officially up and running to date, which obviously degrades its output legitimacy.

Progress on all the initiatives that Tiffany engages with is possible through its partnerships with various NGOs, which include Earthworks and Oxfam with their NDG campaign, and SeaWeb, a marine conservation NGO, with its "Too Precious to Wear" campaign (Tiffany 2012). The Tiffany Foundation provided financial support to a feasibility study for fair trade diamonds and gold in cooperation with FLO and ARM (Madison Dialogue 2007).[14]

The company collaborates with numerous governmental and nongovernmental organizations by participating in and lending public support to their programs. For example, they participate in the Carbon Disclosure Project, the EPA's Climate Leaders program, and the US Coral Reef Conservation Act along with Appendix II of the Convention on International Trade in Endangered Species (CITES) to end trade in coral.

Participation in institution-building offers numerous benefits for the company. While participation may grant the company another dimension of product differentiation by branding Tiffany as a conscientious company, it is perhaps not the greatest benefit to the company. Possibly of greater advantage, Tiffany's engagement gives the company a seat at the table from which to voice its needs and its concerns with any of the proposed elements of the initiative. It also brings environmental groups into their space, giving these groups a stake in the firm's creation of standards. Such benefits allow the company to control the narrative and, in this way, they reestablish their structural power within these industry-based regimes.

By using the instrumental power available to the firm, internal institutional entrepreneurs have altered the political landscape, not only securing the firm's position in the market by reducing its exposure to risk, but also expanding the opportunities for future political action. By creating systems internal and external to the firm, they have lowered the relative cost of compliance with future issues that may arise from within their supply chain. By mainstreaming CSR norms throughout the company and its supply chain, they embed these norms within the corporate culture of the company. By creating and strengthening their CSR department, they raise the profile of social and environmental concerns within the company's operations and establish operating procedures to deal with them. Although such opportunities could always contract, this suggests that continued activist pressure, even in different issue areas, offers a mechanism by which to expand opportunities for institutional entrepreneurs and ratchet up constructive political engagement by the private sector.

Conclusion

Specialty jewelers have created an industry-led, second-party certification initiative in response to the political issues they face throughout their supply chains. For these jewelers, it is predominantly about risk mitigation. So they have organized individually and collectively in an attempt to control the narrative and the non-state institution-building process. By leading the push for industry certification, lead firms and industry groups ensure that their individual reputations along with the shared reputation of the jewelry industry is upheld; that all specialty jewelers are subject to the same standards and related costs; that there are ample quantities of "responsible" gold available; that they forestall any future campaign or state-led pressure; that they maintain control over the processes of agenda-setting and rule-making; and that they are not inadvertently contributing to socially or environmentally irresponsible practices. However, we still needed to explain why Tiffany has pushed so hard while many of the others were slower to respond and less deeply engaged.

Tiffany had strong leadership that cared about the issues and was in a position to implement the directives. The company has taken a very proactive route to engaging with these issues, seemingly because of the intensity of the potential risks to its business model as well as the environmental ethos espoused by a leader with deep influence within the organization. Tiffany clearly has a committed leader in Michael Kowalski, who has the power within the organization to direct the company in ways that align with his assessment of the situation. He not only holds positions within the company that allow him to push chosen policies through, but serves a company that, because of its intangible value, requires the CEO and board of directors to place reputation management at the forefront of their managerial remit.

Once the company committed to a deep engagement, it became a rational strategy, in a market sense, to advocate for strict regulations of mining, because the company would benefit from an elevated reputation of the jewelry industry as a whole, enjoy a wider array of options for sourcing, and force the rest of the industry to pay the slight premium involved in ethical sourcing instead of reaping the benefits of lower prices from using lower standards. In this way, the company levels the playing field, albeit on a higher level.

Through the company leadership's efforts to leverage the firm's power and shape the institutional landscape, Tiffany realigns its practices and interests with the prevailing, post-campaign market forces. The crisis Tiffany experienced with "conflict diamonds" set the stage for their engagement with "dirty gold," enabling the company to extend in-house processes that were already put in place; the opportunity window was wider than it would have been without this history. And through its leadership role on "dirty gold," Tiffany seems to have expanded the opportunities for corporate political engagement with future issues.

While the business case for action is readily apparent for both the ethical and specialty jewelers, this was not the case for the diversified jewelers. The next chapter looks at the diversified category and explores how and why Walmart has become an unlikely leader in tackling "dirty gold."

5

Walmart and the Diversified Jewelers

I arrive in Bentonville, Arkansas (pop. 40,000 or so) late morning, mid-August. The temperature is pushing 104°F. The taxi driver from the airport is my first inquisitor. Detecting an accent not native to the southern United States, he asks if I'm Irish. Not too many Canadians get down to these parts, I guess. The next question: why am I in town? He already knows the answer though. I'm here for the same reason most outsiders come to this out of the way little southern city: Walmart. When I tell him so, he nods knowingly.

I check into the hotel and ask the front desk for directions to Walmart headquarters. They point down the road, asking if I need a taxi. To their clear surprise, I decline. I start walking. A large Ford pickup pulls over to ask if I need help, assuming my car's broken down. I'm fine, I say, and off they drive, clearly bemused. A short while later, the sidewalk ends. It's just trucks and cars now. I walk on the shoulder of the road.

I didn't see any other pedestrians that whole day. There certainly wasn't public transit. I wondered if the sidewalks were simply there for show. Perhaps because somebody figured a town was supposed to have them? Either way, Bentonville was a charming town but, in stark contrast to the Bay Area, it seemed a surprising birthplace for the largest corporate-led sustainability initiative the world has ever known.

Walmart falls into the diversified jeweler category, which includes many of the largest retailers of gold jewelry by value sold annually and, as a group, their share of the market is growing. Since the 2008 financial crisis and the dip in luxury sales, there has been a movement toward consolidation in the industry. The diversified jewelers, who tend to sell products with a lower price point, have been the main beneficiaries of this change in the market (Industry analyst, personal communication, November 22, 2011).

As with the previous cases, I begin by revisiting the expectations for diversified jewelers before focusing in on Walmart as the, perhaps unlikely, leader.

Opportunities Profile and Expectations for Diversified Jewelers

From an opportunities perspective, we should not expect diversified jewelers to actively respond to civil society contestation. They have a low exposure to risk and low reliance on jewelry as part of their overall market strategy; therefore, any latent institutional entrepreneurs within these firms should have a difficult time mobilizing firm resources for engaging in the politics of gold. The high complexity of their supply chains and the high price sensitivity of their customers mean that complying with the demands of civil society activists would be much more costly for the firm than for specialty or ethical jewelers. These companies tend to be publicly traded as well, so managers would need to justify these expenditures to a board of directors overseeing resource use. Overall, we should not expect diversified jewelers to be very deeply engaged in the politics of gold—with any observed variation most likely due to variation along the institutional dimension of the model.

Expectation: Low Level of Engagement and Weak Commitments

The pattern among diversified jewelers largely conforms to these expectations. For the most part, none have opted for the robust, third-party certification, only two of the largest US diversified jewelers have opted

Table 5.1
Opportunities profile for diversified jewelers

Economic dimensions	Institutional dimensions
Exposure to risk	**Corporate culture**
• Level of branding—*Low*	• CSR artifacts—*Mixed*
• Reliance on product—*Low*	• CSR espoused beliefs—*Mixed*
Cost of compliance	**Leadership structure**
• Complexity of supply—High	• Ownership structure—*Public*
• Price sensitivity of consumers—High	• Position of institutional entrepreneurs—*Mixed*

Table 5.2

Profile of non-state initiatives for diversified jewelers

	No Dirty Gold (NDG)	Second-party (RJC)	Third-party (FT/FM)
Argos (UK)	✗	✓	✗
Amazon	✗	✗	✗
Costco	✗	(✓July 2011—not yet certified)	✗
HSC	✗	✗	✗
JCPenney	✓	✓	✗
Macy's	✗	✗	✗
QVC	✓	✗	✗
Sears (and Kmart)	✓	✗	✗
Target	✓	✗	✗
Walmart	✓	✗	✗

for the industry-led certification, and it is a mixed bag as far as signing the Golden Rules. However, there is more diversity in responses evident in this group and not every case meets the expectations of the model. JCPenney and Costco were initially slow to respond to the campaign but, after continued hounding by the NDG activists, JCPenney has signed the Golden Rules and both have opted for RJC membership. Their engagement with the issues has largely stopped there, however. The most intriguing case is Walmart because, despite the low exposure to risk, the company has been very engaged in the politics surrounding its gold jewelry. After a slow start, company representatives have attended a number of significant stakeholder meetings, funded various initiatives and, most surprisingly, launched their own line of ethical jewelry. By showing significant political engagement despite an apparent lack of exposure to risk, Walmart is by far the leader from the diversified category—hence our focus on the company. Contrast this with Macy's—a company that does have a well-branded reputation, albeit not as far as its jewelry. But Macy's is also a company that, to date, has not engaged at all with the politics of gold and has even refused to sign the Golden Rules. Macy's generally enjoys higher margins than Walmart, so it appears to once again come down to differences in corporate culture and leadership as the difference between engagement and resistance. Turning now to Walmart, the largest gold jewelry retailer in the world,[1] I'll attempt to explain why the company has engaged in an issue against the expectations of many—and seemingly against the expectations of the opportunities model.

Company Profile—Walmart

Walmart is an extremely powerful company. Decisions made in its boardrooms have the potential to impact millions of people around the globe. It is far and away the world's largest retailer and one of the world's biggest companies; directly employing 2.2 million people and operating almost 11,000 stores under 65 different names in 28 countries. In fiscal year 2015, these stores served over 260 million customers per week, to whom they sold US$482.2 billion worth of stuff (Walmart 2015).[2]

The company operates three different formats of retail space in the US: "supercenters," discount stores, and neighborhood markets—in descending order of average size. In 2009, there are 2,612 "supercenters," 891 discount stores, 602 Sam's Club stores, and 153 neighborhood markets in the US, in addition to online retailing through its website. The company owns 106 distribution centers and 26 Sam's Club distribution centers, as well as utilizing 15 third-party distributors—and this is just to service the US market (Datamonitor 2009b, 6). In addition to these impressive numbers, Walmart has since added almost 500 stores internationally—per year. Its merchandise consists of both branded and private labels in a wide array of product categories including apparel, groceries, electronics, entertainment, home furnishings, and health and wellness (Datamonitor 2009b, 6). The company sources these goods from an estimated 100,000 suppliers across the globe.

Company History
The company's history and underlying numbers indicate that its core business model is based on high volumes, low profit margins, and continuous expansion. The history of the company is well documented. Sam Walton grew up in the American South during the Great Depression, a time when money was obviously hard to come by. Sam worked in the discount retail industry, working for various large companies before

eventually becoming a franchisee of the Ben Franklin retail chain. But he had a grander plan. He figured that with adequate scale, he could insist on low prices from suppliers and pass these savings on to his customers. He also bet that small, rural communities could sustain the volumes necessary to support this business model. He was right. In 1962, Sam opened Walmart Discount City in Rogers, Arkansas. Within five years he had opened 17 more. From there, Walmarts began popping up in small towns across the southern US, eventually reaching both coasts and beyond.

Wal-mart Stores, Inc. (its official corporate name) was established in 1969 and went public almost immediately, listing on the New York Stock Exchange in 1972. In the 1980s, Walmart diversified into grocery and warehouse formats with Sam's Club opening in 1983, based on the concept initiated by Costco's ancestor, the Price Company of California (Datamonitor 2009b, 8). The 1990s saw rapid expansion as Walmart purchased wholesale distributors in the US and retail chains internationally, including Woolco in Canada, Wertkauf and Interspar in Germany, Lojas Americanas in Brazil, and ASDA in the UK while establishing joint ventures with Cifra in Mexico (Datamonitor 2009b, 8). There was further expansion through 2005 as the company bought a large stake in Seiyu in Japan, bought Supermercados Amigo in Puerto Rico and Bompreco in Brazil outright, and opened 107 new international stores including 2 in Brazil, 22 in Canada, 8 in China, 2 in Germany, 3 in South Korea, 59 in Mexico, 2 in Puerto Rico, and 9 in the UK (Datamonitor 2009b, 8). In the last five years, Walmart has bought, wholly or partially, hundreds more stores in China, Brazil, the US, and Chile (Datamonitor 2009b, 9).

Where Jewelry Fits into the Business Model
Despite being one of the largest jewelry retailers in the US with sales hovering around US$3 billion (National Jeweler 2016), a quick calculation shows that jewelry accounts for significantly less than 1% of Walmart's total revenue. Jewelry has historically seemed almost an afterthought to the company, with display cases nestled inconspicuously among a maze of aisles filled with thousands of apparel items. The company does not publicize its jewelry product lines, perhaps because the economic downturn

has taken a bite out of jewelry sales, as it has done for all categories of discretionary items.

Walmart may be anticipating economic opportunity in the jewelry market, however, as it has been reported that the company is actively moving its jewelry displays to more prominent locations at the front of its stores, improving the training of its jewelry sales people in their retail locations, and moving its jewelry operations from Bentonville to New York (Graff 2009).[3]

Regardless, Walmart limits itself to the retail node of the supply chain, mostly selling popular brands of fashion jewelry as opposed to engagement pieces.

History of Interaction with Civil Society—from Crisis to Response

Crisis—Labor, Katrina, Environment

To recap our previous case studies: with Brilliant Earth, the market for ethical jewelry was really opened up by the conflict diamonds controversy, and the company stepped into fill this gap, further expanding the market through its advocacy and sourcing of ethical gems and metals. Tiffany's business case is based on risk management. The company was caught off guard with the conflict diamonds controversy, but responded by playing to its strengths. By the time gold came along as a concern, Tiffany was prepared for it.

In the case of Walmart, beginning in the late 1990s the company began facing increasing scrutiny from a diverse range of civil society groups, coalescing in a multi-pronged attack on the company. The company that had become the poster child for the evils of corporate America brought much of this on itself by ignoring controversial labor issues. As the company grew, so did the allegations against it. Coalitions opposing Walmart's expansion emerged and deepened. The company's history with these issues is key to understanding its response to the politics of gold. The allegations fall into three broad categories of discontent: labor issues, local economy, and sprawl.

Labor   Labor issues have always been the foremost concern of civil society groups targeting the firm, including allegations that the company pays its workers exceedingly low wages, employs a disproportionate number of part-time workers to avoid paying benefits, outsources jobs by sourcing an increasing proportion of goods from overseas, and engages in systematic gender discrimination.

The accusation is that Walmart pays lower wages than comparable businesses. The company disputes this. Because definitive evidence is lacking and often biased, it is difficult to pass judgment on this issue in any straightforward way.[4] Then there is the charge that the company employs a disproportionate number of part-time workers to avoid paying them the benefits legislated for full-time employees.[5] The effect is a transfer of responsibility from the company to the state as the low-income workers may well be entitled to benefits paid for by taxpayers. Through leaked company documents, the news received international attention (Greenhouse and Barbaro 2005). Unions have rallied against the company for "outsourcing jobs," claiming that by sourcing labor-intensive goods from overseas suppliers, notably China, Walmart is gutting the American manufacturing sector (Jamieson 2012). And the final labor allegation is that Walmart has systematically discriminated against women at every level in the company, consistently paying them less money and promoting them less often than their male counterparts—charges that brought the largest gender discrimination lawsuit in history (Heal 2008; Sage and Stempel 2010; Goudreau 2010).[6] As a result of the company's labor practices, Walmart has experienced increasing opposition to further expansion from various labor groups.

Local Economy An additional concern is centered on the "Walmart effect," the name given to the economic repercussions of the introduction of a Walmart store into a local economy (Fishman 2006). Walmart's ability to bring down consumer prices in all categories is well documented (Basker 2005). The company achieves this by using its purchasing power to squeeze the profit margins of suppliers by rewarding them with large contracts (Javorcik et al. 2006). These sometimes ruthless bargaining tactics are well documented through interviews with former, albeit disgruntled, suppliers (Fishman 2003). Through logistics, scale, and strategy, Walmart has brought down consumer prices and changed the face of the retail sector.

While the effects on local economies are complex and contested, these lower prices have certainly caused many small- and medium-sized local businesses to close shop because they cannot compete with the market power of Walmart. The result has been increasing opposition from local business to the introduction of big box retailers into their communities.

Sprawl   Suburban sprawl is high on the list of environmentalist concerns. The idea is that Walmart superstores, distribution centers, and parking lots take up hundreds of thousands of acres of land, often previously zoned for agricultural use or productive wetlands. Walmart owns thousands of the largest stores most shoppers will ever step into, dozens of distribution centers in which one could fit dozens of stores, and expansive networks of parking lots and feeder roads. It's a major landowner indeed. Add to this the roads and traffic created for shoppers to reach their discount destination and the concerns of environmentalists become clear. The result has been increasing opposition from local environmentalists to the expansion of Walmart.

The company certainly disputes many of these allegations, and I am not going to try to evaluate each of these claims in any great detail. The point is that Walmart has been under fire from a number of societal actors—including labor, local business, and environmental groups—on a number of issues and this has forced the historically recalcitrant company to change its policies and practices.

We have seen that for Tiffany, the crisis moment occurred with the conflict diamonds controversy. For Walmart, this crisis occurred in the early 21st century as the company continued to face persistent criticism and lawsuits, mostly over the workforce-related issues. In addition to the gender discrimination lawsuit mentioned above, the company also faced a number of shareholder resolutions on the aforementioned labor, equal employment, and environmental issues. While one such case resulted in Walmart changing its policy on employment discrimination based on sexual orientation (Vogel 2005, 64), the deeper crisis did not occur until Walmart's business model for growth was challenged directly.

The company was facing increasing resistance to its expansion into urban areas (Mui 2007; Heal 2008). Having conquered the competition in the race to set up shop in smaller, rural communities, Walmart now needed to focus its expansion on urban areas and overseas. Its efforts, however, were increasingly facing resistance from local community groups and city councilors. The company encountered staunch opposition to opening stores in Los Angeles, Chicago, New York, and Washington, DC, in the United States (Heal 2008, 131). In Canada, the city of Guelph, Ontario, put up an unexpectedly strong front, while Vancouver has turned down multiple attempts by Walmart to enter the market.[7] As Geoffrey Heal has noted, many jurisdictions were passing urban planning bylaws that appeared to be tailored for the sole purpose of keeping Walmart and other "big box" retailers out of the market by placing limits on the number of employees, square footage, and product diversification a business can have (Heal 2008, 130). The opposition was based precisely on the grievances laid out at the beginning of this section—concerns over labor issues, local business competitiveness, and suburban sprawl.

This constituted a threat to the company's core business model, which we have seen is based on expansion. If we look at Walmart's key financials, the growth rate of the company has been phenomenal. Gross revenues grew from about US$280 billion in 2005 to about US$374 billion in 2008, US$440 billion in 2012, and a whopping US$469 billion in 2013 (Factiva 2013b; Datamonitor 2009b). Profit margins have remained stable around a very modest 3.52% (five-year average), if anything shrinking slightly over the same period (Factiva 2013b). The extraordinary growth, therefore, is based on aggressive expansion of the company into new regions and markets. Thus, any threat to this expansion is a serious existential threat to the company. There was clearly a business case for engaging with societal demands and a pragmatic response was required. For reasons we will explore later in the chapter, the company chose to champion sustainability.

Walmart's efforts to incorporate sustainability goals into its business model fall into two broad categories: improving the eco-efficiency of its operations and cooperating with external groups from the public and private spheres. We will look at these approaches briefly, as they will help us understand the ways in which the company later mobilized around the issues of gold.

Eco-efficiency in Stores and along Supply Chains   Eco-efficiency initiatives are what are commonly referred to in the business literature as "win-win" solutions to environmental problems. These solutions are based on hunting down wasteful processes and outdated technologies and replacing them with innovative management solutions and cutting-edge technologies. When managers increase the ecological efficiency of their business practices, they also save on operating costs, thereby becoming more "green" *and* more competitive (see, for example, Porter and van der Linde 1995a, 1995b; Porter and Kramer 2002, 2006). Examples from Walmart include fitting doors on the refrigerated food aisles, reducing the energy required to keep the food cool by 70%, and using motion detectors for cabinet lights in 24-hour stores, which cut the time they were on by half (Esty and Winston 2009, 109).

The company is also pushing for increased efficiency along its supply chains, for example, through its plan to reduce the firm's global carbon footprint by 20 million metric tons, or 150 percent of its estimated global carbon footprint growth over the next five years, achieving most of this by asking its approximately 100,000 suppliers to create better products, incorporating sustainability goals into the standing order to make products cheap.

Cooperating with External Actors   Injecting eco-efficiency goals and values into the corporate culture of the firm has paid immediate dividends in terms of opening up space for innovation and cooperation while improving relations with external actors, many of whom used to be ardent critics.

The company is working with the public sector, including signing a memorandum of understanding in 2008 with the Chinese government to raise environmental targets for its suppliers in China (Dauvergne and Lister 2010a, 158). Another example can be seen in the company's agreement with the South Carolina Department of Agriculture to promote locally grown produce (Datamonitor 2009b, 10).

NGOs also seem to be buying in. "By challenging itself and its supply chain, we really believe that Walmart can create a race to the top for environmental benefits," said Gwen Ruta of the Environmental Defense Fund (EDF) in a 2006 interview (Associated Press 2006a, 2006b). In fact, EDF has recently opened up a project office in Bentonville to be closer to the company. "We think their actions demonstrate they are serious about sustainability and the environment," said EDF Executive Vice President David Yarnold. "Being geographically close to Walmart will increase the number of opportunities to advise them on environmental issues" (Associated Press 2006a, 2006b).

The Worldwide Fund for Nature (WWF) is working with Walmart on "phasing out illegal and unwanted wood sources from its supply chain and increasing the proportion of wood sourced from credibly certified sources for US stores" (Market Watch 2008; WWF 2008). Conservation International (CI) has become a partner on many initiatives, including jewelry, and the company hired former Sierra Club president Adam Werbach to launch a sustainability initiative aimed at employees. In fact, Walmart's enthusiasm and actions have altered thinking about the company so much that one prominent activist NGO has apparently decided to not campaign against the company as they no longer make an attractive target (Bendell and Cohen 2006).

Much of this support stemming from civil society is because NGOs like EDF see the potentially positive environmental impact Walmart could have through its influence over its suppliers. "We've come to believe through experience that you really can create environmental progress by leveraging corporate purchasing power. And who's got more corporate purchasing power than Walmart?" asks EDF's Gwen Ruta (Associated Press 2006a, 2006b).

Response of Walmart to "Dirty Gold"

Besides the fact that Walmart had a history of tuning out societal demands on a number of issues, the activists didn't think Walmart customers would much care about the issues. As one activist from Earthworks explained to me, the NDG campaigners were not confident that they could actually muster any real impact on consumer behavior over issues surrounding "dirty gold"—with Walmart or anybody else. While the activists had some doubts about the mid- to high-end jewelry customers, they were even less confident that they would be able to gather a critical mass of Walmart customers willing to interrogate the retail giant about its sourcing. So the campaign only set out to target Walmart halfheartedly. They did not want to risk losing any credibility, and thus the leverage of threat, by hitting companies that they did not think would budge (NDG, personal communication, September 20, 2010). If the company didn't move and there was no bottom-line impact, the jig was up.

They also had very limited resources. The campaign started with a very small niche set of groups, with Earthworks taking the reins initially.

Earthworks was itself just a small organization and this is why they were adamant about getting Oxfam on board. They needed to get a big NGO "of note" and Oxfam had the profile (NDG, personal communication, September 20, 2010). Even once they had Oxfam's name behind them, they still felt they "were much too small and needed to be focused" (NDG, personal communication, September 20, 2010). The idea was to concentrate on the high-end jewelry specialists and hopefully get one or two gold companies on board—or better yet a diversified mining company so they could transfer the impact to other metals as well—and then the entire mining sector. They didn't feel they could get, or really even need, Walmart.

So the NDG campaign against Walmart consisted of sending a few letters. They tried their hand at limited public shaming by including the company's name in lists of laggards on their own site, sites of other networked environmental groups, and any media source that would publish the information.

For years NDG sent letters to Bentonville, calling on Walmart to endorse their campaign and adhere to its principles. The group never got a response, except for one from the communications department (Shin et al. 2008). This minimal response was hardly surprising given the company's history of unresponsiveness on other issues.

The NDG campaigners were not alone in seeing Walmart as just too big to target. Nobody really had a strategy to get Walmart to the table using consumer or public pressure. Despite the company's enormous jewelry sales, the campaigners did not see it as a large enough proportion of its business to be able to leverage (NDG, personal communication, September 20, 2010).

However, the modest campaign pressure from NDG coincided with the intense pressure Walmart was facing on labor initiatives. Lee Scott, the CEO of Walmart at the time, had an epiphany: the company could use its purchasing power to do some good. And so Walmart launched its sustainability initiative, creating 14 sustainability networks—and jewelry was one of them.[8] Each network had to internally set up a goal for achieving sustainability results. This all had little if anything to do with the NDG campaign, which continued to send letters and continued to receive no response. Until, all of a sudden, the phone rang and it was Walmart calling.

The NDG campaign ran a full-page ad in the *New York Times* listing leaders and laggards—and Walmart was on the "companies lagging behind" list.[9] Almost immediately they received that call, and it was Dee Breazeale, Walmart senior vice president, on the other end. Not only that—she was asking them to come down to Bentonville and talk. Pretty much the last thing they had expected. And so, naturally, the campaigners went to Arkansas and began working with Walmart. So what made Walmart respond after all these years? "I am convinced that if they never had the sustainability initiative, they would have never played," says one of the NDG campaign leaders. "Whether somebody could have gotten them … maybe, but not us" (NDG, personal communication, September 20, 2010).

NDG was just too small and lacked the necessary leverage. What turned Walmart was the pressure it was facing on labor issues. "If we ran the ad and there was none of that going on, we would not have gotten the phone call—it wouldn't have happened" (NDG, personal communication, September 20, 2010).

The immediate result of this collaboration was that Walmart publicly joined the NDG campaign by signing on to the Golden Rules in 2007. Soon after signing, the company partnered with CI and launched the "Love, Earth" line of higher-end, sustainable jewelry. Each piece of jewelry comes with a batch number that allows the customer to go online, enter the number, and trace the item all the way back to the mine where it originated. The line features 10-karat gold and sterling silver items at Walmart while Sam's Club carries 14-karat gold and sterling silver—all of which have "earthy" themes like "starfish" and the "tree of life" (Shin et al. 2008). All the materials are responsibly sourced—as defined by the company—from Rio Tinto and Newmont mines (Adler 2008; Smith and Crawford 2012). The plan was to add a collection of ethically sourced diamonds and to have 10% of all jewelry it sells coming from a traceable source by 2010, a goal that the company has not only met, but has exceeded (Adler 2008; Walmart 2010). Eventually, the company claims, all of its jewelry will meet these standards (Shin et al. 2008).

The "Love, Earth" line has been popular with consumers and controversial within the NGO community (NDG, personal communication, September 20, 2010). The media has picked up on both the praise and caution expressed by various groups, including NDG.[10] The charge is that

Walmart is overselling the "responsible" nature of the mining practices, inflating the attributes of their sourcing when there has been neither an agreed definition of what constitutes responsible mining nor third-party verification that the company is even meeting its own standards.[11] In response, the Walmart spokesperson's statement at the time was as follows:

> Walmart's objective is to have a long-term, fundamental and positive influence on the jewelry supply chain by selling jewelery that is made from precious metals and gems that are produced following Walmart's supplier standards and the Jewelry Sustainability Value Network's environmental and social sourcing criteria. (Martin 2008)

The criteria Walmart came up with are closely aligned with current best practices in the industry and, with the help of Assheton Carter from CI, were based on the NDG's Golden Rules pledge (Smith and Crawford 2012). Much of the criticism is based on how the criteria were decided upon. Walmart needed some standard to base its "Love, Earth" line of sustainable jewelry on and this standard had to be compatible with a business climate of needing things urgently (NDG, personal communication, September 20, 2010). According to campaigners, the mining sites that Walmart sources from are relatively good, but still have issues (NDG, personal communication, September 19, 2010). Walmart needed solutions fast and, the fact is, all mining sites have issues. If there are no agreed-upon criteria by which to judge good sites from bad ones, then there are going to be disputes. With the lack of agreed-upon criteria in place, Walmart and a number of environmental groups, including NDG, compromised and hashed out the sourcing criteria Walmart would incorporate into its new line of jewelry.

On top of its "Love, Earth" line, Walmart participates in IRMA, although in practice this amounts to some financial support but not actively taking a seat at the table (NDG, personal communication, September 19, 2010).

It must be said as well that the company has begun distancing itself from NDG since the campaign recently released a "report card" grading companies on their response that included what Walmart considers to be factual inaccuracies (CI, personal communication, September 18, 2010).

We will now return to the model and see if it can shed more light on the company's response.

Opportunities Model Applied to the Diversified Firm—Walmart

Economic Dimensions

Exposure to Risk   While we have seen that a significant proportion of Brilliant Earth's and Tiffany's value is intangible, the same is not true for Walmart. Walmart is noticeably absent from *Businessweek*'s Top 100 Global Brands annual report—perhaps surprising for the world's largest retailer and the only retail company to mingle with the energy giants in company value rankings.[12]

There are three fairly intuitive and very connected reasons for this. First, Walmart is a pure retailer. It does not design or manufacture goods. The "private brands" it does sell are made by small, local contractors in the region where they are retailed, and then sold at a discount—precisely on account of their lack of brand value. The company's model is not based on consumer preference for Walmart goods, but on consumer preference for cheaper goods. Second, Walmart's value is in the infrastructure underlying its business model, which facilitates the delivery of cheaper goods than its competitors. With 8,600 enormous retail locations worldwide, hundreds of colossal distribution centers, thousands of transport trucks, and the most advanced private distribution network in the world, Walmart's infrastructure has very tangible value. Third, and connected to its business model and logistic dominance, is Walmart's market power. Walmart has the power to set the prices at which it will purchase goods from suppliers and then pass on the savings to consumers. It is economies of scale and purchasing power together that add to Walmart's immense, tangible value.

Walmart is extremely diversified in its product and service offerings. The company sells more than 9,000 lines of merchandise, representing every merchandise category (Walmartstores.com). The implication is that Walmart is not heavily invested or dependent on any one product category, including gold jewelry. The fact that it does not rely heavily on any single product category increases its market power and decreases its risk.

Walmart is adept at mobilizing its buying power in the supply chains it dominates as well as transferring risk upstream (Dauvergne and Lister 2010a). A good example of this risk transfer is the way in which Walmart transfers ownership of products between itself and its key partners up and down the supply chain, namely, its suppliers and its customers. Not only does Walmart bargain intensely with its suppliers for favorable terms (allegedly calling them collect to do so) , the company has arrangements with many of its suppliers by which Walmart's legal possession of a good is initiated when the barcode is scanned at the Walmart checkout (Heal 2008, 115). Amazingly, this means that Walmart's obligation to pay the supplier is only activated once a store has already sold the good to the final customer and taken possession of the wholesale cost plus additional markup. While this does not necessarily affect its exposure and dependence on gold as a product category, it demonstrates the power of Walmart over its suppliers and gives an indication of the ease with which it could shed a product line or even product category if it proved to be a security risk.

Notably, no diversified jeweler, including Walmart, has actually dropped gold jewelry due to the threat posed by political controversy. All diversified jewelers were slow to respond to support industry-wide initiatives and reluctant to support them since the political and reputational threat of the "dirty gold" framing does not threaten their core business interests.

Cost of Compliance   Walmart could not initially be so confident about containing its exposure to these issues through its supply chains. This is not to suggest Walmart lacks knowledge of its supply chains. Supply chain management and logistics constitute the major strengths of the company and it's from here they draw much of their competitive advantage. Walmart has managed its exceedingly complex chains by pioneering the movement to bar code scanners, using real-time links with suppliers so they can replenish stocks without communicating with Walmart management, and using the largest computer in the US outside the Pentagon to link its supplier network (Heal 2008, 115). Walmart moves millions of products daily along one of the largest private distribution systems in the world, connecting about 200 million customers per week with the goods of an estimated 100,000 suppliers (Walmartstores.com). The company does this using 40 regional distribution centers, averaging one million square feet each, operating 24 hours a day and seven days a week, to fill the trailers of 7,000 18-wheel transport trucks (Walmartstores.com). However, despite these logistical marvels, knowing the environmental footprint and social impact of all of its products was never part of its remit. The company has been learning on the fly.

When the issue of "dirty gold" arose, Walmart was in no position to verify its supplies. As with most of its products, the company did not factor the environmental and social impacts of gold into sourcing decisions. Its core area of concern was retail, its core metric, price.

When CEO Lee Scott decided that Walmart would not be caught off guard again, as it had been with the fallout from the labor issues, he wanted to know what the next big storm brewing could be. The company held discussions with Conservation International (CI), a moderate environmental NGO with whom Walmart shares a board member, and discussed what types of challenges it may face on this front and how it could counteract any future threats that might emanate from them (CI, personal communication, September 18, 2010).

The initial concern of Walmart was the potential backlash it may face from the effect of Walmart stores on small businesses—the corporate giant undercutting prices and driving the "Mom and Pop" operated retailers out of business (CI, personal communication, September 18, 2010). The people at CI disagreed. They felt that Walmart was most exposed through its complex global supply chains and its potential for negative social and environmental impacts—and, of course, the negative attention this could potentially bring to the company (CI, personal communication, September 18, 2010). The result was that Walmart began working with CI on mapping its supply chains in terms of exposing the potential for risks.

CI was not the only large environmental organization working with Walmart on supply chain issues. As mentioned earlier, EDF, one of the largest environmental NGOs in the US, was also on board—and also has a board connection to Walmart. EDF worked with the company to help develop sustainability "scorecards" for its thousands of suppliers, including the estimated 30,000 in China (EDF 2010).

The customers for diversified jewelers tend to be more sensitive to pricing than consumers within the ethical and specialty jewelry markets. Walmart tends to compete with other large discount retailers. As such, Walmart's major competitors in this market are Target, Safeway, Sears, JCPenney, Kroger, Tesco, Carrefour, Metro, Costco, Amazon.com, and CVS Caremark—only some of which sell a significant amount of gold jewelry (Datamonitor 2009b, 21). As with most of their product lines, those in competition for consumers of gold jewelry compete largely on price.

The significance of this for our study is that these firms operate at very high volumes with very small profit margins. Walmart manages to be successful through sheer volume and manages continuous growth through expansion. Its unparalleled market power allows the company to impose its will up the supply chain, squeezing suppliers for the best price and passing on these savings to its price-conscious clientele. These tight margins leave very little room for absorbing additional overhead costs and even less opportunity for cost sharing with end-use customers. If the price of comparable jewelry rises above that of its discount competitors, Walmart can expect to lose that business. This is not to say the world's largest retailer could not afford to absorb the cost for particular product categories, but it demonstrates that incorporating avoidable costs into the price of a product runs counter to Walmart's business model. As one Walmart executive remarked, "At Walmart, you can't just spend money and not justify it" (Walmart, personal communication, August 16, 2011).

The fact that Target, Sears, JCPenney, Macy's, and Amazon, who all sell large quantities of gold jewelry under comparable business models, have responded much more passively to the issue of "dirty gold" suggests that the business case for Walmart's response was not enough to account for its engagement. For a complete understanding, the analysis must consider additional elements, namely, the emerging culture of sustainability within the company and its leadership.

Institutional Dimensions

Corporate Culture   As with the previous cases, the corporate culture of diversified jewelers will play a significant role in how they respond to the social and environmental issues brought to them. The corporate culture is a reflection of the customer base and marketing strategy of the firm, but treating culture as an indicator in its own right requires an examination of the artifacts and espoused beliefs of the company (i.e., what they do and what they say).

Walmart represents "middle America" and stays true to its Arkansas roots. Not only are its goods attainable but its ethos stems from bringing the prices of goods down so people can afford more of them. Naturally, this leads to very different strategies from those used by the ethical or specialist jewelers when implementing environmental and social directives. For example, while the customers of ethical or specialist labels are buying the brand and everything it represents, Walmart customers are shopping for price. For Walmart, taking a vocal stance against projects with potentially destructive environmental consequences is obviously a much trickier issue than it is for Brilliant Earth, or even Tiffany. While Tiffany's customers may care about these issues and applaud Tiffany's position on them, Walmart's customers may not feel so strongly about them. Many of Walmart's customers work in heavy industry themselves or know people that do. Not only are they, on average, probably less likely to applaud a vocal stance in opposition of a project that could be construed as a stance against heavy industry, they may actually be strongly against it. Walmart tailors the products each store carries to the local population it serves and so in places like Alaska and Nevada, it equips miners with much of the personal gear they need in their work. It would certainly be a tricky issue to publicly back any initiative that appeared to run counter to its clientele's interests.

So, the images of the ethical brands are actually symbiotic with public campaigns decrying the injustices of mining practices worldwide. It is similarly so with the specialist brands. However, Walmart's efforts to tailor outlets to fit the needs of local, working families do not coexist as neatly with campaigning practices. Plus, any vocal stance from Walmart against large-scale extractive projects may elicit strong disapproval from the local governments that approve these lucrative and tax revenue-generating projects. Walmart would need to weigh this against its desire for these same local governments to approve development of new stores in their jurisdictions. This sort of reasoning could go a long way toward explaining why Walmart is changing its practices on the ground, but keeping a lower profile than most of the specialist and ethical jewelers while doing so.

Another aspect of Walmart's corporate culture is its relative insularity—despite the company's huge geographical reach and influence. Located in Arkansas, Walmart has traditionally sat back and had its suppliers come to them, an approach that could only be effective for a company wielding enormous market power. The company's insularity becomes very apparent when one considers the historical reluctance on Walmart's part to translate this economic power into political power of the visible, instrumental sort. In 1998, Walmart had no lobbying operations in Washington, DC, and the company's political contributions were only around US$140,000 total (VandeHei 2000).[13] The company simply did not want to be overtly involved in politics. When considered alongside the potential credibility gap stemming from its ongoing troubles with labor issues, it seems obvious why Walmart has chosen a path of working behind the scenes on public policy issues.

The core ethos of the company from the very beginning has been "saving people money so they can live better" (Walmartstores.com). The company is famous for its frugality too. Desks are packed tight in the corporate offices and executives fly economy—that is, if it's too far to drive (CI, personal communication, September 18, 2010). Squeeze suppliers, maximize efficiency, and keep the operating costs down—these simple principles guide saving. Clearly, expenditures that do not directly further this lean business model run counter to the company's goals. We could expect CSR initiatives that are not firmly aligned with this business model and do not demonstrate positive returns for the company to fall out of favor quickly.

Walmart has always maintained that improving the purchasing power of its customers is a positive contribution to society. When one considers that the average Walmart customer falls into the lower income strata, there is some truth to this. But once the company sought to add sustainability goals to its philosophy, its potential to make a positive contribution to society beyond profit maximization piqued many onlookers' interest.

Walmart has a dedicated, and some might even say eccentric, corporate culture. The workday starts with a Walmart associate (i.e., staff) cheer, bearing more resemblance to a high school pep rally than a major corporation's staff meeting. When the NDG activists flew down to Bentonville to talk to the company about "dirty gold," they told me that the meeting began in this typical Walmart fashion:

Give me a W!
Give me an A!
Give me an L!

Give me a Squiggly!
Give me an M!
Give me an A!
Give me an R!
Give me a T!
What does that spell?
Walmart!
Who's number one?
The customer! Always!
Now what are we going to do about sustainability?!

While efficiency and frugality as core values could have initially slowed the incorporation of sustainability initiatives into its business model, once Walmart decided to embed its particular vision of sustainability into its values, it really knew how to go about it.

It began with the culture. In consultation with former Sierra Club president Adam Werbach, Walmart has created the Personal Sustainability Project (PSP), asking its employees to make a personal pledge to advance sustainability in their own lives (Esty and Winston 2009, 230). Possibly the largest employee program in the world, it asks its 2.2 million employees to pursue their own sustainability quests that have so far ranged from carpooling to helping local schools create recycling programs (Esty and Winston 2009, 230).

While some might object to such a seemingly apolitical and individualized response to environmental issues, arguing it shifts responsibility from leadership to the employees, one could certainly argue that this initiative could have deeper and longer-lasting impacts than at first appears. Not only is it directly challenging 2.2 million individuals to change some aspect of their lives—and at last count well over 500,000 had participated (Esty and Winston 2009, 230), it is also helping to lay a foundation on which to build a corporate culture around environmental sustainability and innovation.

Even the inner corridors of the Bentonville headquarters have gone from gray-washed walls to bright colors splashed with sustainability slogans. Of course this could be seen as simply as a PR stunt, or a form of "greenwashing" (quite literally in this case). But the Walmart executives and even NGO partners I spoke with argue otherwise. They believe the company's commitment to sustainability runs much deeper:

For us, it's integrated in our business; it is part of our operational decision-making now, and it's here to stay. So this isn't a fad. A lot of people ask: "So is this just something Walmart is doing for PR?"... Well if it is just for PR, it sure is integrated into everything we're doing. ... And I think this has a lot to do with the success. (Walmart, personal communication, August 16, 2011)

The company has systematized its interpretation of sustainability and incorporated it into all aspects of its business by creating 14 "Sustainable Value Networks" (SVNs) that correspond to its broad product categories. The networks consist of both outside consulting from interested parties, hand-picked by the company, and executive salespeople from Walmart who steer the process. Together, they find ways to embed sustainability into their operations. Through the jewelry sustainability network Walmart initiated contact with the people from NDG. So when Walmart responded to NDG, the seeds of sustainability were already planted.

Leadership Structure   Why has Walmart become engaged in these issues while other diversified jewelers have remained silent? Macy's, for example, continues to ignore activist prodding despite appearing at least as vulnerable to the politicization of the market as Walmart and other diversified retailers. Activists who've had contact with these companies feel it once again comes down to the differing corporate cultures and leadership (NDG, personal communication, April 24, 2012). We have seen how a culture of sustainability can be manufactured through contestation and collaboration between business and civil society actors. Can the same be said for leadership? Can leadership be created?

As Fligstein (1990) has argued and as we have seen with our cases, it often takes a crisis situation to dislodge status quo routines and create the opportunity for leadership. The market crisis faced by Walmart, based on slowing profits and crippling resistance to its continuing expansion, demanded a pragmatic response. The shape this response took was dictated by the leadership, all of whom seemed to have had personal awakenings of sorts about the role Walmart might play in moving environmental concerns closer to the center of the business world. Whether this amounted to spin or was sincere and altruistic is an open question that will be explored in more detail in the analysis later in the chapter. For now, suffice it to say that Walmart's new leadership role in environmental sustainability was framed as both pragmatism and strategic altruism. It started at the very top of the leadership hierarchy and trickled down through the organization as operational space and resources were made available for the sustainability drive.

Two members of the Walton family—heirs to the family fortune Walmart built—sit on the board of directors for two of the largest environmental NGOs in the US. During the time of increasing civil society pressure on Walmart over labor and community-level issues, the concurrent decline in profits and opposition to expansion, and the exponential increase in Walmart's lobbying activities, S. Robson "Rob" Walton—grandson of the Walmart founder, and chairman of the board of Walmart since 1992—went scuba diving off the Costa Rican coast with Peter Seligmann, the chairman of the board for CI. They had a discussion and the end result was Rob Walton joining the board of CI (Mui 2007). He was introduced to the sustainability consultant, Jib Ellison, whom he, in turn, introduced to Lee Scott, resulting in many of the new sustainability initiatives that now permeate the company's operations (Gunther 2006). Rob Walton continues in his position of chair at Walmart and has since become the chairman of the board at CI.

Another grandson of Walmart's founder, Sam Rawlings Walton—who does not have close links with the daily operations of the company—sits on the board of trustees of EDF. Both CI and EDF work with Walmart on many initiatives, although officers at EDF made a point to mention that Walton recuses himself whenever the Walmart project comes before the board (Associated Press, July 12, 2006; EDF, personal communication, August 16, 2011).

Lee Scott's awakening to the role Walmart might play in pushing for more sustainable business practices is well documented, but diverges slightly from the scuba diving story. This widely acknowledged version traces Walmart's sustainability initiative back to the catastrophe caused by Hurricane Katrina, as Scott himself outlines in the speech he delivered to 7,000 Walmart managers entitled "Twenty-First Century Leadership," which has itself become a key artifact and contribution to the company's espoused beliefs and operational culture.[14]

Scott was deeply moved by the events and extremely proud of his company's response to help Katrina victims. After meeting with many of the company's critics, including EDF, he realized that he needed to change Walmart's strategy for engaging with the issues that they have "been dealing with historically from a defensive posture" (Scott 2005, 3). Scott went on to summarize the goals set by the company to improve its environmental performance, including cutting energy use by 30%, aiming for 100% renewable energy (from wind farms, solar panels, etc.), creating zero waste, and improving the fuel efficiency of its massive shipping fleet of more than 7,000 trucks—with total investment of US$500 million annually (Scott 2005, 6–7).

Naturally, Scott also lays out the business case for such aggressive expenditures and claims in his speech that this "will make us a more competitive and innovative company," while Esty and Winston (2009, 13) note that "in internal meetings, Lee Scott told Walmart executives that their sustainability efforts would help protect the company's 'license to grow.'" This highlights the close alignment of Walmart's CSR strategies to its business model and explicitly links this about face in the company's engagement with civil society on these issues and the threat the company's business model of aggressive expansion was facing.

The central push to internalize this new green initiative into the very fabric of Walmart's operations occurred when Scott ordered all departments to reach goals for sustainability in-house. Essentially they had to start from scratch. Many of those involved did not even understand the concept of sustainability, let alone have any knowledge of the baselines from which they would be working. As one executive confessed, the first thing they did when given the task of creating sustainability policies for the firm was to go home and "Google" sustainability (Walmart, personal communication, August 16, 2011). However, what they did have going for them was a deep understanding of the Walmart business model and its organizational needs. Therefore, the marching orders were purposely vague to begin with. Team leaders were asked to achieve sustainability "wins," which was shorthand for improvements in environmental or social performance of their product or services focus. So while the directives came from the top, it was the salespeople, managers in charge of normal operations, who were to implement the plan.

Both the individuals as well as their position within the company affect the results. An observation that meets the expectations of the opportunities model is that those SVNs led by personnel in more authoritative positions have progressed more rapidly, seemingly experiencing less pushback from middle management as they roll out initiatives (Walmart, personal communication, August 16, 2011).

In the case of Walmart's jewelry operations, those advocating change found an internal champion in Dee Breazeale. I met with Breazeale in a steakhouse in Bentonville. I waited at a table next to a large gathering of sorority sisters, most of whom were well into their twilight years, enjoying what appeared to be a regular reunion. It had been some time since I had visited the American South, and I was soaking it all in.

Breazeale, an aspiring country and western singer when she joined the company, started working the floor in a local Walmart store and rose through the ranks of the company to become the senior vice president of merchandising at Sam's Club, a position she held for almost 20 years. While in this position, Breazeale received word that the company was listed as a laggard by the NDG campaign in their very prominent *New York Times* advertisement. This news would not have sat well with the company when there was a standing directive to make the firm a sustainability leader in all product categories. Breazeale took the challenge and ran with it, quickly realizing she would need to have a chat with the NDG campaigners and get the company off the "laggards list." She phoned Earthworks and invited the activists to come down to Bentonville (Walmart, personal communication, August 17, 2011).

The NDG people went down to Bentonville and met with the jewelry sustainability team, which was made up of regular Walmart managers— not members of a CSR department or outside consultants, the usual types NDG meet when first dealing with large corporations. The team came together, did the cheer, and put their heads together to figure out what the jewelry team was going to do on the issue of sustainability (NDG, personal communication, September 20, 2010). They were not experts on the issues, but worked hard and eventually got there. Going back to the concept of corporate culture, this is revealing. There was very little consulting with outside experts. It was really about the people in the company—the people who were actually doing the work in the product area—who were asked to come up with and implement an appropriate solution for Walmart, and this was different from the approaches taken by other companies the activists had worked with before (NDG, personal communication, September 20, 2010).

Breazeale needed to deliver three sustainability "wins" by a certain date. What exactly these "wins" needed to be was not clearly defined. So the team had boxes to tick and while they were searching for solutions, they saw the *New York Times* advertisement and decided that the NDG organizers may actually be able to help them. This was the rather serendipitous chain of events that led to cooperation between the firm and the NGO.

Breazeale was known as a straightforward, no-nonsense leader. She took part in the Vancouver meetings set up to discuss the prospects for responsible mining practices and the possible creation of some sort of certification institution. It was full of senior CSR people and executives from the big mining companies as well as organizers from the NGO community. According to NDG leadership, it quickly became very analytical and was becoming bogged down in the complexity of the matter. "Dee simply asked, 'Which of your companies can I buy good gold from because that is what I need to know. I will put you in touch with my suppliers tomorrow'—and it totally opened the whole thing up" (NDG, personal communication, September 20, 2010). It was this meeting that eventually delivered the beginnings of IRMA.

So because the sustainability directive was given, and Breazeale needed to tick the sustainability box, it put the whole process in motion and suppliers began to scramble to meet the demand. It was into this directive that Dee Breazeale, with the help of CI's Assheton Carter, drove the "Love, Earth" product line. As one campaign leader explained it: "Dee needed something and the last thing she needed was to be on the 'bad list' when she was trying to come up with three 'wins.' If that context didn't exist we wouldn't have gotten [the response]" (NDG, personal communication, September 20, 2010).

We can see the opportunity window for business actors to engage in the politics of gold was wide open, though framed by the requisites of the business model and enforced by market forces. The final section looks at the ways in which these embedded agents are driving the process forward.

Business Power and Private Governance

This section investigates the ways internal institutional entrepreneurs mobilized firm resources to build institutions inside and outside the firm.

This allows for an empirical analysis of the use of the instrumental power available to business actors embedded in different types of firms. It facilitates an examination of the consequences of different varieties of corporate political mobilization in the non-state sphere and sets the table for a further cross-case comparison in the following chapter.

Walmart has utilized the many forms of instrumental power at its disposal to influence the process, though this is not to say that the actors involved have been able to leverage the latent power of the firm to its full capacity. The ways in which initiatives have been embraced and institutionalized in the firm and along its supply chains have altered the structural opportunities for future political action. The major differences between Walmart's approach and those of Brilliant Earth and Tiffany is that Walmart's is heavily geared toward internal policies that allow it to leverage its immense market power through purchasing criteria. The company frames the issue as a market issue, allowing volunteers from its operations and sales teams to lead, while avoiding the more conventional political activities of philanthropy, membership in external organizations, and vocal advocacy.

Internal

Creation and Maintenance of Institutions Internal to the Firm   Walmart's sustainability initiative is not spearheaded by its public relations or compliance departments, but is carried out by the people working within the core business, such as buyers and others in operations. There are approximately 20,000 associates directly involved in the initiative through its SVNs. The approach seeks to embed sustainability into the corporate culture of the firm by changing mindsets of those in leadership positions and operations, not allowing them the opportunity to "offload" it to a CSR department or the like (Ellison 2006).

Some civil society leaders admit that working with Walmart poses its own unique difficulties despite its salespeople's freedom to innovate. The main difficulty seems to be that people regularly change positions within the company—especially if they are successful. This poses a problem as you "lose some of that institutional memory" (CI, personal communication, September 18, 2010). Both those working inside the firm and those working closely with the firm echoed this sentiment when speaking with me.[15] Relationships forged and information shared between personnel, suppliers, and external consultants suffer with such regular rotation. Also, the company's seasonal contracts with suppliers make investments in environmentally and socially preferable technologies into a risky proposition for producers.

For example, Pam Mortensen took over from Dee Breazeale prior to the launch of the "Love, Earth" line. Assheton Carter, who was working closely with Breazeale, says that despite Mortensen's interest in the issues, and the traceable line, it was like starting over once again (Smith and Crawford 2012). While Mortensen turned out to be an internal champion in her own right, the implication is that you cannot rely on the enthusiasm and drive of individuals, no matter how effective they are. You need to embed the goals and principles as they are established, change practices within the company and allow them to take root. You need to let their potential benefits grow so the process can take on a life of its own. You need to institutionalize them. Walmart is doing exactly that. "In this way," a key civil society leader argues, "we can see real transformation in practices and outcomes, and it is now happening of its own accord" (CI, personal communication, September 18, 2010).

Walmart is working on correcting many of these difficulties across its operations. Typically, people have moved around the company, often with buyers staying on in a network just 12 to 18 months before they are rotated. In areas of its business exposed to tricky ethical issues, the company has now created a longer-term category of buyers so they are able to work with suppliers for a longer period. The company has also switched from strictly seasonal buying to actually offering five-year commitments to incentivize producers to invest in new practices (Ruben 2006).

The core strategy is to change the corporate culture of the firm and the mindsets of leadership so Walmart's business-friendly brand of sustainability becomes a standing order in all the company's operations. As reflected in the opportunities model, it is essential to have leadership on board and many employees and observers credit Walmart's rapid movement toward sustainability to the strong leadership shown by Lee Scott and others at the top of the management team.[16] However, even top management changes eventually and regardless of the depth of mainstreaming, individuals continue to matter—and matter more at the upper echelons of the company. Many observers have noticed a slowdown in the changes being implemented throughout the company as leadership has changed hands (EDF, personal communication, September 7, 2011). For example, Bill Simon, while serving as president and CEO of US operations, attributed Walmart's recent financial slowdown to the company being distracted from its "Everyday Low Prices" mission: "Sustainability and some of these other initiatives," he explained, "can be distracting if they don't add to everyday low cost" (Simon 2011). As one Walmart executive put it to me, "If it costs money, they are going to get rid of it" (Walmart, personal communication, August 16, 2011).

Compliance and Monitoring   While Walmart does have a compliance department, it maintains a sole focus on the retailer's compliance with existing laws in jurisdictions in which it operates and not on the sustainability initiatives undertaken within the company (Ellison 2006). Walmart resists restricting itself by setting hard targets for its initiatives, which makes monitoring a moot point in most cases. There are a couple of exceptions though. Walmart does monitor individual store compliance to company-wide initiatives, such as the initiative committing the company to an internal goal of zero waste. This zero waste initiative has already reached an 80% reduction in store waste from the initial baseline and Walmart is currently negotiating internally whether the next goal will be set at 85% or 90% reduction in the next year (Walmart, personal communication, August 16, 2011). For jewelry, the internal target is an extremely modest 10% traceability of gold through its supply chain and a flexible schedule for meeting this threshold.

The significant point here is that Walmart's targets are internally set and monitored, with the company choosing what the initiatives will be, which results it will announce, and when it will announce them. However, there are opportunities for external actors to influence these decisions. Organizations, such as WWF, EDF, and CI, have the opportunity to bring ideas forward to Walmart and lobby for the ones that they feel have the most promise (EDF, personal communication, August 16, 2011). Walmart benefits from this relationship by avoiding the cost of vetting these new ideas and utilizing the consulting functions of these NGOs. The NGOs benefit from their access to and influence within the largest retail company in the world—gaining valuable knowledge about the retail industry in the process (EDF, personal communication, August 16,

2011). The only way this relationship works is through confidentiality agreements, which are essential for Walmart to be able to share the information necessary for the organizations to take on an effective consultative role (Walmart, personal communication, August 16, 2011; EDF, personal communication, August 16, 2011). An example of the influence NGOs enjoy under this agreement, and an exception to the company's resistance to externally defined targets, is the February 2010 commitment by Walmart—pushed by EDF—to reduce its global carbon footprint in line with the hard targets mentioned above (EDF, personal communication, August 16, 2011).

Therefore, along with the company's new focus on sustainability comes a seemingly new willingness to engage with stakeholders from various spheres of society. Walmart is granting access for interviews to both media and academic researchers. While there has never been a want of interest in the company, new analyses are accompanied by interviews with Walmart executives who have taken to divulging details of their new philosophy and activities. This includes access for researchers, including myself, for whom the company has provided information and face-to-face meetings in its Bentonville home office. By engaging with NGOs and other stakeholders, the company is fortifying its structural power by giving these people and organizations something to lose, namely, a favorable position from which to influence Walmart's investment in sustainability. The company manages to offer these incentives, while maintaining ultimate control over the process.

External
Creation and Maintenance of Institutions Internal and External to the Firm
Walmart is not certified by the RJC or anyone else. While this may initially seem surprising given the company's sustainability goals, it is actually a natural fit with the company's approach and does not mean the company is not quietly involved with RJC in an unofficial capacity.

Recall that Walmart's approach is based on cost-effectiveness. Part of its so-called business approach to sustainability is that the company does not wish to add cost to its operations. While company representatives rightly point out that such an approach has a significant benefit in that it does not change when times are good or bad, financially speaking (Ruben

2006), it also means that they refuse to pay the fees associated with certification membership. The RJC's fees assessment is based on a very small percentage of sales. For many jewelers, this is an acceptable cost for risk mitigation, reputational advantage, and access to the ethical jewelry market. With Walmart, however, one cannot place enough zeros after the decimal point to make this an acceptable cost to the company (CI, personal communication, September 18, 2010; Walmart, personal communication, August 17, 2011).

This approach could also be interpreted as a desire to protect the company's autonomy and not subject its operations to the will of outside partners (see, for example, Sasser et al., 2006). This is a recurring theme for the company. Another example can be found in its new "green buildings," all of which could almost certainly be LEED-certified if Walmart chose this path. The point is, the company strives to maintain its autonomy and refuses to raise costs based on such intangible value.

However, it is not simply cost and autonomy that turns the company away from such initiatives. There is a general feeling within the company that many certifications are in fact pitched too low and may actually restrict innovation (Walmart, personal communication, August 16, 2011). Certifications are often subject to the lowest common denominator among their founding members and do not necessarily incentivize members to ratchet up their standards or look for new approaches to sustainability.

Having said this, Walmart does work closely with many certifying bodies, including the RJC (Rio Tinto, personal communication, August 7, 2011). The question is: how much can Walmart contribute to these certification initiatives from the outside? The answer: a great amount. The company consults with the RJC and has apparently contributed funds to IRMA. It will certainly buy from and even give official preference to certified suppliers; it just will not pay a percentage of its sales for or sacrifice autonomy to it. While there is no official Walmart preference for RJC suppliers to date, there is a precedent being set through the company's procurement practices.

Buying Power and Preferential Procurement   Walmart maintains control over the process by designing its own Supplier Sustainability Assessments (SSAs), asking suppliers to report on a series of questions the company created. The SSAs began quite basic, but are becoming more sophisticated, targeting unique features of different products and creating baselines (EDF, personal communication, September 7, 2011). This represents a big opportunity to gather data and use this data to drive positive change. Walmart states that its goal is to eventually create a sustainability index so consumers can effortlessly choose products that meet their social and environmental expectations. Such an initiative has the potential to be transformational, but it is still very much a long-term goal far from realization.

Thus far, Walmart has managed to shorten its supply chains by cutting out intermediaries. Andy Ruben (2006) recounts a story of cutting packers out of the supply chain by getting the fish mongers to freeze and package fish themselves to sell directly to Walmart. Plambeck and Denend (2008) explain how the company has cut entire countries out of its textiles supply chains by completing more stages in fewer countries. While there are certainly losers in this consolidation, the company cuts costs, reduces its ecological footprint, and tightens its control of its supply chains, reducing its exposure to risk.

Besides developing its own criteria, the company rewards external private governance initiatives with preferential procurement. The company committed to give preference to seafood suppliers certified by the Marine Stewardship Council (MSC). The MSC is the largest seafood certifier and demands that its members adhere to best practices in a number of areas. Although this certifying body enjoys the largest membership in the sector, MSC supply was not nearly enough to supply all of Walmart's seafood needs. Thus, because there were not adequate suppliers of MSC-certified seafood to meet Walmart's demand, the company's commitment meant that if you get certified, you can supply Walmart (Denend and Plambeck 2007, 55) and was therefore a boon to the certifying organization and those who advocate for best practices in the industry. This is really an easy win for Walmart, as the suppliers bear the cost of certification. Despite not bearing the direct cost, the company plays an instrumental role in supporting these efforts and takes care to support the most stringent standards to avoid diluting them (Ruben 2006). It is a clear example of Walmart using its power to shift industry practices and perhaps foreshadows what we will see as relationships develop between the company, the RJC, FT/FM gold, and IRMA, once it is launched.

Similarly, with Walmart we see an alternative approach to supporting the leading advocates against the Pebble Lake Mine—the Alaskan fishermen. Walmart may not publicly support the Alaskan fishery's opposition to the project, which will allegedly damage the fisheries, but its commitment to MSC-certified salmon includes large orders of wild sockeye from the Bristol Bay, Alaska fisheries. The local fisheries were so delighted that they wrote Walmart to thank the company for its support. "It can be nothing but good for the state and the area," said Bob Waldrop of the Bristol Bay Regional Seafood Development Association in an interview with a local newspaper. "You can vote with your fork. You can ask more about the fisheries, Bristol Bay, the threat it faces. It's a really good way to get the word out about Pebble [Mine], and create jobs for people in Bristol Bay and elsewhere" (Associated Press 2008). So it appears that people are buying in to Walmart's approach of leading through market decisions and the company seems content with this less vocal, but seemingly effective, stance on environmental and social issues.[17]

Walking Softly? It hasn't always been the case that Walmart would abstain from taking an overtly political stance on an issue. When Walmart began its sustainability push, it engaged vocally in political debates and advocated for specific environmental policies in Washington. Andy Ruben, who at the time was vice president of strategy and sustainability for Walmart, testified in front of Congress on Capitol Hill in April of 2006, and again in May of 2007, calling for the implementation of carbon regulations and a cap and trade system (Carney 2006; Walmart 2008). Coming from one of the largest and most successful companies in the world, these types of activities add strength, legitimacy, and publicity to such causes and are an invaluable counter to the public skepticism and private lobbying activities of many of industry's biggest players.

However, this vocalism appears to have been short lived. It is difficult to determine specific instances of pushback the company may have felt to its stance on carbon regulation and similarly controversial positions; nonetheless, Walmart observers certainly saw the company backpedal immediately after taking this activist role. The question is: why? While the company continues to hold press conferences in Washington, DC, on "green jobs," as well as the link between sustainability and efficiency, and healthy food and local sourcing, it has backed off the politically charged issues in favor of "the warm, fuzzy kittens of the policy world" (EDF, personal communication, September 7, 2011).

Due to the heavily guarded nature of such political decision-making, it is difficult to know exactly why this decision was made. While there is a certain amount of speculation involved in any outside analysis, most agree this was probably a rational cost–benefit calculation by management. The reality is that their customer base is largely located in the heart of the country, where it is not uncommon to doubt the reality of climate change. Under these conditions, it could be seen as a somewhat risky strategy to be interpreted as being "too far out there" politically and the company would be wise not to put itself in that position.

Besides these strategic, market-based rationales for taking a quiet approach to incorporating sustainability in its operations, the narrative put forward by the sustainability gurus in working both with and within the company offers another explanation. If Walmart vocally pushes sustainable products, it risks creating a niche. If the company instead works toward creating better products long-term, everybody will want these products regardless of the individual customer's commitment to conscientious consumption (Ellison 2006).

This line of argument can be easily seen as a type of discursive power being wielded by a very influential organization, effectively domesticating calls for sustainable consumption by aligning it with their business interests and delegitimizing approaches that may cost the company money or market share. However, the company also has a point. Walmart brandishes such immense market power that simple changes in the products and services it offers—and how it frames these—have ripple effects throughout the industry. Decisions made within the company, even those involving the allocation of shelf space within stores, set the agenda for change and can quietly make or break entire sectors.

So with the Walmart case, we seem to be observing another example of business actors mobilizing the political power of their firm by taking advantage of the opportunities created by civil society contestation, but contestation that originated from earlier issues. The response to the politics of "dirty gold," in turn, should continue the momentum and expand opportunities for future political action. Walmart has been creating elaborate systems to integrate sustainability goals into its operations, and the company has been entrenching its particular understanding of social and environmentally responsible business into its organizational culture. By creating incentives along its supply chains for suppliers to do the same, Walmart leverages its considerable market power to expand opportunities for latent institutional entrepreneurs in diverse industries. While the company never seemed very exposed to any tangible risk from the NDG campaign, institutional entrepreneurs took advantage of the opportunities created by past cooperation and conflict and have helped expand this window even further.

Conclusion

The core business interests of the diversified jewelers were never severely threatened by the specter of "dirty gold," since the jewelry these companies sell is not branded in-house and they only have a very small stake in the industry relative to their total sales. As a group, diversified jewelers responded fairly passively, if at all, to the issue of "dirty gold." Very few diversified jewelers joined the RJC and most were slow to sign on to the NDG's Golden Rules, because these companies appear unwilling to relinquish either their autonomy or the membership fees to external certifications.

While Walmart has also declined joining the RJC, it remains in discussions with the group as well as with IRMA. Walmart has signed the Golden Rules and has opted to create its own, first-party certification in the "Love, Earth" line. There appears to only be a small market for ethical jewelry among its customers, so it created this niche line that may be expanded upon if it remains profitable. What then explains how Walmart has become a lead firm among diversified jewelers in the politics of gold?

Its interest in the sector appears to be more driven by the requisites of its larger sustainability push than by pressure exerted by activists or consumers interested in gold. So, in the end, it was the desire to meet the directives handed down from the company's leadership that drove its approach as the issues surrounding jewelry did not constitute a direct threat to its business model, a claim buttressed by the fact that its main competitors, operating according to similar business models, have responded much more passively. Note that the larger, company-wide sustainability initiative was partially driven by risk mitigation and a threat to the firm's business interests—it was simply not the threat it faced by the issue of "dirty gold."

Walmart's approach is arguably more process-oriented than the approach of the retailers in the other categories we've looked at. It allows the market to set the pace for change. This is not to say that Walmart has refused to take a stand altogether. The company has signed on to the guiding principles of the activist groups and is moving toward internalizing them, building systems around the general guidelines that should lubricate ongoing transformation. While the corporate political mobilization of the diversified jewelers may be more market-oriented and individualized than those of the ethical and specialty jewelers, it is important to note that none of the jewelers in any category have thus far relinquished their operational autonomy.

The Walmart case also demonstrates the cross-cutting effect of issue areas—an experience in one issue area, labor, has driven change in another, the environment. It seems the politicization of one aspect of a company's operations has led to deep change in another. This is an example of a company tailoring its political mobilization to its business model; instead of focusing on labor issues, it focuses on sustainability. While there are clearly economic reasons for this, corporate culture and leadership have also played a role, both in filtering out labor concerns and injecting environmental concerns.

Furthermore, this cross-cutting suggests changes in sustainability may change the culture and decision-making processes in all aspects of the company's operations. These wider changes should bleed into other areas—including the possibility of feeding back into the initial area of concern, namely, labor issues. This highlights the importance of breaking a problematic status quo. A crisis moment expands the opportunity window and allows for change to the inner functioning and culture of the firm and, with enormous firms such as Walmart, it can spread to the operational culture of multiple industries. As these corporate leaders leverage their power and influence, they may end up changing not only the competitive and cognitive dynamics of their firm, but also those along their supply chains.

Table 5.3
Corporate political mobilization—*Walmart*

	Economic	Institutional
Internal	✓ Translating regulations into actionable practices	✓ Creation and maintenance of institutions internal to the firm
External	✗ Donations ✓ Strategic investments ✓ Buying power and preferential procurement ✗ Paying membership fees	✗ Lobbying and advocacy ✓ Issue framing ✓ Creation and maintenance of institutions external to the firm ✓ Acting as a role model for others to benchmark

6

The Causes and Consequences of Corporate Leadership

With the opportunity model, one must understand both its mechanics and the claims it makes. The economic and institutional dimensions of opportunity structures, and the indicators used to approximate their value, are not *driving* firm responses, per se. They are *opportunities* that offer business actors within firms an increased chance of successfully mobilizing the firm's resources for political purposes. They are opportunities for corporate executives to exercise their political agency and initiate private governance.

Leadership has been a key variable in all of the principal firms investigated, and one seemingly missing from those that have not responded to activist pressure. Without leadership, opportunities are more likely to remain dormant. In this chapter, I bring the cases together, summarizing what the findings can tell us about variation within and across categories of firms; in other words, I offer an explanation as to why lead firms lead, why they lead in different ways, and the impacts these leaders might have.

Why Lead Firms Lead

A crisis is an opportunity, a moment for profound agency. In a world where actions are channeled through socioeconomic structures, crises introduce uncertainty, scrambling societal codes and expectations. This allows for the remaking of these structures through the directives of convincing agents. In such a moment, leadership is key.

Activists supply such a moment when they target industries directly. They fracture the structural constraints imposed by market forces by introducing conflict. Conflict creates risk, and markets, through the aggregate decisions of individual investors, punish risk. The structural forces in the market shift slightly as activists open opportunity windows for the political mobilization of firms by recalibrating the interests of firm managers. Those managers now have incentives to act to reduce their exposure to risk and avoid being disciplined by the market. Whereas pre-campaign, firm managers would not have the space or economic rationale for these political activities, post-campaign, these managers are incentivized, or at least given the opportunity, to mobilize and shift practices to where they will once again enjoy the protection of structural forces and not be sanctioned by the market.

Our findings have shown that the threat leveraged by activists was very intangible indeed. While there is no evidence to suggest that activists have affected the bottom line of jewelers in any measurable way, what they have done is expose the companies to risk. Risk, by nature, is difficult to calculate and, therefore, must be interpreted; past experiences, in turn, inform interpretations.

All of the case firms examined in this book exhibited leadership above and beyond those of their peer firms because they had systems in place, had the right people in the right positions, and were informed by past experience with civil society groups. The fact all three firms so clearly built upon their past experience with civil society in other issue areas suggests the significance of having a history of interaction with activists and points to the importance of learning in expanding the opportunity structures for political mobilization.

Establishing ethical brands is a particular, but increasingly common, private sector response to the politicization of markets by activists. Brilliant Earth and the ethical jewelers are filling a perceived gap in the market and catering to those conscientious consumers who were beginning to demand ethically sourced jewelry in the wake of activist efforts. As with most of the ethical jewelers, Brilliant Earth based the way they approach gold on the lessons learned from the earlier and higher profile issues surrounding diamonds. In fact, it is highly doubtful that without this previous civil society contestation there would be much of a market for ethical jewelry at all. The company was designed to avoid irresponsible practices along its supply chains and, therefore, when new issues arise, it is prepared to meet the challenge. While the company has investors, leadership at all levels would be well-aware of the need for an ethical firm to stay out front of supply chain issues.

Tiffany was able to be extremely proactive with its response to the issue of "dirty gold" as they learned from their experience with conflict diamonds and quickly consolidated their supply chain, identifying an appropriate mine site from which the company could trace the gold to its own manufacturing facilities. The company also has a strong CSR department, established at the height of the conflict diamonds controversy, which holds considerable sway within the company and interfaces with the operations managers daily (Luxury jeweler, personal communication, September 16, 2010). Investor expectations would surely have been impacted by the conflict diamonds controversy as well, offering management increased leeway to confront the politics of gold. The fact that most specialty jewelers would have also been exposed to the conflict diamonds experience explains the proactive response of the entire sector while Tiffany's internal institutional entrepreneurs account for the company's extraordinary depth of engagement.

Again, with Walmart, proactive political leadership can be explained through a combination of an economic case for a wider sustainability initiative with strong leadership backing this initiative. The company faced civil society contestation targeting its labor practices, its contribution to urban sprawl, and its negative effect on local businesses. These issues led to a broad-based sustainability push within the company, which created the room for action on the gold issue. Walmart's leadership, from the founding family and ownership group to the CEO and chair, all got behind this broader sustainability drive. The internal champions that pushed the "Love, Earth" initiative through this opportunity window did so under these general directives. The fact that no other diversified jeweler has come close to the level of engagement underscores the importance of past experience, systems, and leadership in accounting for the company's response.

Let's be a little more specific about the ways in which prior activist contestation expands the opportunities for future political mobilization by business actors. Along the economic dimension of the opportunities model, prior civil society campaigns inform the risk analysis of firms when dealing with new issues as they have either seen or experienced the power activists can bring to bear. An even more tangible effect of past pressure is its impact on the institutions and mechanisms of the firm and industry. Past civil society contestation also created opportunities for business actors to mobilize the resources of the firm, creating institutions with which to mitigate the risk—or in the case of ethical jewelers, fill the gap—associated with the particular issues. This means when new issues arise, the systems are in place, or at least the knowledge of how to deal effectively with activist contestation, and so the marginal cost of engagement is reduced. Along the institutional dimension, the corporate culture has changed as past experiences have led business actors to embed social and environmental concerns within the operational culture of the firm; in effect, raising the profile of these concerns within the hierarchy of organizational interests. Relatedly, as these issues become seen as increasingly important to the interests of the firm, they become part of the remit of the organization's leadership, further enhancing the profile of social and environmental concerns within the company. CSR departments are created, people are hired, and their power in organizational decision-making increases. So all four dimensions of the opportunities model are expanded from past experience. This also demonstrates one of the key consequences of the *present* political mobilization of the firm's resources in response to civil society contestation, namely, the further expansion of these structural opportunities for *future* private sector engagement in social and environmental issues.

The cases suggest the political roles these firms have taken on would be very difficult to explain without an understanding of the history of civil society contestation in their markets. The importance of past experience and institutional learning cannot be overestimated and the opportunities model assists in understanding the mechanisms by which this experience translates into leadership. While a history with civil society contestation is clearly a key factor explaining present corporate engagement, the firm resources available to leaders and the ways in which they mobilize these resources also impact upon the opportunity window for future political engagement.

Business power has generally been considered a defiant force opposed to the emergence of robust regulation; but the cases investigated in this book suggest business actors can exercise this power to build institutions that expand the opportunity window for, and therefore the likelihood of, proactive engagement with social and environmental issues. Firms exert their instrumental power to fortify their new position in markets and realign their operations with market forces. It is at this stage where we can observe the mechanisms by which institutional entrepreneurs expand the economic and institutional dimensions of the opportunity window for future action. Specifically, they exert their instrumental power to create or alter institutions both internally and externally to the firm. Internally, preferences are institutionalized throughout an organization via a process of mainstreaming, or embedding, norms and practices while ensuring operations are compliant through a system of monitoring and evaluation. Externally, firm preferences are diffused instrumentally through market power, agenda-setting, and discursive framing. Through these actions, business actors alter the institutional landscape, contributing to the creation of collective institutions, building coalitions with like-minded firms and civil society groups, and tightening their control over their supply chains. All of these actions can have a positive effect on the likelihood of corporate political engagement with social and environmental issues.

Building Institutions

Business actors exercise the instrumental power of the firm to help create internal and external institutional environments conducive to their interests, thereby expanding the opportunities for future political action. These institutions are created to reduce the firm's exposure to risk, especially in the case of the specialty jewelers. Firms will tend to avoid losing any operational autonomy during this process, as joining an initiative in which civil society groups share decision-making power could constitute an even greater risk than doing nothing at all (see also Sasser et al. 2006). At the same time, building and supporting regulatory systems, even at arm's length, reduces costs and reinforces norms.

Business actors attempt to control the process of private institution-building in a variety of ways by mobilizing firm resources to operationalize and institutionalize their preferences. They do so by choosing between rival institutions, supporting those they approve of by either joining them, lending their vocal support for them, consulting with them, offering preferential purchasing to them, or contributing to the cost of their formation. Institutions and organizations that firms do not approve of are ignored, publicly criticized, or boycotted. In these ways, firms steer the process of institution-building and shape the governance landscape in which they operate. Business actors not only take advantage of opportunity structures, they also help create them.

The case chapters highlighted many specific instances in which these practices have been undertaken with regards to private initiatives. Walmart opts for the highest certification standards, demonstrated through its support of the MSC in seafood certification, as the company does not want to bring standards down and wants to avoid controversy. This seems to be a rather easy decision to make as the company does not need to meet the criteria of these standards themselves, but simply offers purchasing priority to those suppliers that do. When sufficient standards did not exist in the jewelry industry, the company opted to create its own which, by all accounts, constitute best practices in the industry despite concerns the standards cover only a small percentage of their jewelry sales and the company may be "overselling" the assurances beyond its ability to manage the practices down the chain. While Walmart does not subscribe to any particular external certification, the company does work with the institutions in an informal, consultative capacity. Tiffany is not only a member of the RJC, but devoted significant time and resources to its development. They also support the continued efforts to launch IRMA, the main goal of which is to certify the mines themselves. Brilliant Earth advocates for ethical consumption by way of recycled gold, but is a strong supporter of FT/FM gold from Oro Verde, which the company helped develop, and backs up this support with purchasing priorities. Additionally, all three firms support various organizations working to develop regulatory initiatives in other issue areas through funding and philanthropic activities.

Tiffany and Brilliant Earth are staunch advocates for reforming the KPCS, which they find is inadequate in its definition of conflict diamonds and in its ability to quash the entrance of these diamonds into the supply chain. They feel it may do more harm than good through the complacency it breeds. Brilliant Earth is a critic of the RJC; the company feels the RJC lacks legitimacy through its narrow and industrial membership, which Brilliant Earth claims has led to serious deficiencies in the standards themselves.

Building Partnerships and Coalitions
Business actors will often handpick their partners when building coalitions with civil society groups. As they control the process to a large

extent, many firms will avoid formalized arrangements with the most contentious groups and opt instead for informal discussions. Deeper cooperation is more likely with the more business-friendly groups, who are usually the biggest NGOs with the most resources to contribute and a history of corporate partnerships. While this also reduces the immediate risk to the firm by finding solutions to pressing issues and adding the legitimacy that comes with civil society partnerships, it also expands the opportunity window for future political engagement by reducing the cost, through cost sharing, while further embedding norms and moving social and environmental concerns up the leadership hierarchy within the firm.

When institutions or organizations do not meet the criteria necessary for a firm to cooperate, firms either shut them out (for example, Walmart and NDG), act unilaterally (for example, Tiffany and Zimbabwean diamonds), or vocally oppose them (for example, Brilliant Earth and the RJC). They are influencing the agenda for industry change and setting the parameters of possibility for what can be asked of them. NGOs working with them are supplied with funding, information, and vocal accolades. Those that do not play by the rules are marginalized. This goes for organizations that appear to be asking too much in the eyes of particular firms (for example NDG and Walmart) as well as those organizations that ask too little (for example, KPCS and Tiffany/Brilliant Earth). Those espousing positive messages are rewarded (for example, MSC and Walmart) while those adopting critical positions are sidelined (for example, NDG and Walmart).

There is no consensus among jewelers as to which organizations and initiatives to support and how to do so. However, there are striking agreements of approach in that they all exert their influence over the institutional architecture of the industry while carefully guarding their autonomy. Walmart refuses to become certified, but consults with and supports those initiatives that fit the company's economic needs and cultural preferences. Tiffany has committed itself to becoming certified, but by an organization that it helped develop and is intimately involved with. Brilliant Earth has been directly involved in the development of the only certified gold it will buy and differentiates itself from other "responsible jewelers" by refuting the claims made by the main industry group. In these ways, firms attempt to maintain control of the process.

These divergent strategies have led to three types of firm-NGO coalitions in the jewelry industry, which could be categorized as free market, regulatory, and niche market, in character. Free market coalitions involved the less exposed firms who joined forces with mainstream NGOs to help devise, implement, and add legitimacy to market-based solutions. Regulatory coalitions included more exposed firms who sought more institutionalized, external solutions to protect their interests. Once institutionalized, these firms were less vulnerable to direct-targeting campaigns, were able to defend against less palatable regulation by taking a seat at the table and, by getting like firms to also join, avoided suffering a competitive disadvantage from implementing these higher standards. The niche market coalitions involved the firms who stepped into the gap in the market for ethical goods and had the luxury, due in part to their relatively small scale, and the need, due to their business model relying on product differentiation, to form coalitions with NGOs representing the highest ethical standards in the market. Although different in character, all three types of coalitions constitute learning networks that should make proactive political mobilization more likely.

Tightening Control over Supply Chains

Firms are responding to activist pressure by tightening control over their supply chains. This reduces their exposure to risk and also the cost involved when making future commitments, further expanding their opportunity window for future action.

Brilliant Earth and the other ethical jewelers have responded to the political issues facing the jewelry industry with tightly controlled supply chains from inception. Their value is largely built upon the ability to trace and control processes along their modest and carefully regulated supply chains. They undertake much of their production in-house and fabrication is done locally in the US. It must be said that they have recently expanded their sourcing to include mining cooperatives overseas, but this has been done using tightly controlled, third-party certification.

In the case of Tiffany, the company is vertically integrating its processes. The company has consolidated its control over its diamond supply chain by buying shares in mines and is instituting preferential purchasing policies for specific cutting and polishing facilities. The company implemented similar changes with its gold supply chain, sourcing the vast majority of its gold from the Kennecott copper mine in Utah, which maintains high standards, is part of an established mining community, has onsite refining, is a local (US) source, and mines gold as a by-product of its copper production. Tiffany favors in-house melting, molding, and fabrication that also takes place in the US. This significantly reduces their supply chain risk. As Tiffany learned from its experience with conflict diamonds, integrating supply chains can not only lead to cost savings and a secure supply, but has the added benefit of being traceable. This allows the company to become a first-mover when social and environmental issues arise.

Walmart has also been exercising its influence, using different means toward similar ends. The company is reducing the number of intermediaries by encouraging and assisting its suppliers to integrate processes downstream into its operations. The case chapter showed how the company is cutting out middlemen and helping producers further downstream in the supply chain meet its evolving standards, finding cost savings and consolidating the chain. In some cases, this has resulted in cutting out entire countries from the production process, significantly shortening the length of the supply chain. The main tactic of the company thus far appears to be diversifying the tasks that suppliers undertake instead of diversifying suppliers themselves. This is a significant departure from the traditionally complex supply chains and arm's length supplier relationships the company has maintained in the past.

When activists target industries, they seek to shed light on what Peter Dauvergne (2008, 5–6) has called the "ecological shadows of consumption," referring to how globalized production allows industry "to displace the environmental costs of producing, transporting, using, and replacing consumer goods" onto the poorest in society. With firms reacting by shortening these chains and integrating upstream processes into their companies, it appears that these campaigns are consolidating the geographic, economic, and social distance for these products as well.[1] These findings suggest one of the effects of direct targeting appears to include the *defragmentation* of global production chains, which constitutes a minor reversal to one of the major elements of economic globalization—the transnationalization of production.

Why They Lead in Different Ways

Interpreted through the lens of structured agency, we expected ethical firms to be deeply engaged, as the only reputational risk they really faced was not using the highest standards available. They are generally small firms built for niche sourcing and traceability, so the marginal cost of compliance with new standards is relatively low. Their political engagement is built into their business model and the more politicized the market, the better for their political goals and their brand. The corporate culture should reflect both their core ethos and business model; therefore, we expect it to be clearly receptive to engaging in the politics of gold. Their leadership structure is generally one of owner-operator and so those with the original vision are running the company and have fewer, if any, investors to answer to.

The large opportunity window available to executives in specialty jewelers explains their high levels of engagement and strong commitments. Specialty jewelers are highly exposed to reputational risk due to their branding and reliance on gold jewelry. While they require too much gold as inputs to simply source from niche, ethical suppliers, their supply chains should be much less complex than the diversified jewelers and traceability could eventually become a cost-effective option. They enjoy high profit margins due to their branding and design; therefore, the companies should be able to either absorb the costs associated with compliance or be able to pass it along to consumers in the form of higher prices. Their corporate culture and leadership structures will differ and so some variation is to be expected based on these institutional dimensions but, based largely on opportunities along the economic dimensions, their opportunities profile suggests they will act individually and collectively to protect their reputation.

The small opportunity window faced by actors working within diversified jewelers explains their very low levels of engagement and weak commitments. Diversified jewelers were also targeted, but never faced the same levels of exposure to risk as the specialty firms. They compete in the market based on price more than brand and are not reliant on jewelry sales for their future success. They have highly complex supply chains and are less involved with their suppliers down the chain. Their profit margins are small and their customers are price sensitive. Their corporate cultures and leadership structures are mixed. However, we could expect general trends toward frugal cultures stemming from their business model and most will be publicly traded due to their size and capital requirements for expansion.

The ethical jewelers tend to develop their own elaborate, first-party standards while sourcing gold from the highest (and only available) third-party certified suppliers. There is little variation along either the economic or institutional dimensions of their respective opportunities profiles, and little variation in their mobilization. The specialized jewelers, especially the luxury brands, have almost all signed on to both the NDG's Golden Rules as well as the second-party, RJC certification. The diversified jewelers have been generally less responsive with many ignoring activists altogether, some signing on to the NDG's Golden Rules, a few opting for the RJC, and really only one becoming more deeply engaged and developing their own first-party certification. So there is some variation present in both the specialized and diversified categories and, because like-firms should face similar risk and costs, we should expect to be able to account for inter-category variation through the institutional dimensions of their opportunity window.

The patterns we have seen suggest two general findings. First, the fact that there are different strategies employed among firms operating with relatively similar business models, ranging from deep engagement to no engagement, suggests that there are factors other than their business model, which also must be considered to account for this type of variation. Second, the fact that the majority of jewelers within each of the three categories seem to eventually respond in a similar way as the leaders within their respective category, and different from those found in the other two categories, suggests this type of variation remains closely connected to their shared business model and market.[2]

So where does all this leave us? The final section pushes the analysis toward an understanding of how these combinations of business power and preference are impacting the governance of gold, both in the short and long term.

Impact of Corporate Leadership

Institutional entrepreneurs' political power is limited by both the resources of their firm and their ability to mobilize them. As these resources and opportunity windows vary among firms, different types of firms bring different elements of business power to the private institution-building process, leading to a range of contributions.

Brilliant Earth and the Ethical Jewelers

Small, ethical jewelers clearly cannot garner the market power of their larger counterparts. However, they do possess the ability to lead with their voice. While statements made by larger specialized companies, such as Tiffany, probably carry more weight in that their consumer base is much larger and the firm is more established, there are certainly some benefits enjoyed by these ethical companies. The major advantage is that because they utilize the highest possible standards for their product sourcing and manufacturing processes, they are able to be the industry voice for raising standards without fear of appearing hypocritical. When taking a stand on a particular issue, firms often subject themselves to increased scrutiny. Walmart's "Love-Earth" line could be interpreted in this light as it sometimes seemed activists were lining up to critique the initiative. The issue is with firms "overselling" their commitment to sustainability. By using best practices in the industry, the small ethical jewelers are able to advocate for the highest standards without fear of reputational reprisal.

Ethical jewelers are business enterprises with a social mission. This mission can be summarized in four parts. First, they strive to make high quality, ethical jewelry to meet the demand from ethical consumers and to translate this previously latent demand into economic incentives for ethical practices upstream in the jewelry supply chain. Second, they attempt to increase this demand for ethical jewelry by raising consumer awareness of the issues surrounding gold and diamond mining. Third, they advocate for change within the industry and the creation of more purposeful regulatory frameworks surrounding the industry. Fourth, they act as a role model for other firms in the industry, especially the larger jewelers that wield significant market power, in order to demonstrate that sourcing ethical metals is not only possible, but desirable (Ethical jeweler, personal communication, October 10, 2011).

Ethical jewelers can have an impact disproportionate to their financial turnover. Many feel that smaller companies are more innovative and are not held hostage to the structural constraints that appear to lock the larger jewelers into a particular model that makes the larger jewelers much more resistant to change and innovation (Ethical jeweler, personal communication, August 7, 2011). This study has certainly uncovered many of the structural constraints faced by these larger jewelers, but it has also shown these constraints can be overcome through a combination of strong and committed leadership along with innovative reforms to sourcing strategies that are aligned with the business models of the firms. All the same, the ethical jewelers do appear to be leading the industry in both advocacy and innovative sourcing.

Eric Grossberg at Brilliant Earth explained to me how they were ridiculed early on when discussing the possibility of a traceable, ethical supply chain for gold (Ethical jeweler, personal communication, August 1, 2011). They were told this was not the way it had been done and will never be the way it is done, as it is logistically impossible to trace. But the Oro Verde project and similar FT/FM projects seem to be proving these sceptics wrong, at least on a small scale, as they have succeeded in becoming fully traceable. However, he noted that the critiques have not gone away, but have simply switched to claims that this is a niche market, there are no margins, and it cannot be done on a large scale (Ethical jeweler, personal communication, August 1, 2011). How salient these critiques prove to be remains an open question.

The greatest contribution of ethical jewelers is creating and maintaining the highest possible standards and not needing to dilute these standards to fit a previously existing business model. As small and specialized companies, they are in a somewhat unique position to do so. They are limited by their lack of market power, but make an important contribution with their soft power. By not participating in industry governance initiatives that do not meet their very high standards for ethically sourced commodities, they deny themselves a seat at the table, but provide themselves with the opportunity to hold these institutions to account as an external critic.

Tiffany and the Specialty Jewelers

Specialty jewelers tend to have less direct market power than the more diversified retailers. But the largest have powerful brands, so are especially suited to leading. With Tiffany, the company sources great quantities of gold, but it mostly originates from one relatively benign mine in

Utah. It did not need to shift their supply chain for social or environmental reasons; its campaigning stance will not have much of a direct, economic effect on mining companies. However, it is a very well-known and well-respected company and so its opinions and actions carry significant weight in the industry and marketplace. Tiffany's work in promoting responsible gold mining is helping to define and stigmatize irresponsible practices. The company is contributing to the institutionalization of governance structures and setting the stage for a potential long-term shift in the normative structure of the mining industry.

Internally, Tiffany responded to the "dirty gold" issue in a similar manner to conflict diamonds. The company increased its control and monitoring ability by vertically integrating its supply chains. We have seen the benefits for the company, including risk mitigation and financial rewards, but how does this contribute to the governance of gold?

First, this approach strengthens the responsible mining movement by rewarding good practice with the money allocated to purchase the metals and minerals (while denying poor practices). It also contributes to governance indirectly by offering a model of good practice that other firms may imitate. Immense value derives from industry leadership that demonstrates how things can be done differently. Such an approach has significant limitations as well. In contrast to the Walmart approach, Tiffany has essentially shut out suppliers that cannot guarantee the provenance of their gold. This eliminates any direct incentive that Tiffany could have offered them through its purchasing power.

The second major contribution the company has made to the governance of the supply chain stems from the conferences and collaborations Tiffany has nurtured. Through its work organizing stakeholder meetings and through its collaborations with NGOs, even the most contentious ones, the company is building "learning networks" and developing criteria for responsible mining, a necessary first step to effective governance, as concepts must be defined before policy is devised (see, for example, Ruggie 2002). This has the added benefit of giving these groups a stake in the process and helps ensure the input legitimacy of resulting institutions.

The third aspect of Tiffany's contribution is its direct involvement in institution-building. The company was a founding member of the RJC and has been closely involved in the development of IRMA. This is a vital role as they have lent their expertise and reputational legitimacy to these groups, not only helping to create serviceable standards, but also bringing other companies into the process. These certification institutions help protect the reputation of the industry and provide a baseline for best practices. It allows the company a seat at the table while these standards are being defined. By contributing to institution-building directly, Tiffany can use its instrumental power to enhance its structural power by ensuring their input into shaping the debate's parameters.

There are, however, downsides to these governance institutions. Certification institutions are often subject to the lowest common denominator for standards among their founding members. This is true for any voluntary, membership-based organization. While there will almost certainly be intense bargaining involved when devising the standards, certification institutions have trouble asking firms to contribute past the ability of the member with the lowest appetite for standards. A related concern voiced by industry and non-profit organizations alike is that certification may stifle innovation on sustainability. Variation among firms means individual firms face their own unique circumstances, and standardization processes may have the perverse effect of dis-incentivizing institutional entrepreneurship within companies.

Walmart and the Diversified Jewelers

Diversified retailers competing on price do not carry the same relative, intangible value in their brands as specialty jewelers. What they do have is market power and lots of it.

These firms have the latent ability to shift processes in multiple supply chains; they lead with their procurement policies. Walmart, through a history of conflict on labor issues, probably does not possess the persuasive voice that Brilliant Earth and Tiffany do on social and environmental issues. But the persuasiveness of its market policies is unrivalled. Its market power relative to their suppliers is perhaps the greatest the world has ever known (Fishman 2003). This asymmetrical relationship allows the company to dictate practices in virtually every product range they carry. By harnessing this market power and steering it toward sustainability, this could constitute a coup for the goals of the environmental movement. "What you have to understand about Walmart," explains one executive, "is that when [we] make a decision, we can change an industry" (Walmart, personal communication, August 16, 2011).

There are, of course, many downsides to such a unilateral approach. The processes at the input stage of defining their sustainability initiatives in general, and the criteria for the "Love, Earth" line of jewelry in particular, is opaque and exclusive. While the output of these efforts, such as the "Love, Earth" sustainability criteria, are quite innovative and effective in many instances, they will have trouble gaining widespread support due to this lack of input legitimacy.

Walmart responded to the political environment surrounding gold mining in line with its wider sustainability movement. This maintains the goal of creating a culture of sustainability throughout the company's vast network of suppliers and retail outlets. One could wish Walmart was pushing its suppliers harder for faster change in certain areas, but by bringing them along instead of simply forcing them out, the company is utilizing its market power and considerable resources to shepherd change across industries. Additionally, its unapologetic business approach to sustainability increases the likelihood these improved processes stay intact even when times are economically challenging—because the processes are based on discovering value and not creating costs.

Walmart's approach to supply chain control transfers cost and risk upstream by fostering competition among potential suppliers while preserving the company's autonomy. By driving change in the direction demanded by society, Walmart's engagement with social and environmental issues is protecting the company from accusations of negligence, yet it is also insulating the company from any hard limits exogenously imposed. In this way, Walmart avoids changes that might put its competitive advantage at risk and preserves control over the process and the resulting costs of mitigation.

Although the company claims its business approach avoids simply creating niche markets for higher priced, sustainable goods, the reality of Walmart's flagship sustainable jewelry line is exactly this—a niche line of environmentally and socially responsible jewelry. The "Love, Earth" line is not available in all stores and the remainder of Walmart's jewelry continues to be largely untraced and unevaluated against these higher standards. In its defense, this is a starting point in a longer-term goal to bring the majority of Walmart's jewelry in line with best practices once the company improves upon its supply chain traceability.

Another challenge concerns Walmart's ability to embed sustainability throughout its operations in a way that makes these higher standards irreversible. Changes in leadership at the top of the company may put this to a test. At one point, the head of US operations, Bill Simon, publicly signaled his view of sustainability as sometimes "distracting" from its core business model of bringing products to market at the lowest price possible. His comments indicate he does not believe all of the company's sustainability initiatives have created value. But, he wasn't ultimately tapped to take over the top job of CEO of Walmart International in 2014. Doug McMillon was. And the company's commitment to sustainability has so far endured through this transition. But, it serves as a reminder that opportunity windows may also contract through changes in the economic or institutional environment and, importantly, how leadership interprets these changes.

The different types of firms studied in this book all had leadership willing to drive the process forward and, critically, all these leaders had opportunities to mobilize the firm's resources within the structural constraints of their organizational environments. While limited in different ways, all three cases demonstrate a multifaceted capacity to contribute to the creation of private governance institutions, resulting in a division of labor of sorts. The hope for both business and civil society actors alike is that this piecemeal approach, leading to a diverse array of initiatives, might somehow fit together someday, offering comprehensive coverage of the social and environmental issues facing the industry.

Conclusion

Despite the very intangible nature of the civil society threat, it enabled proactive executives to drive the private regulatory process forward. Leadership was a key element and this leadership was nurtured by past experience with civil society contestation,[3] Past engagement created systems and embedded norms that expanded the prospective window for political mobilization and enhanced the political agency of the institutional entrepreneurs.

Institutional entrepreneurs have the potential to not only act as role models, but also change the calculations for other industry actors. They increase the risk for those companies that resist civil society demands by delegitimizing this resistance and increasing the likelihood these outliers will be directly targeted in the future. At the same time, they increase the opportunities for other business actors to mimic their political engagement by reducing the risk for late-comers as far as potential backlash or wasted resources. They reduce the cost to followers who can now skip the experimentation stage and implement similar policies with cost certainty. And these leaders expand institutional opportunities by increasing the legitimacy of corporate political mobilization on these issues and others, diffusing norms of engagement through learning networks, benchmarking, and isomorphic pressures.

However, the findings also speak to the limitations of what society can expect from firms regarding their willingness and ability to contribute positively to the regulation of global supply chains. Crises, or issues that threaten the core business interests of firms, can enable institutional entrepreneurs to change the practices of their firm, but even deep changes seem to conform to the requisites of each firm's business model.

7
Conclusion

When I arrived at Walmart headquarters in Bentonville that stifling August day, I showed my ID at the front desk. They checked their computer screens, made some calls, and handed back my passport. They then passed me a Walmart nametag. It was a sticker with my name and the company logo, blue and yellow. I peeled off the back and attached it to my lapel while the woman at the counter contacted the executive I was there to meet.

I could hear the enthusiastic voices of people around me, engaged in animated conversation. When I focused in on a small group near me, I realized they were salespeople—come to pitch their products to the Walmart buyers inside. No wonder they sounded excited. If they could get Walmart on board, their business success would be all but guaranteed. Such is the market power of the world's biggest retailer.

The woman at the desk hung up the phone and politely instructed me to head toward the guard at the door to the building's inner chambers. He stood beside a metal detector and was holding a wand, the type you see at a store checkout. He scanned the barcode that I hadn't yet noticed on my nametag. I passed through, processed.

Walmart's senior director of sustainability and compliance, Vonda Lockwood, greeted me on the other side. Though friendly, she had an air that demanded respect. She led me through the halls past rows of large rectangular windows on either side. Behind each window was a room containing a single table surrounded by chairs. These were the rooms in which Walmart buyers met with suppliers. Where the suppliers made their pitches and the Walmart people decided their futures. She led me into one.

Inside was another Walmart executive who worked on "innovations and sustainability"—a position that did not even exist only a few years previous. With him was Michelle Harvey, a representative from the Environmental Defense Fund, one of the largest and wealthiest environmental organizations in the US. Like other environmental groups, EDF had set up a small field office in Bentonville to work with Walmart on the company's sustainability initiative. Harvey is one of two EDF staff members located in Bentonville and she leads their "onsite corporate partnership" with the company (EDF 2015). I had originally arranged to meet Harvey and the Walmart executive separately, but they had called back and suggested we all meet together to discuss what they were working on. Times had changed.

After our meeting I was given a short tour of the building by Harvey, the EDF representative—rather than the Walmart staff themselves. That was some sign of cooperation, I thought. We walked through the vast halls of this nondescript, utilitarian building. Only a few years ago the interior was painted gray throughout, she explained, meeting the expectations for a company built on practical frugality. It had always been the sales that were important, not the décor. Expanding sales, nothing else.

Now the halls were painted a variety of colors with slogans stenciled throughout. Upon closer inspection, the slogans were predominantly related to sustainability. Quotes from Lee Scott's inspirational 2005 speech dominated. These painted walls were a reflection of cultural change and a mechanism for more of it.

We rounded a corner and I was led into an enormous theater-like hall. Again, the walls were adorned with Walmart's sustainability slogans. This was the hall in which Scott delivered his speech to the gathered Walmart executives. The speech has taken on historical proportions (for the company anyway), and is treated with apposite reverence. Rightly so. It had changed the company's direction, politically at least.

The changes I saw during my visit were striking. Only five years ago, it would have been highly unusual for me, as a researcher, to be invited here and given a tour around. It would have seemed extraordinary that our meeting would take place with an environmental activist in the room, let alone that the Walmart and NGO representatives would be taking turns explaining different aspects of their partnership to me. That the walls would be painted bright, with Walmart's commitment to the environment declared throughout, would have been almost unimaginable. But here we were. Leaders within the company were changing the culture of the place, and this culture change was being reflected in its practices. They were building institutions that would help solidify the company's commitment to sustainability. They were paving the way toward the company's expanded role in global environmental governance, albeit a role on its own terms.

Walmart is a unique company, but similar stories are being written across industries. Proactive executives are not only changing how their companies do business, but are also changing the governance landscape around them. With the help of activists, business actors have carved out new and impactful roles in global environmental governance. Through the story of gold jewelry retailers, this book has explored when, why, and how different companies have expanded their mandates and, in doing so, have expanded the opportunities for others to follow.

But what effect are proactive retailers having on the actual gold mining industry itself? Is retail-led governance changing the practices of the mining companies? Our findings suggest retailers can have a positive impact on their suppliers, though not necessarily due to their economic clout.

There is a big difference between getting retailers on board and getting miners on board, or actually changing mining practices. We cannot *force* widespread changes in gold mining through the market leverage of retailers alone. The threat of economic sanctions in the form of canceled orders with branded buyers rarely drives substantive change along supply chains. This has been the case across industries in which activists have targeted retailers, including the well-known campaigns targeting popular apparel brands like Nike.[1] This appears to be especially the case when dealing with natural resource supply chains. The market power of retailers is rarely sufficient to force hard compliance across the industries that supply them.

Such is the case with gold. In order to make a clear link between gold jewelry demand and gold mining practices, activists have stressed that 80 percent of end-use demand comes from gold jewelry (NDG n.d.). While this may be true for end-use consumer demand, this figure leaves out demand for gold as an investment asset.

If we include demand for physical bars, coins, ETFs, and official sector purchases, then jewelry accounts for about half of the worldwide demand for gold (WGC 2015). This adds an additional market, which would need to be politicized by activists to prevent it from reducing their market

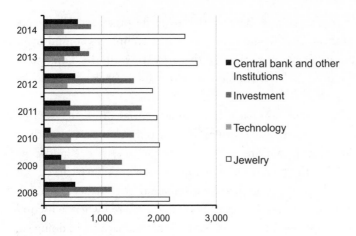

Figure 7.1

Gold demand by sector (WGC 2015)

leverage. The existence of multiple markets offers "exit options" to gold mining companies that might want to avoid the dictates of branded buyers.

Even the gold jewelry market itself is not a single market. Gold jewelry is sold in multiple countries, often by traders without recognizable brands. Consumer leverage is located where the money is; thus, targeting retailers in rich countries has been a favored strategy for activists. This is one of the reasons why consumer campaigns in the gold commodity chain have focused not on the jewelry market in general, but rather on the US jewelry market. However, while the US is the largest developed country market for jewelry, it is not the largest market for gold. The US and EU markets together only account for just under 10% of world demand for gold destined for jewelry (WGC 2012c). In 2014, the three biggest markets for gold were India (842.7 tonnes), China (813.6 tonnes), and then the US (179.2 tonnes). The last 10 years have seen a 71% increase in the demand volumes of India and China combined (WGC 2015), with China's demand for gold having more than doubled over the course of just a few years (WGC 2012c; Statista 2015). And these patterns are reflected in the global demand for jewelry, with India (662.1 tonnes) leading the way, China (623.5 tonnes) a close second, and the US (132.4 tonnes) a distant third (WGC 2015). Clearly, the combined buying power of India and China reduces the overall market power of US jewelers vis-à-vis their

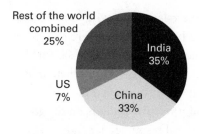

Figure 7.2

Gold jewelry demand by country, 2014 (WGC 2015)

global suppliers. Indeed, China and India together accounted for fully 68% of the 2,152.9 tonnes of gold destined for the jewelry sector in 2014 (WGC 2015).

In these large Asian markets, activists may not even be able to garner the very limited leverage through brands they have realized in the US market. The Chinese market, for example, is very different than the US or EU markets in that the mark-ups for adornment are not there. The market for jewelry is less based on emotive marketing and more closely linked to investment. Jewelry is bought by quality and weight; there are much smaller mark-ups for design and branding (WGC, personal communication, July 18, 2012). The cultural significance of gold in India would be another hurdle for activists. For example, gold passed down through families acts as an important financial security instrument, especially for women. So much so that major banks in the country accept jewelry as collateral for short-term loans, a practice that has been going on for generations, and a practice that some commercial banks were recently legislated to continue (Larmer 2009, 58).

But activists face limitations even when we consider only the US jewelry market. The jewelry industry itself is highly fragmented, with the US market alone composed of about 28,000 specialty stores, although the top 50 chains account for almost half of sales and consolidation of large retailers appears to be increasing (Hoovers 2011; *National Jeweler* 2016). The fact remains that the thousands of small, independently operated designers and retailers are not directly targeted by the NDG campaign and are generally far less active in the politics of gold.

But if there is one thing we've learned from the case of jewelry retailers it is that industry change is not explained through economic leverage alone. Activists seldom *force* change—there is rarely a visible impact on the bottom line of retailers, as evidenced by the lack of repercussions for firms like Rolex and Macy's. Instead, activists create the space for dialogue and change by loosening the restrictions of the market. It is a process of learning and leadership that drives institutional change.

The same can be said for the effects of proactive retailers on the governance of gold, and the governance of natural resources generally. We can expect any changes in extraction through retailer-led governance to be driven by entrepreneurial executives within the mining companies. This is not to say that economic incentives don't play a part. The case of gold jewelers suggests that changing buying criteria and expectations of gold buyers should reduce the perceived risk of being sanctioned for institutional entrepreneurs working within mining companies.

Hard, state regulation has a role to play here as well. In fact, it remains absolutely necessary and desirable when well-conceived. While it is difficult to identify changes in mining practices that can be directly attributed to the NDG campaign or retailer initiatives, there is potential for a ripple effect. Through dialogue and learning, certain practices, while legal in some jurisdictions, are being stigmatized. Through the work of individuals from civil society and industry, an understanding of the impacts of market decisions is being improved—as is transparency along industry supply chains. These changes make further improvements cheaper and easier. With more companies on board, one could optimistically expect less business power to be used to resist regulation, and some to even be directed toward supporting stronger regulation—even if this is only driven by competitive pressures to keep the playing field level for those companies already implementing higher standards. In other words, the jewelry cases demonstrate that private governance and state regulation can be complementary.

The impact of retailer-led governance, not unlike that of activist direct-targeting, has the potential to be greater than its direct economic impact. The power of actors from both industry and civil society works through multiple dimensions. Sometimes they can create immediate changes in corporate policy by altering economic incentives. But, this is not where their power ends. Their political actions can open the door to further innovation, leadership, and change. While understanding the actual impacts of retailer-led initiatives on the practices of gold miners remains a tad speculative at this stage, there are a number of more concrete lessons that can be gleaned from the experience of gold jewelers.

Ten Takeaways

So what core lessons can we learn about business power and agency in global governance from the experiences of gold jewelry retailers? We can pick out ten key insights from the preceding pages that can further our understanding of why businesses have seemingly expanded their role in global environmental governance and the ways that activists have influenced their practices.

1. Activists create opportunities and empower executives.
2. Business power can also expand the opportunity window.
3. Cross-fertilization expands opportunities across issue areas.
4. Business actors may control the process, but are not always defiant.
5. There is a division of labor within civil society, within industry, and between the two.
6. Variation in firm responses may lead to comprehensive coverage.
7. Risk need not be tangible to incentivize industry to respond.
8. Once lead firms are on board, others will probably follow.
9. There may be trade-offs involved in both collaboration and contestation.
10. Repeated or sustained contestation can help ratchet up private governance mechanisms.

1. Activists create opportunities and empower executives

During the non-state institution-building process, activists *create* the political space for business actors to later fill. There has been a tendency in the social movement literature to treat political opportunities as already existing structural conditions. But this study has shown that activists can construct opportunities through issue framing, placing social and environmental concerns on the business agenda. Activists need only breathe word of a potential campaign to create risk and, in so doing, empower forward-thinking executives to respond proactively.

Crisis is a key mechanism by which regulatory initiatives emerge outside of state institutions. Leaders from the jewelry industry have shown that business actors can be earnest political players outside of state institutions, mobilizing the resources of the industry for political purposes, with tangible results to show for these efforts. However, these efforts are enabled by activist contestation. Fledgling governance institutions would surely not have emerged without the concerted efforts of these civil society actors. These actors created the crisis, or exogenous shock, necessary to destabilize the regulatory equilibrium in the market. In effect, they empowered industry executives by offering them a business case to act politically, expanding their room to move.

2. Business power can also expand the opportunity window

The other key mechanism driving the creation of private governance is the leadership of industry actors. The difference between those that have led the process and those that have either followed or resisted altogether comes down to leadership. Civil society actors create the opportunity to act, but there needs to be leadership present within the industry to power the process.

Throughout this book, I have stressed that the engine powering these processes has been the instrumental power of firms. The findings suggest that activists may be the impetus behind corporate political mobilization, but the direct mechanism for expanding the opportunity window was business power wielded by people within the firm.

Activists bring the issues to industry, but business actors translate these issues into policies and actionable practices. Institutional entrepreneurs exercise the instrumental power of the firm to realign the firm's interests and practices with the new expectations of the market. They develop systems that reflect these new interests and practices, expanding the opportunity window for future leadership. Mitigation technologies and practices are constructed and the marginal cost of future compliance declines. Social and environmental norms are institutionalized throughout the company, reducing the potential for future resistance. Norms climb the leadership ladder to senior management or those that are tasked with these issues (like CSR departments) become more influential themselves. Overall, the presence of leadership poised to take advantage of these opportunities becomes more likely.

3. Cross-fertilization expands opportunities across issue areas

The findings suggest the cumulative effect of activist pressure is not restricted to the immediate issue of concern. Cross-issue learning can take place. Systems created by activists and business actors may translate across issue areas. The cases have clearly shown this potential for cross-fertilization as activist pressure in other spheres of industry activity expanded the opportunities for proactive political mobilization in response to "dirty gold."

Perhaps the starkest example came from Walmart. Civil society contestation focused on labor issues gave rise to action on environmental issues, moving from wages and unionization to eco-efficiency and supply chain risk. We witnessed something similar in the other two cases, with both categories of companies driving their responsible gold strategies into the systems and markets created by "conflict diamonds."

The separate issue of "conflict gold" is now also being driven through the opportunity window created by "conflict diamonds" and "dirty gold." While activist action on "dirty gold" has not yet led to an across-the-board mobilization of mining companies, the issue of "conflict gold" has gotten the attention of the miners. Through their political organization, the WGC, the world's major mining companies are attempting to distance themselves from "conflict gold" and are developing their own chain-of-custody system. The seemingly robust traceability mechanisms being developed come from a recognition that these conflicts are going to keep arising, in different regions and different issue areas, and WGC members need a more universal system that is transferable and will protect them (WGC, personal communication, July 18, 2012).

So, we have ample evidence from the cases of the cross-issue and cumulative effect of activist contestation. While we must be careful not to exaggerate the potential of these activities, the opportunities model has demonstrated the mechanisms by which institutional learning and operational systems reduce the marginal cost of future engagement and build a culture around social and environmental responsibility.

4. Business actors may control the process, but are not always defiant

There can be a temptation to conflate industry control over the process with weak regulation. While there are some good reasons to make such assumptions, the result is a tendency to underestimate the contribution of business actors to global governance. While the political efforts of institutional entrepreneurs certainly include a healthy element of self-interest, this does not negate the fact that these efforts can also be valuable contributions toward improving the social and environmental performance of industry.

All of the jewelers have avoided relinquishing any policy or operational autonomy to activists. Ethical jewelers have filled the gap by only procuring what they see as the highest standard materials, specialty jewelers rushed to create an industry-led certification to organize politically and neutralize the threat, and diversified jewelers have either done nothing or created a niche line of jewelry as they were never really at risk. In this way, the cases appear to confirm findings from different industries that suggest one of the main goals of firms is to maintain their autonomy while reducing the risk to their business interests (see, for example, Gereffi et al. 2001; Sasser 2003; Sasser et al. 2006). Even Tiffany, a firm led by a CEO who seems to share the deep social and ecological commitments of the activists, helped found the RJC, which shut NGOs out of the inner policy circle.[2]

While no firms in the industry have relinquished autonomy to the activists, the autonomy of institutional entrepreneurs within these firms continues to be limited by market forces. While it may appear that business actors have controlled the private institution-building process, their actions have been channeled by the structural constraints present in the market. The extent to which business actors were able to mobilize industry resources for political purposes certainly involved significant agency, but this agency was subject to the opportunities available to them within their particular type of firm—an assertion backed up by the patterns present between and within categories of firms. When these market constraints are underestimated, the autonomy of business actors and their ability to control the private institution-building process can be severely exaggerated. It is this lack of autonomy that limits the potential impacts of proactive corporate political mobilization. And these findings resonate with studies emphasizing the limits to CSR (Vogel 2005) as well as those highlighting the difficulty managers face when attempting to balance their responsibilities to shareholders with their often conflicting responsibilities to the wider society (Mason and O'Mahony 2008).

While business has been largely able to control the process, and those leading the charge are themselves limited by markets, this does not necessarily negate progress toward robust regulation. The next two lessons drive this point home.

5. There is a division of labor within industry, within civil society, and between the two

There appears to be a division of labor taking shape, among actors working within the private sector, within civil society, and between the two. They all contribute in different ways to the tapestry of governance.

That different firms have different opportunities to contribute to global governance should be clear. Business actors have limited autonomy for political action when working within markets and this should temper expectations for what can be accomplished through these non-state initiatives.

The story of gold jewelers has also included a division of labor among activists. Some create risk, others provide information. Some leverage buying power, while others lobby government, the public, or corporations directly. There is an array of groups, each employing a variety of tactics. One of the starkest divisions is between the "attack dogs" of the activist world and the groups that focus on "corporate partnerships." While the former include groups like Earthworks (though they aren't as aggressive as the Rainforest Action Network or even Greenpeace, for example) the latter refers to groups like EDF and CI. The former open up the space for proactive corporate engagement while the latter help business actors fill that space. Though this is not necessarily part of an overarching strategy by these groups, the result is a division of labor that helps spur the process.

So contrary to the conventional narrative of activists relentlessly attacking firms and these firms reactively defending against this perceived threat, this book has shown instances of civil society activists actually facilitating the political mobilization of business actors. This has taken place through the political space that activists create for corporate executives, but also through organizing meetings between business actors and critiquing, though not trashing, the responses that industry actors innovate. The result is an incomplete and often imperfect array of private governance initiatives. But there is also evidence supporting a case for cautious optimism.

6. Variation in firm responses may lead to comprehensive coverage

Any type of firm can contribute to the non-state regulatory architecture, albeit in different ways. The results witnessed along the gold supply chain support this; lead firms are creating or supporting a variety of initiatives covering different dimensions of gold governance. The hope is that these diverse regulatory contributions might eventually link together and form comprehensive coverage for the industry. There appears to be some evidence to this effect. Certainly the impact of leadership among business actors becomes amplified when ideas and practices diffuse through organizations, among organizations, and across industries. But there are also clear signs that groups working on different elements of the industry, those within their respective spheres of interests and influence, are contributing to different aspects of what might result in something more comprehensive over time.

Along the gold commodity chain, IRMA hopes to certify mine sites and the WGC is working on a chain of custody from mine to refiner. The RJC has a chain of custody from refiner to jeweler and there is now an additional program, the Global e-Sustainability Initiative (GeSI), which is working from refiner to the electronics industry. ARM is working on different ways to expand the market for FT/FM gold, working with FLO in Europe and Fairtrade USA in the US, while also negotiating pending agreements to link into the RJC chain of custody and industrial consumer base. There remains much work to be done, but the evolving standards certainly indicate there is both a ratchet-up effect to existing standards and the possibility they will fit together at some point in the future.

So perhaps, in this case at least, it is less accurate to think of these initiatives as competing with one another and more fruitful to think of them as potentially complementary dimensions of an evolving regulatory landscape.

7. Risk need not be tangible to incentivize industry to respond

Through the politicization of markets, activists do not necessarily need to create a tangible threat. Merely being exposed to a *potential* threat is often enough to open the opportunity window. Activists created the crisis in the jewelry industry through a very intangible threat. However, risk is inherently intangible and markets tend to discipline those exposed to it. Simply the threat of exposure is often sufficient to expand the opportunity window enough for entrepreneurial executives to drive the private governance process forward.

It is the intangible nature of risk that necessitates interpretation and it is this interpretative element that grants institutional entrepreneurs significant discretionary power in policymaking. The lesson is that if activists create risk by politicizing the market, simply by threatening to target firms within it, often there will be a latent leader ready to champion necessary change.

8.   Once lead firms are on board, others will probably follow

It appears all campaigners really need is to get one lead firm on board and others will follow. So if they can get one latent leader, occupying the right position in the right firm, it has the potential to be a game changer for the industry.

An opportunities approach helped us understand the mechanisms by which lead firms increase the opportunities for others to follow in their footsteps while the empirical findings improved our understanding of the model itself by detailing the mechanisms underpinning the theory. Along the economic dimension, lead firms increase the risk of resisting, decrease the risk of engaging, and reduce the costs of implementation by offering a model to mimic. Along the institutional dimension, they increase the legitimacy of proactive policies while disseminating social and environmental norms through learning networks, benchmarking, and isomorphic pressures. Thus, lead firms can amplify the cumulative effects of activist contestation by diffusing these practices and norms across the industry.

Activists have partners—in fact, *need* partners—within the business community. These cases have revealed a symbiotic relationship. Only when people from civil society and industry work together do they create and act upon opportunities to mobilize private sector resources for political purposes. Activists are necessary to not only bring the issues to the attention of business actors, but to give latent leaders the business case they need to escape the structural constraints of market requisites. And only through the effort of internal champions within firms is this intangible risk transformed into corporate engagement. The firms that lacked this leadership either did not move or moved much more slowly. The same can be said for those that lacked the business case.

9. There may be trade-offs involved in both collaboration and contestation

The findings remind us that there are trade-offs involved in private institution-building through the cooperation and contestation of firms and NGOs. Some scholars have voiced concerns over the creation of interdependence between firms and NGOs that could lead to a domestication or taming of radical campaign strategies and values that do not easily mesh with a market-oriented logic (Falkner 2003; Ford 2005; Taylor 2005; Klooster 2010; Dauvergne and LeBaron 2014). It is easy to see the potential for this in the jewelry supply chain. NGOs that have bought into Walmart's market-driven sustainability initiative have been rewarded with insider knowledge and influence. Although NGOs working with Walmart, such as EDF, made it clear to me that they do not accept funding from the company (EDF, personal communication, August 16, 2011), the relationship allows them to deliver "wins" to their funders and so there is certainly an indirect financial benefit to this relationship. Although Walmart cannot use its instrumental power to compel favorable treatment from these NGOs, they wield enormous structural power in the relationship. These NGOs have significant resources invested in their association with the company and its willingness to work closely with them. Walmart has shown that NGOs that do not play by its rules are shut out, which is exactly what happened when the NDG campaigners gave Walmart a low score on their report cards and criticized the company's "Love, Earth" line of jewelry. Another reading of the NDG example, however, demonstrates the willingness of many NGOs to break away from this cozy relationship and retract the civil society legitimacy the companies so desire.

10. Repeated or sustained contestation can help ratchet up private governance mechanisms

Continued or repeated activist pressure incentivizes business actors to develop more elaborate systems for dealing with social and environmental issues. These systems become a cost-effective way of protecting their interests, as opposed to quick-fix solutions that would need to be repeated as new issues arise. This implies that, along with the cumulative effect of activist pressure, a key mechanism to ratchet up private governance and industry practices is to keep the market politicized so institutional entre-preneurs from civil society and industry might leverage the risk into further opportunities and action.

The findings indirectly suggest that when the market lacks this politi-cized element and when the risk dissipates, either through a discontinua-tion of activist pressure or a disinterest by business actors and consumers, the business case for mitigating the impacts of corporate activity in the sector also disappears. Once the risk dissipates, the fissure that appeared in the structural constraints of the market will be filled with industry-led directives and a regulatory equilibrium will again be reached. When this happens, we can expect the opportunity window for business actors to contract, as the market again demands less expenditure on political issues. If the goal is to engage the resources of the private sector to bolster the social and environmental regulatory architecture in the industry, activists need to keep these structural constraints fractured. They need to keep the market politicized. Only while politicized will business actors retain the mandate to engage in the institution-building process.

Concluding Thoughts

There is good reason to be skeptical of corporate-led environmental gov-ernance. Many firms across industries have a long history of willful igno-rance on environmentalism, disingenuousness, or even ruthless practices to combat environmental movements. The immediate impact of Walmart's sustainability initiative, for example, does not make up for the unsustain-able nature of continuous expansion, selling more and more goods for cheaper—and encouraging more and more consumption of Earth's finite resources.

Peter Dauvergne and Jane Lister (2013), in their important work on "big brand" sustainability, rightly note that much of the change we are seeing in business practices is incremental and will not offset the environ-mental damage, or the unequal distribution of this damage, driven by the mass consuming, discount economy. If left to its own devices, the expan-sion of business engagement in global governance may simply reinforce a hierarchy of priorities that privileges short-term market interests over environmental ones, while consolidating the business power and authority that underpins it. Activists and academics alike must remain vigilant, which only underscores the importance of taking these actors and initiatives seriously. Continued collaboration (and confrontation) between states, activists, and industry is necessary. Linking state regulation to private initiatives is desirable. Working on the political and economic structures that channel unsustainable practices is critical.

There certainly appears to be substantial change taking place in the jewelry industry. There is evidence of past action on environmental issues, by both activists and business actors, leading to more action—even in other issue areas. There is evidence that the private initiatives in the jewelry industry are linking up with one another and forming more comprehensive coverage. There is evidence there could be more to come—that activists and proactive executives are expanding the opportunities for future action on these issues and others. And businesses in other industries, as well as those along their supply chains, may follow suit. There is even a suggestion that this could also expand opportunities for an expansion of traditional "hard" regulation by states. People are shifting industry practices. But, more importantly, they are building institutions that shift the parameters for environmental action.

This last point is extremely important—and the one I want to leave you with. These so-called market-based initiatives are political. This is not a case of the market mechanism providing solutions for environmental problems. This is a case of people acting politically within the market.

The examples I offer in this book are certainly *not* examples of "the invisible green hand" (*Economist*, July 4, 2002) of the market at work. They are the exact opposite. They are the work of a collection of very visible hands. They are examples of political agency at work.

There is a case for cautious optimism here, but not one that stems from "win-win" solutions within existing market structures. It stems from the people acting upon these market structures, and changing them. This is where I see the potential for meaningful change.

Appendix: Research Methods and Design

Process tracing is a within case study technique that pays particular attention to process, as the name suggests, seeking to identify the causal pathways linking independent variables to outcomes. In so doing, it lends itself to uncovering the layers of complex multi-causality present in social phenomena, including the organizational decision-making and the political action of corporate actors.[1] As Steven Brint and Jerome Karabel (1991, 346) argue, "A key task of the institutional analyst is to specify [the power structures and opportunity field] faced by decision-makers and to show how they shape and constrain the pattern of development of organizations operating within a particular field. Since organizational forms develop over time, such an analysis will almost necessarily be historical in character."

What's more, as Jacob Hacker and Paul Pierson (2002) have previously argued, analyses of firm behavior must not simply infer firm preferences and influence from a *post hoc* correlation between the observed outcomes and a preconceived notion of the firm's interests. Interests change with the evolution of institutions and policies, positions may be strategic rather than reflect actual preferences and, therefore, outcomes can end up anywhere along a continuum between their initial position and the negotiated result (Hacker and Pierson, 2002). All social interaction is influenced by previous events, encounters, and interpretations; an historical approach helps capture the interplay between economic and institutional opportunities, the effects of learning and the development of policies through trial and error, imitation and innovation (see also Hobden 1998).

Importantly, process tracing allows for agency. While a key component of an "opportunities" approach is to recognize that agents are embedded in socioeconomic structures that channel their actions, process tracing leaves conceptual space for actors to not only work within these structures, but also upon them. My goal is to be sensitive to structures changing over time and so escape the trap of privileging and naturalizing the current *status quo*, which is always a danger when separating case from context.

So when I interpret firm preference formation, decision-making, and influence I begin with an analysis that considers the history of each firm, its past interactions with political issues, and the evolution of its response to the issue at hand.

Using historical process tracing makes sense if we are to take agency seriously, but there is a trade-off to be made. Context-specific, historical analysis of this kind does not lend itself to producing widely generalizable and parsimonious theories (Checkel 2006, 2007; Lake and McCubbins 2006)—nor does it attempt to. Instead of identifying single and independent causal variables as necessary or sufficient (see for example, King, Keohane, and Verba 1994), it produces causal narratives that fall somewhere in between generalizable laws and thick description (Elster 1998).

By using this approach, I accept the trade-off. However, I do leverage my findings by incorporating a comparative approach within the controlled environment of the US jewelry industry. By comparing across different types of gold jewelry retailers, I attempt to overcome some of the limitations of historical process tracing. Imposing a kind of "structured agency" (more on this in chapter 2) allows me to generate findings and identify patterns that can contribute to the development of a more generalizable theory from the particulars of the case; namely, the firm-level opportunities that structure business actor agency when responding to civil society contestation.[2]

This approach falls largely in line with what is sometimes referred to as "theory-guided process tracing" (see, for example, Faletti 2006; Faletti and Lynch 2009), which has been usefully characterized by Ronald Aminzade (1993, 108) as requiring "theoretically explicit narratives that carefully trace and compare the sequences of events constituting the process." Here, I organize the case narratives around firm-level variables, derived in chapter 2, which facilitates the later comparison between cases. This allows me to probe the plausibility of the model and to generate additional insights (see also Büthe 2002, 489). As Aminzade (1993, 108) notes, "by comparing sequences, we can determine whether there are typical sequences across [cases] ... and can explore the causes and consequences of different sequence patterns."

I do realize that the focus on lead firms introduces the potential for bias. Results will skew toward an emphasis on proactive firms and away from intransigent firms. The jewelry industry includes a number of as-yet obdurate players. While their disinterest is documented and explored here, there are inherent difficulties in including these firms in a more comprehensive manner. One problem is that there is often by definition not much activity to report on and, even though this in itself may be of interest to analysts, business actors that do not engage in these issues also tend not to engage in research attempting to explain why this might be the case. However, the pattern of firm commitments over time shows significant similarities between like firms. This suggests that either the responses of lead firms, though they tended to be first-movers and engage more deeply with the issues, are either representative of most firms in their category or, alternatively, that they have influenced their peers to the point of imitation. Either way, for our purposes, and given the necessity of investigating only a very small number of firms to conduct the historical process tracing, a focus on lead firms remains our best option. When possible, I reference observed differences across firms *within* each category, but because of time and space constraints, as well as the difficulty in gathering data on unresponsive firms, I leave the deep study of unresponsive firms for another day.[3]

In essence, this is a within-case analysis with a comparative case dimension involving a small number of cases. It represents only one industry, and—although the campaign has a global focus, the corporations have global reach, and the effects of the governance initiatives have global implications—the protagonist organizations all hail from one country, which quite obviously limits the extent to which the findings can be generalized across institutional settings. But, it should be clear that my goal for this book is to develop and refine a more sophisticated model of corporate engagement with activists, and the social and environmental issues associated with their particular industry. Rigorous theory-testing projects, with cases chosen to vary the explanatory variables across industries and firms, could be conducted at a later time, which should allow for stronger causal inferences on the individual variables themselves.

Notes

Chapter 1

1. Robert Falkner (2003, 72–73) has usefully defined private governance as emerging from "the interactions among private actors, or between private actors on the one hand and civil society and state actors on the other, give rise to institutional arrangements that structure and direct actors' behavior in an issue-specific area." See also Clapp 1998; Cutler et al. 1999; Cutler 1999, 2002, 2003, 2009, 2010; Hall and Biersteker 2002; Haufler 1993, 1999, 2000, 2001; Webb 2008 for a range of perspectives on the emergence of "private authority" in the global economy. In the most recent contribution, Green (2014) distinguishes between the emergence of different forms of private authority: one form being delegated by the state at the other initiated and institutionalized by non-state actors themselves.

2. See, for example, Pattberg and Dingwerth 2007; Gulbrandsen 2010; Auld 2014; Green 2014.

3. There are some excellent recent contributions that buck this trend. Büthe and Mattli (2011) have written on how global private governance initiatives are created, across sectors and issue areas, envisioning them as a result of political contests linked to the domestic context of firms. Pattberg (2005), Bartley (2007), and Auld (2014) see the emergence of private governance mechanisms explained through a combination of market solutions and political contests between firms and NGOs, a perspective that resonates strongly with the findings in this book. Additionally, scholars have offered valuable insights into the role international organizations (Abbott 2012; Abbott et al. 2012) and states (Schleifer 2013; Overdevest and Zeitlin 2014) play in orchestrating the creation and maintenance of private governance initiatives.

4. I use the term "corporate political mobilization" throughout the book to change the focus from "the firm" to the actors within the industry who attempt to mobilize firm and industry resources for the purpose of influencing their institutional environment in the face of countervailing forces. Nedelmann (1987, 181) has usefully defined "political mobilization" as "the actors' attempt to influence the existing distribution of power." As a concept, corporate political mobilization better captures the active and collective nature of industry responses to political

contestation than the idea of corporate political "strategy" or "activity" as it emphases the process of building support for initiatives while centering on the role of power and the struggles inherent in the process. In other words, it captures the ways in which firms sometimes act like social movements and become political agents of change (see Soule 2012 for a useful review of some recent literature). In favoring this language, I am in good company. Edward Walker and Christopher Rea (2014, 284) have placed their scholarly authority behind using the language of mobilization "to highlight the move by contemporary scholarship to extend concepts from the study of social movements, revealing continuities between the political actions of business and those made by other actors seeking to maintain or destabilize institutionalized practices within fields of strategic action" (see also Fligstein and McAdam 2012).

5. This example is adapted from Solomon and Nicholls 2010, 6.

6. These politics have been playing out in various industries, including forestry (Cashore 2002; Bernstein and Cashore 2000, 2007; Cashore, Auld, and Newsom 2004; Pattberg 2005b), fisheries (Constance and Bonanno 2000; Cummins 2004; Gale and Haward 2004, 2011; Ponte 2008; Gulbrandsen 2009), biotechnology (Skogstad 2001; Falkner 2000; Bail, Falkner and Marquard 2002; Schurman 2004), coffee (Muradian and Pelupessy 2005; MacDonald 2007; Auld 2010a), e-waste (Renckens 2013), and palm oil (Schleifer 2015).

7. Philipp Pattberg (2006, 243) has written on the multiple ways by which to categorize private regulation based on who develops the standards, the focus of the standards, and how these standards are verified and enforced. First, we might make a distinction based on whether the rules originated from the public or private sector or, more relevant to a study focused on private regulation, whether the standards were developed by industry, civil society, or through a multi-stakeholder process including broad representation from both groups. Second, we might distinguish between regulation that industry groups have traditionally been associated with, such as that focused on quality, health, and safety issues of the product itself versus the increasingly common regulation based on the process by which a product comes to market, accounting for management practices that impact upon the social and environmental externalities of the industry. Third, we might make a distinction based on who monitors and enforces the rules and, specifically, if this is done by the firm itself, an industry group representing multiple firms, or by an independent, third-party auditor. With these options in mind, the typology used here is focused on private, process-oriented regulatory initiatives, but is based on both who sets the rules as well as who verifies compliance.

8. Regulatory systems gain this legitimacy through the perceived effectiveness of their procedures and results. Building from Scharpf's (1999) input-oriented and output-oriented dimensions of democratic legitimacy, input legitimacy is a procedural element that refers to how well the regulatory process incorporates the preferences of its stakeholders. It is about the perceived legitimacy of the regulatory process. In contrast, output legitimacy considers the functional elements of a regulatory system and is based on the effectiveness of the outcomes or, as Scharpf (1997, 19) has put it, "achieving the goals that citizens collectively care about." See also Mattli and Woods (2009) for the distinction between the "proceduralist"

and "idealist' school of legitimacy, which roughly parallels the input–output distinction. Additionally, Beisheim and Dingwerth (2008) link the success of non-state regulatory initiatives to procedural legitimacy based on a case study of the Global Reporting Initiative (GRI).

9. Some second-party initiatives are attempting to fill this gap as they ratchet up their standards in response to external criticism (see, for example, Cashore et al. 2007; Overdevest 2010; Bloomfield 2012). See Pattberg 2006 for a nice breakdown of the ways in which we could categorize private governance.

10. Fairtrade International was formerly the Fair Labour Organisation.

11. More information about IRMA is available at responsiblemining.net. You can also view part of the framework draft developed in Vancouver at the International Mining (n.d.) website, http://corporate.im-mining.com/Articles/TheInitiativeforResponsibleMiningAssurance.asp.

12. I adopt the term "ethical jeweler" when referring to the boutique jewelers who have differentiated themselves based on their social and environmental commitments and the impacts of their business practices. I am using the term for convenience, and so it should not be taken to imply that jewelers who are not in this category are not ethical.

13. This includes Sterling Jewelers, which places second to Walmart with annual sales at about US$2.557 billion (Hoovers 2011). However, Sterling is actually the parent company of Kay's, Jared's, and 10 additional store brands in the US. Its size is, therefore, a function of it representing 12 retail store brands. It is also a fully-owned subsidiary of Signet Jewelers in the UK, making it somewhat of a unique company and a less than perfect choice to represent US specialty jewelers.

14. Early adopters of organizational innovations may do so to improve performance or mitigate risk, but these new processes may become infused with value that goes beyond the technical requirements and strategic motivations behind the task at hand (Selznick 1957, 17; Powell and DiMaggio 1991, 65). As organizational sociologists have shown, innovation that may have originally been adopted for strategic reasons can spread to other firms who then adopt these innovations not for strategic reasons, but because adoption provides legitimacy or a normatively sanctioned model they can copy in the face of uncertainty (Meyer and Rowan 1977; Powell and DiMaggio 1991, 65). Or, from a more economic perspective, other firms may follow once they benchmark best practices and run a cost–benefit evaluation of their options based on the responses of their competitors (Porter 1996; Dobbin and Baum 2000).

15. Institutional entrepreneurs are "actors who have an interest in particular institutional arrangements and who leverage resources to create new institutions or to transform existing ones" (Maguire, Hardy, and Lawrence 2004, 657). The term seems to have originated with Paul DiMaggio (1988, 14), when he argued that "new institutions arise when organized actors with sufficient resources see in them an opportunity to realize interests that they value highly."

16. While there are many thousands of independent designers and retailers of jewelry in the US market, they have not been targeted directly by activists and have generally been much less involved in the politics of gold.

17. By "institutional dimensions" I mean dimensions of the social, organizational, and political environment in which agents operate.

Chapter 2

1. Hacker and Pierson (2002) provide a wonderful discussion on the significant divergence within each camp, splitting theoretical positions into instrumentalist and more structural perspectives to locate areas of overlap in the field—specifically identifying the positions of Block and Lindblom as one such area of overlap.

2. The "faces of power" debate among scholars within the fields of political science and sociology is well-known with Dahl (1957) perhaps the best example of the first face of power, which was behavioral in approach and was limited to observable and, therefore, measurable, instrumental forms of power. Bachrach and Baratz (1962, 1963, 1970) added a second face of power, which took into account the power over agenda-setting and the role of non-decisions in power relations that could suppress conflict and bias debate in favor of those wielding this power. This second face of power straddles the division between instrumental and structural power as laid out in this book. The third face of power was added by Lukes (1974, 11) who argued for a structural form of power—similar to what Barnett and Duvall (2005a, 2005b) call "productive power"—one which could "prevent people, to whatever degree, from forming grievances by shaping their perceptions, cognitions and preferences in such a way that they accept their role in the existing order of things."

3. In this way, structural power as defined here is similar to Gill and Law's (1988, 73) concept referring to "material and normative aspects, such that patterns of incentives and constraints are systematically created." In contrast, instrumental power involves "agents' decisions and non-decisions in pursuing their interests" (see Guzzini 1993, 463 on the implicit differentiating criterion in Gill and Law 1988).

4. Naturally, unintentional effects could be seen as approaching the analytical territory of structural power, which they enter once these unintentional effects become deep-rooted and systematically influence expectations (see also Strange 1988; and Guzzini 1993).

5. Barnett and Duvall (2005a, 2005b) have created a useful typology that includes structural power, but they consider compulsory, institutional, and productive power as categories in their own right. While this is a useful exercise for clarifying certain analytical distinctions, the authors create divisions that are ultimately unnecessary for the study at hand and may confuse the division between instrumental and structural power and their economic and institutional manifestations as defined in this study.

6. Doris Fuchs (2005a, 2005b, 2007) maintains "discursive power" as a category unto itself, emphasizing this often hidden component of business power (other authors adopting a similar framework include: Barnett and Duvall 2005a, 2005b; Falkner 2008; Clapp and Fuchs 2009a, 2009b; Meckling 2011a, 2011b). This has been a necessary corrective to approaches that did not offer appropriate recogni-

tion of the discursive dimension of power. However, I see no reason to analytically separate it from other institutional dimensions of instrumental and structural power, which allows us to make the important distinction between its instrumental and structural variants. For example, discursive power is a particular form of instrumental power when it is deployed by identifiable actors to exert their influence over others and structural when it is deeply entrenched and accepted as appropriate by those actors it affects, similar to the idea of a "logic of consequences" giving way to a "logic of appropriateness" (March and Olsen 1996). The instrumental dimension can be mobilized to reinforce or change the structural dimension while the structural dimension can strengthen or weaken the instrumental dimension, depending on the latter's fit with the former.

7. This appears, in fact, to be one of the great misquotes of our time. It is based on the recollection of one senator that was at a US Senate hearing held in 1953 and attributed to the CEO of GM, Charles Wilson, who was being investigated for a potential conflict of interest. Nevertheless, it makes for a well-known, if potentially inaccurate, example of discursive power wielded by big business to curry political favor. I am grateful to one of the anonymous reviewers for this example.

8. To avoid any confusion between categories, institutional creation and maintenance are considered instrumental power. Only the partly autonomous and unintentional effects of deep-seated institutions, in the broadest sense of the concept, are considered structural in nature.

9. Therefore, it can be thought of as a kind of impersonal power (see Ward 1987).

10. The structural variant of discursive power is similar to Barnett and Duvall's (2005a, 2005b) category of productive power; however, their concept of productive power is distinct from their concept of structural power in that it refers to a prior constitutive step of identity and interest formation. Instead of creating a productive power category, the approach taken here analytically separates productive, or discursive, forms of power into instrumental and structural variants. While "framing" is the instrumental use of discursive power, a taken-for-granted cultural or ideational "frame" is the structural variant.

11. In addition to Leca et al. (2006, 2008), see also Garud, Hardy, and Maguire (2007) for a comprehensive review of the "institutional entrepreneur" literature.

12. Studies emphasizing the divergent policy preferences of different types of firms have been prevalent in the IPE literature and include Rogowski 1987; Freiden 1988; Milner 1988a, 1988b; Hiscox 2001; Falkner 2008, 2010a.

13. The market itself, of course, could also be considered an institution, but again, it is not created or maintained by a discreet and identifiable group of actors; therefore, the force of the myriad decisions made by independent agents acting within it is considered a structural force. Likewise, one could argue that there is a capitalist class or group of elites that maintain these structural forces, but this is where the difference between the theoretical underpinnings of the "elite" theories—especially those of conventional Marxist thought—and the position I take here becomes clear.

14. See, for example, Eisinger 1973; Tarrow 1994, 1996, 1998; McAdam 1996; McAdam, McCarthy, and Zald 1996; Meyer 2003, 2004.

15. Likewise, principle-agent theorists have adopted a similar perspective that views agents as operating semi-autonomously within an "authorising environment" (Chwieroth 2008a, 484; 2008b) or "outer structural constraint" (Woods 2006, 4).

16. Reputation management was found to be a significant driver of CSR and other private governance mechanisms in a number of core studies, including Vogel 2005; Potoski and Prakash 2005; Green 2014).

17. While economic-based explanations of corporate political behavior have also stressed factors such as the size of the firm (Schuler and Rehbein 1997; Cook and Fox 2000), its organizational slack (Bourgeois 1981; Meznar and Nigh 1995), and its capital structure (Rubin and Barnea 2005), these factors tend to find their explanatory power in measuring unsolicited corporate political behavior and instances of over-compliance in social or environmental issue areas (see Hillman et al. 2004 for an in-depth review). The contention here is that the *risk-cost ratio* is of primary concern when responding to external threats and this relationship is more directly related to and observable through the specific costs of risk mitigation for each type of firm; indicators related to the general availability of resources for political activity would constitute secondary indicators.

18. Hillman, Keim, and Schuler (2004) have shown that firm age has been used for a proxy in many studies for "visibility of firm" (Hansen and Mitchell 2000), "reputation" (Baron 1995; Boddewyn and Brewer 1994; Keim and Baysinger 1988), and "experience" or "credibility" (Hillman 2003; Hillman and Hitt 1999), which could all conceivably be linked to the susceptibility of the firm to NGO pressure, and certainly to its potential political impact; however, the level of branding is a more direct indicator of the firm's exposure to risk as branding is a purposive strategy to differentiate the firm, create intangible value and, therefore, constitutes a conscious and often costly element of the firm's business model and market strategy. In contrast, there are many old and established firms that remain insulated from reputational threats, especially those that are not consumer facing.

19. This would be akin to Gereffi's (1994, 2001) "buyer-driven" commodity chain model.

20. We can consider a corporation to be a type of formal institution and corporate culture to be an institutional framework of sorts. An institutional framework is a social construct that allows an organization to, as Scott says, "define the ends and shape the means by which interests are determined and pursued" (1991, 164, cited in Powell and DiMaggio 1991, 28). Powell and DiMaggio concur: "Cultural frames thus establish approved means and define desired outcomes. ..." (1991, 28).

21. Basic underlying assumptions are the unconscious, or taken for granted, beliefs and values that will inform the other two aspects of culture and so ultimately determine behavior, perception, thought, and feeling of the agents within the firm. This is the most deep-seated of the three elements of culture and roughly correlates with the idea of the worldview of the agents within an organization. As

such, this is probably the most difficult to measure, but for the analysis at hand it is simply a matter of interpreting the combination of artifacts along with espoused beliefs and values. There are no neat lines drawn between these levels in the real world, but it will be important to keep these analytical categories in mind as we attempt to interpret the role that corporate culture plays in influencing firm responses.

22. For reference, Tarrow (1994, 18) defines political opportunity structures as "dimensions of the political environment which either encourage or discourage people from using collective action" of which he identifies four, namely, the degree of openness and closure of the polity, the stability or instability of political alignments, the presence or absence of allies and support groups, and division within the elite and its tolerance or intolerance of protests.

23. To reiterate, while this is not a theory-testing analysis, strictly speaking, but rather an exercise in theory development and refinement, being explicit about the expectations of the model will help focus the analysis, evaluate the expectations in their ability to explain these particular cases, and facilitate a more structured comparison across cases in chapter 6.

Chapter 3

1. They are also participating in the Madison Dialogue, source their diamonds from Canada, and source some of their precious gemstones from the Tanzania Women Miner's Association mining cooperative (Bario Neal 2016).

2. Ethical jeweler, personal communication, August 1, 2011; Ethical jeweler, personal communication, October 10, 2011; Ethical jeweler, personal communication, August 8, 2012.

3. A note on sources: dozens of individuals were extremely generous with their time and expertise during the writing of this book. In order to maximize the protection of these individuals, direct quotes and paraphrased passages simply refer to either an individual's generic position in the industry or their specific organization, where appropriate.

4. See, for example, Global Witness 2000; Smillie, Gberie, and Hazleton 2001; Le Billon 2008; Smillie 2014.

5. Global Witness has also withdrawn their support for the KPCS after voicing serious concerns over the certification's unwillingness to take on broader human rights issues and its inability to take effective action without an independent technical capacity and more efficient decision-making process (see http://www .globalwitness.org/library/global-witness-leaves-kimberley-process-calls-diamond -trade-be-held-accountable for more information on their stance).

6. In the Canadian system, the Government of the Northwest Territories—the regional government for the territory in which the mining takes place—does not have the rights enshrined in the Canadian Constitution that allows full-fledged provinces rights over natural resources. Instead, the Government of Canada owns the mineral rights and negotiates the environmental impact agreements with the

mining companies directly, leaving only the socioeconomic impacts within the jurisdiction of the territorial government. While payments by the mining companies find their way directly to Ottawa, some of the value makes its way back to the local communities through transfer agreements with the Federal Government and socioeconomic agreements with the local government and aboriginal authorities. Despite this quirk in the Canadian political system, the legal framework in place assures buyers of Canadian diamonds that best practices are being employed and the local community benefits from extraction of the resource.

7. The exchange can be viewed on the Brilliant Earth blog at: http://www.brilliantearth.com/news/the-one-percent-myth-the-diamond-industry-responds-to-brilliant-earth.

8. As one expert on the luxury market has conveyed to me, the middle market consumer, which is the one that the luxury market has been targeting for the last twenty years, shops at both big box stores and luxury boutiques. It is a high-low equation, like in many other areas of consumption today. This is why traditionally middle market businesses, such as JC Penney, Sears and Liz Claiborne, to name a few, are all suffering—because they are in the middle. People save money shopping at Walmart so they can spend it at Louis Vuitton (Luxury market analyst, personal communication, August 22, 2012). However, while many customers may shop at both stores—in this case Walmart and Tiffany—they are not necessarily buying their gold jewelry from both. In other words, they are probably still not directly competing with one another in luxury product markets, even though they may share customers.

9. See blog.brilliantearth.com.

10. For more on the Responsible Care program, see King and Lenox (2000); Prakash (2000a, 2000b); and Gunningham (2008).

Chapter 4

1. Associated Press, April 27, 2004.

2. Ibid.

3. *Washington Post,* March 25, 2004.

4. Tiffany's direct marketing division consists of Internet and catalog operations, through which it markets over 3,500 items online and via mailing lists (Datamonitor 2009a, 5).

5. Tiffany has recently expanded into other luxury items, such as eyewear, while also operating other retail outlets through its subsidiaries, including Iridesse, which specializes in the design and retail of pearl jewelry (Datamonitor 2009a, 5).

6. Information was compiled from Tiffany.com, Bloomberg (2012a), and Datamonitor (2009a).

7. In addition to its major operating segments, the wholesale diamonds that were obtained in bulk, but failed to meet its in-house quality standards, are sold by its wholly-owned subsidiary, Laurelton Diamonds.

8. Other examples include the fur trade and, of course, diamonds.

9. The National Geographic ad can be found at http://www.tiffany.com/csr/ responsiblesourcing/PDF/National%20Geographic_Dec_2010_cropped.pdf.

10. Tiffany's net profit margin for 2013 was 11.08% (10.49% five-year average) on US$3,794.25 million in sales (Factiva 2013a).

11. Again, Tiffany's net profit margin was 10.49% (five-year average) compared to 3.52% (five-year average) for Walmart (Factiva 2013b).

12. Silver is another by-product of copper mining at Bingham Canyon, about half of which is also bought by Tiffany (Lee 2012).

13. http://www.frameworkforresponsiblemining.org/pubs/Framework_20051018 .pdf.

14. This particular initiative is still in its draft stage. It is called "Standard Zero" and can be viewed at the ARM website: http://communitymining.org/index.php/ en/standard-zero.

Chapter 5

1. See the "Jewelry Network Fact Sheet" available at Walmartstores.com.

2. The company operates in in three business segments: Walmart US, Sam's Club and the international segment. Additionally, Walmart has a fourth, non-operating segment generating revenues from financial services, rent from tenants, and Sam's Club membership fees (Datamonitor 2009b, 6).

3. However, rumor has it that these offices are now being moved back to Bentonville.

4. See, for example, Global Insight (2005) for a company-sponsored study and go to walmartwatch.com for the watchdog group tracking a comprehensive collection of issues associated with the company.

5. For a quick view, see http://walmartwatch.com/wp-content/blogs.dir/2/files/ pdf/2006_02_20_WM_HC.pdf.

6. The lawsuit was recently blocked in the US Supreme Court as the court ruled in Walmart's favor, effectively defeating the claim (*Washington Post* 2011; Goudreau 2011).

7. For a first-hand account of the reasoning given for opposing Walmart from a Guelph activist, see http://www.bbc.guelph.org/goliath/folios.PDF

8. More on Scott and the awakening of Walmart's leadership when we apply the opportunities model later in the chapter.

9. To see the advertisement, go to http://www.nodirtygold.org/pubs/ LeadersLaggards_lores.pdf; to see the accompanying letter to the companies, go to http://www.nodirtygold.org/laggard_ltr.cfm.

10. See the NDG official statement at http://www.nodirtygold.org/loveearth.cfm and check the pressroom for media coverage.

11. CI, personal communication, September 18, 2010; NDG, personal communication, September 20, 2010; NDG campaign leader, personal communication, September 19, 2010.

12. See *Bloomberg Businessweek* (2010) for top brands. See FTGlobal500 (2012), CNN (2010), and Forbes (2010) for global company value rankings.

13. However, there was a significant spike in Walmart's spending on lobbying 2008–2009 as it wielded its financial power in Washington, DC, in the face of Obama's healthcare reform, which would certainly affect the company's bottom-line (see, for example, Mui 2007; Sherwell 2007; Sarkar 2008; Bloomberg 2010; as well as Opensecrets.org, a website that tracks lobbying in Washington).

14. In fact, key quotes from the speech were also sprinkled around the company's headquarters in large letters. Transcripts of the speech are readily available at both Walmartstores.com and Walmartwatch.com.

15. CI, personal communication, September 18, 2010; Walmart, personal communication, August 16, 2011; EDF, personal communication, August 16, 2011.

16. Walmart, personal communication, August 16, 2011; Walmart, personal communication, August 16, 2011; EDF, personal communication, September 7, 2011.

17. Unravelling the puzzle of why Walmart has not signed the petition to halt mining in Bristol Bay is a difficult task as it is certainly multi-causal and very sensitive in nature. The first possible cause was that those pushing for support to halt the Pebble mine development, including the NRDC and NDG, didn't reach out to Walmart to any great extent because they didn't think they would get a response. Second, it may be because many politicians in Alaska favor the development and so the company would have felt political pressure to abstain from the conflict. Third, a company as big as Walmart relies on regular supplies of large amounts of goods; the Pebble mine is a giant copper and gold mine run by an industry giant, Anglo American, and cutting off supplies from this or like projects may not have appeared to be in Walmart's best interest. Fourth, the company certainly wouldn't want to alienate its customers, who are—generally speaking—more likely to be involved in heavy industry than environmental movements. Lastly, the company's sustainability philosophy is to make greener products that people want because they are better, not to create a niche market for environmentally friendly goods, which it argues would be the result if the company took a more vocal approach instead of focusing on the business case.

Chapter 6

1. See Thomas Princen's (1997, 2002) work for more on the "distancing" of consumers from the environmental impacts of their consumption decisions.

2. The opportunities perspective does not explain whether firms sharing the same business model and market came to respond in the same way through independent analysis of the issues, benchmarking, or isomorphism. The focus on lead firms rules out the latter two explanations—for these principle cases at least.

3. These findings resonate with those of past studies emphasizing the impact of private actor politics on social learning and norm diffusion (see, for example, Keck and Sikkink 1998; Risse et al. 2002; Pattberg 2005a, 2006; Schleifer 2010).

Chapter 7

1. See, for example, Bartley 2005; Marx 2008; Locke et al. 2009; Locke 2013; Marx and Wouters 2015.

2. The RJC invited interested parties to multiple consultative meeting and considered their concerns, but the fact remains that industry controls the process and, perhaps understandably, is loath to become subject to the whim of these NGOs. In fact, we can see that signing on to an NGO initiative may in fact increase the risk exposure of the firm from the perspective of those in the market.

Appendix

1. There are many in-depth analyses of the process tracing approach available: see, for example, George and Bennett 2005; Collier 2011; and Bennett and Checkel 2014.

2. Comparing across lead firms introduces an element of selection bias to the analysis (see, for example, Geddes 1990), but these limitations are overcome to a certain extent through a combination of counterfactual analysis and limited comparison to "non-leaders" occupying the same category.

3. The methodologically astute reader will note that selecting only leaders from each category necessarily limits the causal claims I can make, as there is a lack of variation on the dependent variable. This is a conscious trade-off I have made. The selected cases show the range of outcomes in firm responses across the industry, which lines up with each category of jeweler. This allows me to explore the precise links between their various firm-level structures and their responses to the politicization of the market. It also allows me to explore the implications of the different types of responses. On the leadership question, the research is a bit trickier for the reasons given in the main text above. To address this element of the study, I use a more inductive version of process tracing, which is appropriate since we know less about leadership on these issues to begin with (see Bennett and Checkel 2014, 18 on inductive process tracing). Additionally, the patterns we have observed—specifically, the differences among firms within each category of jewelers—implies that the explanation will go beyond differences in the business model (although not unconnected to them, which will become clear over the course of the book). As such, the explanations can be expected to contain elements of managerial preference formation, feedback mechanisms, and significant agency. Thus, it makes sense for the investigation to be historical in character, for all the reasons given in the main text above, as long as the claims made throughout fit within these parameters.

References

Abbott, K. W. 2012. Engaging the public and the private in global sustainability governance. *International Affairs* 88 (3): 543–564. doi:10.1111/j.1468-2346 .2012.01088.x.

Abbott, K. W., P. Genschel, D. Snidal, and B. Zangl. 2012. Orchestration: Global governance through intermediaries. *Available at SSRN 2125452*. Retrieved from http://papers.ssrn.com/sol3/papers.cfm?abstract_id=2125452.

Abbott, K. W., and D. Snidal. 2009a. The governance triangle: Regulatory standards institutions and the shadow of the state. In *The Politics of Global Regulation*, ed. W. Mattli and N. Woods, 44–88. Princeton, NJ: Princeton University Press.

Adler, C. 2008, November 8. FT.com / UK—Clean campaign gathers traction. Retrieved September 23, 2012, from http://www.ft.com/cms/s/0/621fe068-ad35 -11dd-971e-000077b07658.html#axzz27GnewAuo.

Akard, P. J. 1992. Corporate mobilization and political power: The transformation of U.S. economic policy in the 1970s. *American Sociological Review* 57 (5): 597–615. doi:10.2307/2095915.

Aminzade, R. 1993. Class analysis, politics, and French labor history. In *Rethinking Labor History*, ed. L. Berlanstein, 90–113. Urbana: University of Illinois Press.

Amoore, L., and P. Langley. 2004. Ambiguities of global civil society. *Review of International Studies* 30 (1): 89–110.

Andree, P. 2005. The genetic engineering revolution in agriculture and food: The "biotech bloc." In *The Business of Global Environmental Governance*, ed. D. L. Levy and P. J. Newell, 135–166. Cambridge, MA: MIT Press.

Aronson, D. 2011, August 7. How Congress devastated Congo. *New York Times*. Retrieved September 23, 2012, from http://www.nytimes.com/2011/08/08/ opinion/how-congress-devastated-congo.html.

Associated Press. 2004, April 27. Dirty gold? Jewelers urge miners to clean up— US news—Environment | NBC News. Retrieved September 26, 2012, from http:// www.msnbc.msn.com/id/4607954/ns/us_news-environment/t/dirty-gold-jewelers -urge-miners-clean/#.UGJPvVGgHMo.

Associated Press. 2006a, July 12. First green group opens near Wal-Mart. *The Spokesman Review*. Retrieved September 23, 2012, from http://www.spokesman.com/stories/2006/jul/12/first-green-group-opens-near-wal-mart.

Associated Press. 2006b, July 12. Green group opens near Wal-Mart. *Fox 16 News*. Retrieved September 23, 2012, from http://www.fox16.com/news/story/Green-Group-Opens-Near-Wal-Mart/Lua0LRd-nkKUNOy6tsxiDw.cspx.

Associated Press. 2008, November 23. Alaska salmon bound for Wal-Mart freezers. *Arkansas Online*. Retrieved September 23, 2012, from http://www.arkansasonline.com/news/2008/nov/23/alaska-salmon-bound-wal-mart-freezers.

Atkinson, R., and J. Flint. 2001. Accessing hidden and hard-to-reach populations: Snowball research strategies. *Social Research Update* 33 (1): 1–4.

Auld, G. 2010a. Assessing certification as governance: Effects and broader consequences for coffee. *Journal of Environment & Development* 19 (2): 215–241.

Auld, G. 2010b. Non-state certification and the problems of institutional fit. *American Political Science Association*. Retrieved September 23, 2012, from http://papers.ssrn.com/sol3/papers.cfm?abstract_id=1642665.

Auld, G., L. H. Gulbrandsen, and C. L. McDermott. 2008. Certification schemes and the impacts on forests and forestry. *Annual Review of Environment and Resources* 33:187–211.

Auty, R. M. 1993. *Sustaining Development in Mineral Economies: The Resource Curse Thesis*. New York: Routledge.

Bachrach, P., and M. S. Baratz. 1962. Two faces of power. *American Political Science Review* 56 (4): 947–952.

Bachrach, P., and M. S. Baratz. 1963. Decisions and nondecisions: An analytical framework. *American Political Science Review* 57 (3): 632–642.

Bachrach, P., and M. S. Baratz. 1970. *Power and Poverty: Theory and Practice*. New York: Oxford University Press.

Bail, C., R. Falkner, and H. Marquard. 2002. *The Cartagena Protocol on Biosafety: Reconciling Trade in Biotechnology with Environment and Development?* London: Earthscan.

Banerjee, S. B. 2008. Corporate social responsibility: The good, the bad and the ugly. *Critical Sociology* 34 (1): 51–79.

Bario Neal. 2016. Sustainability. Bario Neal. Retrieved August 1, 2016, from http://bario-neal.com/sustainability.

Barnett, M., and R. Duvall. 2005a. *Power in Global Governance*. Cambridge: Cambridge University Press.

Barnett, M., and R. Duvall. 2005b. Power in international politics. *International Organization* 59 (1): 39–75. doi:10.1017/S0020818305050010.

Baron, D. P. 1995. Integrated strategy: Market and nonmarket components. *California Management Review* 37 (2): 47–65.

Baron, D. P. 2001. Private politics, corporate social responsibility, and integrated strategy. *Journal of Economics & Management Strategy* 10 (1): 7–45.

Baron, D. P. 2006. *Business and Its Environment.* 5th ed. Upper Saddle River, NJ: Pearson/Prentice Hall.

Baron, D. P. 2007. Corporate social responsibility and social entrepreneurship. *Journal of Economics & Management Strategy* 16 (3): 683–717.

Bartley, T. 2003. Certifying forests and factories: States, social movements, and the rise of private regulation in the apparel and forest products fields. *Politics & Society* 31 (3): 433–464.

Bartley, T. 2005. Corporate accountability and the privatization of labor standards: Struggles over codes of conduct in the apparel industry. *Research in Political Sociology* 14. doi:10.1016/S0895-9935(05)4007-8.

Bartley, T. 2007. Institutional Emergence in an Era of Globalization: The Rise of Transnational Private Regulation of Labor and Environmental Conditions. *American Journal of Sociology* 113 (2): 297–351. doi:10.1086/518871.

Basker, E. 2005. Selling a cheaper mousetrap: Wal-Mart's effect on retail prices. *Journal of Urban Economics* 58 (2): 203–229.

Battilana, J., B. Leca, and E. Boxenbaum. 2009. How actors change institutions: Towards a theory of institutional entrepreneurship. *Academy of Management Annals* 3 (1): 65–107.

Beckert, J. 1999. Agency, entrepreneurs, and institutional change. The role of strategic choice and institutionalized practices in organizations. *Organization Studies* 20 (5): 777–799.

Beckert, J. 2003. Economic sociology and embeddedness: How shall we conceptualize economic action? *Journal of Economic Issues* 37 (3): 769–787.

Beisheim, M., and K. Dingwerth. 2008. Procedural legitimacy and private transnational governance: Are the good ones doing better? Retrieved September 23, 2012, from http://edoc.vifapol.de/opus/volltexte/2008/617.

Bendell, J., and J. Cohen. 2006. *Tipping Frames: Lifeworth Annual Review.* Sheffield: Greenleaf Publishing. Retrieved September 23, 2012, from http://www .lifeworth.com/2006review/pdfs/tippingframes-2006review.pdf.

Bennett, A., and J. Checkel. 2014. *Process Tracing: From Metaphor To Analytic Tool.* Cambridge: Cambridge University Press.

Bernstein, P. L. 2000. *The Power of Gold: The History of an Obsession.* New York: John Wiley & Sons.

Bernstein, S. 2001. *The Compromise of Liberal Environmentalism.* New York: Columbia University Press.

Bernstein, S., and Cashore, B. 2000. Globalization, four paths of internationalization and domestic policy change: The case of ecoforestry in British Columbia, Canada. *Canadian Journal of Political Science/Revue canadienne de science politique, 33*(1), 67–99.

Bernstein, S., and B. Cashore. 2007. Can non-state global governance be legitimate? An analytical framework. *Regulation & Governance* 1 (4): 347–371.

Betsill, M., and E. Corell. 2007. *NGO Diplomacy: The Influence of Nongovernmental Organizations in International Environmental Negotiations.* Cambridge, MA: MIT Press.

Biernacki, P., and D. Waldorf. 1981. Snowball sampling: Problems and techniques of chain referral sampling. *Sociological Methods & Research* 10 (2): 141–163.

Biermann, F. 2008. Earth system governance. A research agenda. In *Institutions and Environmental Change: Principal Findings, Applications, and Research Frontiers,* ed. O. R. Young, L. A. King and H. Schroeder, 277–302. Cambridge, MA: MIT Press.

Biermann, F. 2014. *Earth System Governance: World Politics in the Anthropocene.* Cambridge, MA: MIT Press.

Biermann, F., M. Betsill, J. Gupta, N. Kanie, L. Lebel, L. Liverman, H. Schroeder, B. Siebenhuner, and R. Zondervan. 2010. Earth system governance: A research framework. *International Environmental Agreement: Politics, Law and Economics* 10:277–298.

Block, F. 1977. The ruling class does not rule: Notes on the Marxist theory of the state. *Socialist Revolution* 33:6–28.

Bloomberg. 2010. 2010 Top 100 brands. *Businessweek.* Retrieved September 23, 2012, from http://images.businessweek.com/ss/06/07/top_brands/index_01.htm.

Bloomberg. 2012a. TIF: New York stock quote, Tiffany & Co. *Bloomberg Online.* Retrieved September 9, 2012, from http://www.bloomberg.com/quote/TIF:US.

Bloomberg. 2012b. Tiffany & Co. (TIF:New York): Insider trading and share prices. *Businessweek.* Retrieved September 9, 2012, from http://investing .businessweek.com/research/stocks/ownership/ownership.asp?ticker=TIF.

Bloomberg. 2012c). Michael Kowalski: Executive profile and biography. *Businessweek.* Retrieved September 23, 2012, from http://investing.businessweek .com/research/stocks/people/person.asp?personId=163645&ticker=TIF.

Bloomfield, M. J. 2012. Is forest certification a hegemonic force? The FSC and its challengers. *Journal of Environment & Development* 21 (4): 391–413. doi:10.1177/1070496512449822.

Bloomfield, M. J. 2014. Shame campaigns and environmental justice: Corporate shaming as activist strategy. *Environmental Politics* 23 (2): 263–281.

Blowfield, M. 2005a. Corporate social responsibility: Reinventing the meaning of development? *International Affairs* 81 (3): 515–524.

Blowfield, M. 2005b. Corporate social responsibility: The failing discipline and why it matters for International Relations. *International Relations* 19 (2): 173–191. doi:10.1177/0047117805052812.

Blumentritt, T. P. 2003. Foreign subsidiaries' government affairs activities. *Business & Society* 42 (2): 202–233.

Boddewyn, J. J., and T. L. Brewer. 1994. International-business political behavior: New theoretical directions. *Academy of Management Review* 19 (1): 119–143.

Bourgeois, L. J., III. 1981. On the measurement of organizational slack. *Academy of Management Review* 6 (1): 29–39.

Braithwaite, J., and P. Drahos. 2000. *Global Business Regulation*. Cambridge: Cambridge University Press.

Brilliant Earth. 2012a. Canadian diamonds. *Brilliant Earth*. Retrieved September 25, 2012, from http://www.brilliantearth.com/canadian-diamonds.

Brilliant Earth. 2012b. Why Brilliant Earth? *Brilliant Earth*. Retrieved September 25, 2012, from http://www.brilliantearth.com/ethical-brilliant-earth.

Brilliant Earth. 2012c. Ethical sapphires. *Brilliant Earth*. Retrieved September 25, 2012, from http://www.brilliantearth.com/ethical-sapphires.

Brint, S., and J. Karabel. 1991. Institutional origins and transformations: The case of American community colleges. In *The New Institutionalism in Organizational Analysis*, ed. P. DiMaggio and W. Powell. Chicago: University of Chicago Press, 337–360.

Burris, V. 2005. Interlocking directorates and political cohesion among corporate elites. *American Journal of Sociology* 111 (1): 249–283.

Burris, V. 2001. The two faces of capital: Corporations and individual capitalists as political actors. *American Sociological Review* 66 (3): 361–381.

Bustillo, M. (2011, March 21). With sales flabby, Wal-Mart turns to its core. *Wall Street Journal*. Retrieved September 23, 2012, from http://online.wsj.com/article/SB10001424052748703328404576207161692001774.html.

Büthe, T. 2002. Taking temporality seriously: Modeling history and the use of narratives as evidence. *American Political Science Review* 96 (3): 481–494.

Büthe, T., and W. Mattli. 2011. *The New Global Rulers: The Privatization of Regulation in the World Economy*. Princeton, NJ: Princeton University Press.

Campbell, J. L. 2005. Where do we stand?' In *Social Movements and Organization Theory*, eds. G. Davis, D. McAdam, W. R. Scott, and M. N. Zald, , 41–48. Cambridge: Cambridge University Press.

Campbell, J. L. 2007. Why would corporations behave in socially responsible ways? An institutional theory of corporate social responsibility. *Academy of Management Review* 32 (3): 946–967.

Carney, T. 2006, September 5. Welcome to Washington, Wal-Mart. *Competitive Enterprise Institute*. Retrieved September 23, 2012, from http://cei.org/op-eds -and-articles/welcome-washington-wal-mart.

Cashore, B. 2002. Legitimacy and the privatization of environmental governance: How non-state market-driven (NSMD) governance systems gain rule-making authority. *Governance: An International Journal of Policy, Administration and Institutions* 15 (4): 503–529.

Cashore, B., and I. Vertinsky. 2000. Policy networks and firm behaviours: Governance systems and firm responses to external demands for sustainable forest management. *Policy Sciences* 33 (1): 1–30.

Cashore, B., and, J. Lawson. 2003. Private policy networks and sustainable forestry policy: Comparing forest certification experiences in the US Northeast and the Canadian Maritimes. *Canadian American Public Policy*, 53.

Cashore, B., G. Auld, and D. Newsom. 2003. Forest certification (eco-labeling) programs and their policy-making authority: Explaining divergence among North American and European case studies. *Forest Policy and Economics* 5 (3): 225–247.

Cashore, B., G. Auld, and D. Newsom. 2004. *Governing through Markets: Forest Certification and the Emergence of Non-State Authority*. New Haven: Yale University Press.

Cashore, B., G. Auld, S. Bernstein, and C. McDermott. 2007. Can non-state governance "ratchet up" global environmental standards? Lessons from the forest sector. *Review of European Community & International Environmental Law* 16 (2): 158–172. doi:10.1111/j.1467-9388.2007.00560.x.

CASM. 2011. *Communities and Small-scale & Artisanal Mining: A Global Partnership for Action*. Washington, DC: CASM. Retrieved September 23, 2012, from http://www.artisanalmining.org/UserFiles/file/CASMbrochure_Updated.pdf.

Cerny, P. G. 2010. *Rethinking World Politics: A Theory of Transnational Neopluralism*. Oxford: Oxford University Press.

Checkel, J. T. 2006. Tracing causal mechanisms. *International Studies Review* 8 (2): 362–370.

Checkel, J. T. 2007. Process tracing. In *Qualitative Methods in International Relations: A Pluralist Guide*, ed. A. Klotz and D. Prakash, 114–130. New York: Palgrave MacMillan.

Choyt, M. (2009, July 1). Making the Responsible Jewelry Council (RJC) responsible. *Fair Jewelry Action*. Retrieved September 23, 2012, from http://www.fairjewelry.org/making-the-responsible-jewelry-council-rjc-responsible.

Christian Aid. 2004. Behind the mask: The real face of corporate social responsibility. *Christian Aid*, 1–66.

Chwieroth, J. M. 2008a. Organizational change "from within": Exploring the World Bank's early lending practices. *Review of International Political Economy* 15 (4): 481–505. doi:10.1080/09692290802260498.

Chwieroth, J. M. 2008b. Normative change from within: The International Monetary Fund's approach to capital account liberalization. *International Studies Quarterly* 52 (1): 129–158. doi:10.1111/j.1468-2478.2007.00494.x.

CIA. 2012. The world factbook: Country comparison by area. Central Intelligence Agency. Retrieved September 23, 2012, from https://www.cia.gov/library/publications/the-world-factbook/rankorder/2147rank.html

Clapp, J. 1998. The privatization of global environmental governance: ISO 14000 and the developing world. *Global Governance* 4 (3): 295–316.

Clapp, J., and D. Fuchs. 2009a. Agrifood corporations, global governance, and sustainability: A framework for analysis. In *Corporate Power in Global Agrifood Governance*, ed. J. Clapp and D. Fuchs, 1–15. Cambridge, MA: MIT Press.

Clapp, J., and D. A. Fuchs. 2009b. *Corporate Power in Global Agrifood Governance*. Cambridge, MA: MIT Press.

CNN. 2010. Fortune 500 2010: Annual ranking of America's largest corporations from Fortune magazine. Retrieved September 23, 2012, from http://money.cnn.com/magazines/fortune/fortune500/2010/index.html.

Coen, D. 2005. Environmental and business lobbying alliances in Europe: Learning from Washington? In *The Business of Global Environmental Governance*, ed. D. Levy and P. Newell, 197–220. Cambridge, MA: MIT Press.

Collier, D. 2011. Understanding process tracing. *PS, Political Science & Politics* 44 (4): 823–830.

Collins, J., and J. Porras. 1994. *Built to Last*. New York: HarperCollins.

Conroy, M. 2007. *Branded!: How the "Certification Revolution" Is Transforming Global Corporations*. Gabriola Island, BC: New Society Publishers.

Constance, D. H., and A. Bonanno. 2000. Regulating the global fisheries: The World Wildlife Fund, Unilever, and the Marine Stewardship Council. *Agriculture and Human Values* 17 (2): 125–139.

Cook, R. G., and D. Barry. 1995. Shaping the external environment. *Business & Society* 34 (3): 317–344.

Cook, R. G., and D. R. Fox. 2000. Resources, frequency, and methods. *Business & Society* 39 (1): 94–113.

Copping, N. 2009, September 14. Political correctness: Cartier provides the new gold standard. *Financial Times*. Retrieved September 23, 2012, from http://www.ft.com/cms/s/0/46f296c4-9d9d-11de-9f4a-00144feabdc0.html#axzz25jL9OA20.

Cox, R. W. 1996. *Business and the State in International Relations*. Boulder, CO: Westview Press.

CRB. 2009. *The Commodity Research Bureau Commodity Yearbook 2009*. Revised ed. New York: John Wiley & Sons.

Cummins, A. 2004. The Marine Stewardship Council: A multi-stakeholder approach to sustainable fishing. *Corporate Social Responsibility and Environmental Management* 11 (2): 85–94.

Cutler, A. C. 1999. Locating "authority" in the global political economy. *International Studies Quarterly* 43 (1): 59–81.

Cutler, A. C. 2002. Private international regimes and interfirm cooperation. In *The Emergence of Private Authority in Global Governance*, eds. R. H. Hall and T. J. Biersteker, 23–42. Cambridge: Cambridge University Press.

Cutler, A. C. 2003. *Private Power and Global Authority: Transnational Merchant Law in the Global Political Economy*, 90. Cambridge: Cambridge University Press.

Cutler, A. C. 2009. Constituting capitalism: Corporations, law, and private transnational governance. *St. Antony's International Review* 5 (1): 99–115.

Cutler, A. C. 2010. The legitimacy of private transnational governance: Experts and the transnational market for force. *Socio-economic Review* 8 (1): 157–185.

Cutler, A. C. 2011. The privatization of authority in the global political economy. In *Relations of Global Power: Neoliberal Order and Disorder*, ed. G. Teeple, 41–59. Toronto: University of Toronto Press.

Cutler, A. C., V. Haufler, and T. Porter. 1999. *Private Authority and International Affairs*. New York: State University of New York Press.

Dahl, R. A. 1957. The concept of power. *Behavioral Science* 2 (3): 201–215.

Dahl, R. A. 1961. The behavioral approach in political science: Epitaph for a monument to a successful protest. *American Political Science Review* 55 (4): 763–772.

Dahl, R. A., and C. E. Lindblom. 1976. *Politics, Economics and Welfare: Planning and Politico-Economic Systems Resolved into Basic Social Processes*. Chicago: University of Chicago Press.

Dahl, R. A. 2005. *Who Governs?: Democracy and Power in an American City*. 2nd ed. New Haven, CT: Yale University Press.

Dashwood, P. H. S. 2012. *The Rise of Global Corporate Social Responsibility: Mining and the Spread of Global Norms*. Cambridge: Cambridge University Press.

Dashwood, H. S. 2014. *The Rise of Global Corporate Social Responsibility: Mining and the Spread of Global Norms*. Cambridge: Cambridge University Press.

Datamonitor. 2009a. Company profile: Tiffany & Co. (January 27). Retrieved September 23, 2012, from datamonitor.com.

Datamonitor. 2009b. Company profile: Wal-Mart Stores, Inc. (September 14). Retrieved September 23, 2012, from datamonitor.com.

Datamonitor. 2009c. Industry profile: Jewelry & Watches in North America. (September). Retrieved September 23, 2012, from datamonitor.com.

Dauvergne, P. 1997. *Shadows in the Forest: Japan and the Politics of Timber in Southeast Asia*. Cambridge, MA: MIT Press.

Dauvergne, P. 1998a. Reforming multinational loggers in Solomon Islands. *Pacific Economic Bulletin* 13 (1): 106–115.

Dauvergne, P. 1998b. Corporate power in the forests of the Solomon Islands. *Pacific Affairs* 6 (1): 524–546.

Dauvergne, P. 2005. The environmental challenge to loggers in the Asia-Pacific: Corporate practices in informal regimes of governance. In *The Business of Global Environmental Governance*, ed. D. Levy and P. Newell, 169–196. Cambridge, MA: MIT Press.

Dauvergne, P. 2008. Globalization and the environment. In *Global Political Economy*. 2nd ed., ed. J. Ravenhill, 448–478. Oxford: Oxford University Press.

Dauvergne, P. 2008. *The Shadows of Consumption: Consequences for the Global Environment*. Cambridge, MA: MIT Press.

Dauvergne, P., and J. Lister. 2010a. The power of big box retail in global environmental governance: Brining commodity chains back into IR. *Millennium* 39 (1): 145–160.

Dauvergne, P., and J. Lister. 2010b. The prospects and limits of eco-consumerism: Shopping our way to less deforestation? *Organization & Environment* 23 (2): 132–154.

Dauvergne, P., and J. Lister. 2011. *Timber*. Cambridge: Polity Press.

Dauvergne, P., and J. Lister. 2013. *Eco-Business: A Corporate Take-Over of Sustainability*. Cambridge, MA: MIT Press.

Dauvergne, P., and G. LeBaron. 2014. *Protest Inc.: The Corporatization of Activism*. Cambridge: Polity Press.

Davis, G. F., and T. A. Thompson. 1994. A social movement perspective on corporate control. *Administrative Science Quarterly* 39 (1): 141–173. doi:10.2307/2393497.

Davis, G. F., and M. N. Zald. 2005. Social change, social theory, and the convergence of movements and organizations. In *Social Movements and Organization Theory*, ed. G. F. Davis, D. McAdam, W. R. Scott and M. N. Zald, 335–350. New York, NY: Cambridge University Press.

Deephouse, D. L. 1996. Does isomorphism legitimate? *Academy of Management Journal* 39 (4):1024–1039.

DeMarco, A. 2011, November 4. All that glitters is beauty and business. *Forbes*. Retrieved September 23, 2012, from http://www.forbes.com/sites/anthonydemarco/2011/04/11/all-that-glitters-is-beauty-and-business/.

Denend, L., and E. Plambeck. 2007. Wal-Mart's sustainability strategy. *Stanford Graduate School of Business Case OIT* 71:1–50.

DiMaggio, P. 1988. Interest and agency in institutional theory. In *Institutional Patterns and Culture*, ed. L. Zucker, 3–22. Cambridge, MA: Ballinger Publishing Company.

DiMaggio, P., and W. Powell. 1983. The iron cage revisited: Institutional isomorphism and collective rationality in organizational fields. *American Sociological Review* 48 (2): 147–160.

Dingwerth, K. 2007. *The New Transnationalism: Transnational Governance and Democratic Legitimacy*. New York: Palgrave Macmillan.

Dingwerth, K. 2008. Private transnational governance and the developing world: A comparative perspective. *International Studies Quarterly* 52 (3): 607–634.

Dobbin, F., and A. C. Baun. 2000. Introduction: Economics meets sociology in strategic management. In *Economics Meets Sociology in Strategic Management* (Advances in Strategic Management, Volume 17), eds. F. Dobbin, A. C. Baun, Bingley, UK: Emerald Group Publishing, 1–26. doi:10.1016/S0742-3322(00)17001-9.

Doremus, P., W. W. Keller, L. W. Pauly, and S. Reich. 1999. *The Myth of the Global Corporation*. Princeton, NJ: Princeton University Press.

Dowding, K. 2006. Three-dimensional power: A discussion of Steven Lukes' Power: A Radical View. *Political Studies Review* 4 (2): 136–145.

Earthworks. 2009, December 21. Mining and jewelry industry self-certification system falls short, groups say. Retrieved September 23, 2012, from http://www.earthworksaction.org/media/detail/mining_and_jewelry_industry_self-certification_system_falls_short_groups_sa.

Economist. 2002, July 4. The invisible green hand. *The Economist*. Retrieved from http://www.economist.com/node/1200205.

Eden, L. 1991. Bringing the firm back in: Multinationals in International Political Economy. *Millennium* 20 (2): 197–224.

EDF. (n.d.). Walmart announces goal to eliminate 20 million metric tons of greenhouse gas emissions from global supply chain. Environmental Defense Fund. Retrieved August 29, 2012, from http://www.edf.org/news/walmart-announces-goal-eliminate-20-million-metric-tons-greenhouse-gas-emissions-global-supply.

EDF. 2010. Walmart: Our seven areas of focus. Environmental Defense Fund. Retrieved September 23, 2012, from http://business.edf.org/projects/walmart/walmart-our-seven-areas-focus.

Edwards, L. 2008. How to start a green business without raising money. *Ecopreneurist*. Retrieved July 9, 2012, from http://ecopreneurist.com/2008/01/24/how-to-start-a-green-business-without-raising-money.

Eisinger, P. K. 1973. The conditions of protest behavior in American cities. *American Political Science Review* 67 (1): 11–28.

Ellison, J. 2006. Promoting Environmental Sustainability. Talk given at Stanford Graduate School of Business, Centre for Social Innovation, Stanford, CA. Retrieved September 23, 2012, from http://sic.conversationsnetwork.org/shows/detail3199.html.

Elster, J. 1998. A plea for mechanisms. In *Social Mechanisms: An Analytical Approach to Social Theory*, ed. P. Hedström and R. Swedberg, 45–73. Cambridge: Cambridge University Press.

EPA. 2015. Toxic releases inventory. *United States Environmental Protection Agency*. Retrieved December 21, 2015, from www.epa.gov/tri.

Esty, D. C., and A. S. Winston. 2009. *Green to Gold: How Smart Companies Use Environmental Strategy to Innovate, Create Value, and Build Competitive Advantage*. New York: John Wiley & Sons Inc.

Factiva. 2013a. *Factiva Company Report for Tiffany & Co*. New York: Dow Jones.

Factiva. 2013b. *Factiva Company Report for Walmart Stores, Inc*. New York: Dow Jones.

Falleti, T. G. 2006. Theory-guided process-tracing in comparative politics: Something old, something new. *Newsletter of the Organized Section in Comparative Politics of the American Political Science Association*, 17(1). Retrieved September 23, 2012, from http://www.polisci.upenn.edu/~falleti/Falleti-CP-APSANewsletter06-TGPT.pdf.

Falleti, T. G., and J. F. Lynch. 2009. Context and causal mechanisms in political analysis. *Comparative Political Studies* 42 (9): 1143–1166.

Falkner, R. 2000. Regulating biotech trade: The Cartegena Protocol on Biosafety. *International Affairs* 76 (2): 299–313.

Falkner, R. 2003. Private environmental governance and international relations: Exploring the links. *Global Environmental Politics* 3 (2): 72–87.

Falkner, R. 2005. The business of ozone layer protection: Corporate power in regime evolution. In *The Business of Global Environmental Governance*, ed. D. Levy and P. Newell, 105–134. Cambridge, MA: MIT Press.

Falkner, R. 2008. *Business Power and Conflict in International Environmental Politics*. New York: Palgrave Macmillan.

Falkner, R. 2010a. Business power and business conflict in climate change politics: A neo-pluralist perspective. In *Business and Global Governance*, ed. M. Ougaard and A. Leander, 99–117. London: Routledge.

Falkner, R. 2010b. Globalization, neopluralism, and multinodal politics: Review of Cerny, P. G. (2010). Rethinking World Politics: A Theory of Transnational Neo-pluralism. Oxford University Press. *Journal of Power* 3 3): 452–458. http://personal.lse.ac.uk/Falkner/_private/Falkner_2010_Globalisation_Neopluralism.pdf.

Finnemore, M., and K. Sikkink. 1998. International norm dynamics and political change. *International Organization* 52 (4): 887–917.

Fishman, C. 2003. The Wal-Mart you don't know. *Fast Company,* 77. Retrieved September 23, 2012, from pf.fastcompany.com/magazine/77/walmart.html.

Fishman, C. 2006. *The Wal-Mart Effect: How the World's Most Powerful Company Really Works—and How It's Transforming the American Economy.* London: Penguin Press.

Fligstein, N. 1990. *The Transformation of Corporate Control.* Cambridge, MA: Harvard University Press.

Fligstein, N. 1996. Markets as politics: A political cultural approach to market institutions. *American Sociological Review* 61 (4): 656–673.

Fligstein, N. 1997. Social skill and institutional theory. *American Behavioral Scientist* 40 (4): 397–405.

Fligstein, N. 1999. Fields, power and social skill: A critical analysis of the New Institutionalisms. Retrieved September 23, 2012, from http://escholarship.org/uc/item/89m770dv.pdf.

Fligstein, N. 2001. Social skill and the theory of fields. *Sociological Theory* 19 (2): 105–125.

Fligstein, N. 2002. *The Architecture of Markets: An Economic Sociology of Twenty-First-Century Capitalist Societies.* Princeton, NJ: Princeton University Press.

Fligstein, N., and D. McAdam. 2012. *A Theory of Fields.* New York: Oxford University Press.

Flohr, A., L. Rieth, and S. Schwindenhammer. 2007. Transnational corporations as norm-entrepreneurs? A conceptual framework. *DACS Review* 1, Darmstadt.

Retrieved September 23, 2012, from http://www.politikwissenschaft.tu-darmstadt.de/fileadmin/pg/Sektionstagung_IB/090707_CSR_Project_TU_DA_AF_LR_SaS_draft_version.pdf.

Forbes. 2010. The global 2000. *Forbes.* Retrieved September 23, 2012, from http://www.forbes.com/lists/2010/18/global-2000-10_The-Global-2000_MktVal.html.

Ford, L. H. 2003. Challenging global environmental governance: Social movement agency and global civil society. *Global Environmental Politics* 3 (2): 120–134.

Ford, L. H. 2005. Challenging the global environmental governance of toxics: Social movement agency and global civil society. In *The Business of Global Environmental Governance*, ed. D. Levy and P. Newell, 305–328. Cambridge, MA: MIT Press.

Fransen, L., and B. Burgoon. 2012. A market for worker rights: Explaining business support for international private labour regulation. *Review of International Political Economy* 19 (2): 236–266. doi:10.1080/09692290.2011.552788.

Fraser, B. 2011, August. New label boosts mine practices—and prices. *EcoAmericas,* Retrieved September 23, 2012, from http://www.communitymining.org/attachments/131_EcoAmericas_AUGUST_2011_Centerpiece.pdf.

Frieden, J. 1988. Sectoral conflict and foreign economic policy, 1914–1940. *International Organization* 42 (1): 59–90.

Friedland, R., and A. Robert. 1991. Bringing society back in: Symbols, practices, and institutional contradictions. In *The New Institutionalism in Organizational Analysis*, eds. P. DiMaggio and W. Powell, 232–266. Chicago: University of Chicago Press.

Friedman, V. 2008, May 28. Michael Kowalski: Tiffany parades its new voluntary standards. *Financial Times.*

FTGlobal500. 2012. *Financial Times Global 500 2012.* Retrieved September 23, 2012, from http://media.ft.com/cms/a81f853e-ca80-11e1-89f8-00144feabdc0.pdf.

Fuchs, D. 2005a. *Understanding Business Power in Global Governance.* Berlin: Nomos.

Fuchs, D. 2005b. Commanding heights? The strength and fragility of business power in global politics. *Millennium* 33 (3): 771–801.

Fuchs, D. 2007. *Business Power in Global Governance.* Boulder, CO: Lynne Rienner.

Fuchs, D., and A. Kalfagianni. 2010. The causes and consequences of private food governance. *Business and Politics* 12 (3): 5.

Fuchs, D., A. Kalfagianni, J. Clapp, and L. Busch. 2011. Introduction to symposium on private agrifood governance: Values, shortcomings and strategies. *Agriculture and Human Values* 28 (3): 335–344.

Fuchs, D., A. Kalfagianni, and T. Havinga. 2011. Actors in private food governance: The legitimacy of retail standards and multistakeholder initiatives with civil society participation. *Agriculture and Human Values* 28 (3): 353–367.

Gale, F., and M. Haward. 2004. Public accountability in private regulation: Contrasting models of the Forest Stewardship Council (FSC) and Marine Stewardship Council (MSC). *Australasian Political Studies Association Conference, University of Adelaide* (Vol. 29). Retrieved September 23, 2012, from https://www.adelaide.edu.au/apsa/docs_papers/Pub%20Pol/Gale-Haward.pdf.

Gale, F., and M. Haward. 2011. *Global Commodity Governance*. London: Palgrave Macmillan.

Gamson, W. 1975. *The Strategy of Social Protest*. Homewood, IL: Dorsey Press.

Garud, R., C. Hardy, and S. Maguire. 2007. Institutional entrepreneurship as embedded agency: An introduction to the special issue. *Organization Studies* 28 (7): 957–969.

Geddes, B. 1990. How the cases you choose affect the answers you get: Selection bias in comparative politics. *Political Analysis* 2 (1): 131–150.

George, A., and A. Bennett. 2005. *Case Studies and Theory Development in the Social Sciences*. Cambridge, MA: MIT Press.

Gereffi, G., and M. Korzeniewicz. 1994. *Commodity Chains and Global Capitalism*. Westport, CT: Praeger Publishers.

Gereffi, G. 2001. Beyond the producer-driven/buyer-driven dichotomy: The evolution of global value chains in the internet era. *IDS Bulletin* 32 (3): 30–40.

Gereffi, G., R. Garcia-Johnson, and E. Sasser. 2001. The NGO-industrial complex. *Foreign Policy* 125 (4): 56–65.

Gerstein, B. 2008, January 24. How to start a green business without raising money. Interviewed by L. Edwards for *Ecopreneurist*. Retrieved September 23, 2012, from http://ecopreneurist.com/2008/01/24/how-to-start-a-green-business-without-raising-money/.

GFMS. 2010. *Gold Survey 2010*. London: Thomas Reuters GFMS Limited.

GFMS. 2014. *Gold Survey 2014*. London: Thomas Reuters GFMS Limited.

Gill, S., and D. Law. 1988. *The Global Political Economy: Perspectives, Problems, and Policies*. Baltimore: Johns Hopkins University Press.

Gill, S., and D. Law. 1989. Global hegemony and the structural power of capital. *International Studies Quarterly* 33 (4): 475–499.

Gilpin, R. 1987. *The Political Economy of International Relations*. Princeton, NJ: Princeton University Press.

Global Insight. 2005. The economic impact of Wal-Mart. *Global Insight Business Planning*. Retrieved September 23, 2012, from http://www.ihsglobalinsight.com/publicDownload/genericContent/11-03-05_walmart.pdf.

Global Witness. 2000. *Conflict Diamonds: Possibilities for the Identification, Certification and Control of Diamonds: A Briefing Document*. London: Global Witness.

Goodwin, J., and J. M. Jasper. 1999. Caught in a winding, snarling vine: The structural bias of political process theory. *Sociological Forum* 14:27–54.

Goudreau, J. 2010, April 27. Walmart faces the largest sex discrimination lawsuit in US history. *Forbes.* Retrieved September 23, 2012, from http://www.forbes.com/sites/work-in-progress/2010/04/27/wal-mart-faces-the-largest-sex-discrimination-lawsuit-in-u-s-history.

Goudreau, J. 2011, June 6. Wal-Mart wins Supreme Court ruling in historic sex discrimination suit. *Forbes.* Retrieved September 23, 2012, from http://www.forbes.com/sites/jennagoudreau/2011/06/20/wal-mart-wins-supreme-court-ruling-in-historic-sex-discrimination-suit.

Graff, M. 2009, June 25. Wal-Mart gives prime placement to fine jewelry. *National Jeweler.*

Graff Zivin, J., and A. Small. 2007. A Modigliani-Miller theory of altruistic corporate social responsibility. *B.E. Journal of Economic Analysis & Policy* 5 (1). http://works.bepress.com/jgraffzivin/1.

Graz, J. C., and A. Nölke. 2008. *Transnational Private Governance and Its Limits.* New York: Routledge.

Green, J. F. 2014. *Rethinking Private Authority: Agents and Entrepreneurs in Global Environmental Governance.* Princeton, NJ: Princeton University Press.

Greenhouse, S., and M. Barbaro. 2005, October 26. Wal-Mart memo suggests ways to cut employee benefit costs. *New York Times.* Retrieved September 23, 2012, from http://www.nytimes.com/2005/10/26/business/26walmart.ready.html.

Grossberg, E. 2010, February 15. Interviewed by Aster, N. for *Triple Pundit.* Retrieved September 23, 2012, from http://www.triplepundit.com/2010/02/interview-brilliant-earth-diamonds.

Gulbrandsen, L. H. 2009. The emergence and effectiveness of the Marine Stewardship Council. *Marine Policy* 33 (4): 654–660.

Gunningham, N. 2008. Environment, self-regulation, and the chemical industry: Assessing Responsible Care. *Law & Policy* 17 (1): 57–109.

Gunther, M. 2006. The green machine. *Fortune Magazine* 154:42–57.

Guzzini, S. 1993. Structural power: The limits of neorealist power analysis. *International Organization* 47 (3): 443–478.

Hacker, J. S., and P. Pierson. 2002. Business power and social policy: Employers and the formation of the American welfare state. *Politics & Society* 30 (2): 277–325.

Hall, R. B., and T. J. Biersteker. 2002. *The Emergence of Private Authority in Global Governance.* Cambridge: Cambridge University Press.

Hamann, R., and N. Acutt. 2003. How should civil society (and the government) respond to'corporate social responsibility'? A critique of business motivations and the potential for partnerships. *Development Southern Africa* 20 (2): 255–270.

Hamann, R., N. Acutt, and P. Kapelus. 2003. Responsibility versus accountability. *Journal of Corporate Citizenship* (9): 32–48.

Hamann, R., and P. Kapelus. 2004. Corporate social responsibility in mining in southern Africa: Fair accountability or just greenwash? *Development* 47 (3): 85–92.

Hansen, W. L., and N. J. Mitchell. 2000. Disaggregating and explaining corporate political activity: Domestic and foreign corporations in national politics. *American Political Science Review* 94 (4): 891–903.

Hasenclever, A., P. Mayer, and V. Rittberger. 1997. *Theories of International Regimes*. Cambridge: Cambridge University Press.

Haufler, V. 1993. Crossing the boundary between public and private: International regimes and private actors. In *Regime Theory and International Relations*, ed. V. Rittberger and P. Mayor. Oxford: Oxford University Press.

Haufler, V. 1999. Self-regulation and business norms: Political risk, political activism. In *Private Authority and International Affairs*, ed. A. C. Cutler, V. Haufler and T. Porter, 199–222. Albany, NY: SUNY Press.

Haufler, V. 2000. Private sector international regimes. In *Non-State Actors and Authority in the Global System*, ed. R. A. Higgott, R. D. Underhill and A. Bieler, 121–137. London: Routledge.

Haufler, V. 2001. *A Public Role for the Private Sector: Industry Self-Regulation in a Global Economy*. Washington, DC: Carnegie Endowment.

Haunschild, P., and C. Beckman. 1998. When do interlocks matter? Alternate sources of information and interlock influence. *Administrative Science Quarterly* 43 (4): 815–844.

Heal, G. M. 2008. *When Principles Pay: Corporate Social Responsibility and the Bottom Line*. New York: Columbia Business School Publishing.

Hewitt, A., T. Keel, M. Tauber, and T. Le-Fiedler. 2015. *The Ups and Downs of Gold Recycling: Understanding Market Drivers and Industry Challenges*. London: World Gold Council and Boston Consulting Group.

Higgott, R. A., R. D. Underhill, and A. Bieler. 2000. *Non-State Actors and Authority in the Global System*. London: Routledge.

Hildebrandt, A. 2009, July 22. The Kimberley Process: A rough cut? *CBC News*. Retrieved September 23, 2012, from http://www.cbc.ca/news/world/story/2009/07/22/f-blood-diamonds.html.

Hillman, A. J. 2003. Determinants of political strategies in US multinationals. *Business & Society* 42 (4): 455–484.

Hillman, A. J., and M. A. Hitt. 1999. Corporate political strategy formulation: A model of approach, participation, and strategy decisions. *Academy of Management Review* 24 (4): 825–842.

Hillman, A. J., G. D. Keim, and D. Schuler. 2004. Corporate political activity: A review and research agenda. *Journal of Management* 30 (6): 837–857.

Hinton, J., M. Veiga, and C. Beinhoff. 2003. Women and artisanal mining: Gender roles and the road ahead. In *The Socio-Economic Impacts of Artisanal and Small-Scale Mining in Developing Countries*, ed. G. Hilson. Leiden, Netherlands: Swets Publishers.

Hiscox, M. J. 2001. Class versus industry cleavages: Inter-Industry factor mobility and the politics of trade. *International Organization* 55 (1): 1–46.

Hiscox, M. J., and S. J. Rickard. 2002. Birds of a different feather? Varieties of capitalism, factor specificity, and interindustry labor movements. Harvard University and University of California, San Diego. Retrieved September 23, 2012, from http://dev.wcfia.harvard.edu/sites/default/files/HiscoxRickard2002.pdf.

Hobden, S. 1998. *International Relations and Historical Sociology: Breaking Down Boundaries*. Oxford: Psychology Press.

Hoovers. 2011. Jewelry stores report. *Hoovers*. Retrieved September 23, 2012, from http://www.hoovers.com/industry-facts.jewelry-watch-retail.1540.html.

Hudson, J. 2015. What next for Fairtrade Gold? *Fairtrade Gold*. Retrieved January 23, 2016, from wordpress.p20126.webspaceconfig.de.

Humphreys, D. 2006. *Logjam: Deforestation and the Crisis of Global Governance*. London: Earthscan.

Hysing, E. 2010. *Governing Towards Sustainability : Environmental Governance and Policy Change in Swedish Forestry and Transport* (doctoral dissertation). Örebro universitet. Retrieved September 23, 2012, from http://umu.diva-portal.org/smash/record.jsf?pid=diva2:285179.

IDEX. 2011. *IDEX Magazine: Full Story*. Retrieved September 3, 2012, from http://idexonline.com/portal_FullMazalUbracha.asp?id=35292.

International Mining. n.d. *The Initiative for Responsible Mining Assurance*. Retrieved September 23, 2012, from http://corporate.im-mining.com/Articles/TheInitiativeforResponsibleMiningAssurance.asp.

ISEAL. 2012. New full ISEAL member: Responsible Jewellery Council. *ISEAL Alliance*. Retrieved September 23, 2012, from http://www.isealalliance.org/online-community/news/new-full-iseal-member-responsible-jewellery-council

Jamieson, D. 2012, June 6. Walmart outsourcing depresses wages in U.S. warehouses: Report. *Huffington Post*. Retrieved September 20, 2012, from http://www.huffingtonpost.com/2012/06/06/walmart-outsourcing-depresses-wages_n_1573885.html

Javorcik, B., W. Keller, and J. Tybout. 2006. Openness and industrial response in a Wal-Mart world: A case study of Mexican soaps, detergents and surfactant producers. *World Bank Policy Research Working Paper, 3999*.

Jenkins, J. C., and C. M. Eckert. 2000. The right turn in economic policy: Business elites and the new conservative economics. *Sociological Forum* 15 (2): 307–338. doi:10.1023/A:1007573625240.

Jessop, B. 1982. *The Capitalist State: Marxist Theories and Methods*. Oxford: Martin Robertson.

Josselin, D., and W. Wallace. 2001. *Non-State Actors in World Politics*. London: Palgrave MacMillan.

Kaplinsky, R., and M. Morris. 2001. *A Handbook for Value Chain Research*. Ottawa: International Development Research Centre.

Kantz, C. 2008. *Precious Stones, Black Gold and the Extractive Industries: Accounting for the Institutional Design of Multi-Stakeholder Initiatives* (doctoral dissertation), London School of Economics and Political Science, London, UK.

Keck, M. E., and K. Sikkink. 1998. *Activists Beyond Borders: Advocacy Networks in International Politics*. Ithaca, NY: Cornell University Press.

Keim, G., and B. Baysinger. 1988. The efficacy of business political activity: Competitive considerations in a principal-agent context. *Journal of Management* 14 (2): 163–180.

Keohane, R., and J. Nye. 1977. *Power and Interdependence: World Politics in Transition*. New York: Little, Brown and Company.

Keohane, R. O. 1984. *After Hegemony: Cooperation and Discord in the World Political Economy*. Princeton, NJ: Princeton University Press.

Khagram, S., J. V. Riker, and K. Sikkink. 2002. *Restructuring World Politics: Transnational Social Movements, Networks, and Norms*. Minneapolis: University of Minnesota Press.

King, A. A., and M. J. Lenox. 2000. Industry self-regulation without sanctions: The chemical industry's responsible care program. *Academy of Management Journal* 43 (4): 698–716.

King, B. 2008. A Social Movement Perspective of Stakeholder Collective Action and Influence. *Business & Society* 47 (1): 21–49. doi:10.1177/0007650307306636.

King, G., R. O. Keohane, and S. Verba. 1994. *Designing Social Inquiry: Scientific Inference in Qualitative Research*. Princeton, NJ: Princeton University Press.

Kingdon, J. W. 1995. *Agendas, Alternatives, and Public Policies*. 2nd ed. New York: HarperCollins College Publishers.

Kitschelt, H. P. 1986. Political opportunity structures and political protest: Antinuclear movements in four democracies. *British Journal of Political Science* 16 (1): 57–85.

Klandermans, B. 1997. *The Social Psychology of Protest*. New York: John Wiley & Sons.

Klein, N. 1999. *No Logo: Taking Aim at the Brand Bullies*. New York: Picador.

Klooster, D. 2010. Standardizing sustainable development? The Forest Stewardship Council's plantation policy review process as neoliberal environmental governance. *Geoforum* 41:117–129.

Koopmans, R. 1999. Political. Opportunity. Structure. Some splitting to balance the lumping. *Sociological Forum* 14 (1): 93–105.

Kosich, D. 2004, November 11. And, now, a few words from Tiffany & Co. Interview with Kowalski, M. for *Mineweb.com*. Retrieved September 23, 2012, from

http://www.mineweb.com/mineweb/view/mineweb/en/page39?oid=3232&sn
=Detail.

Kosich, D. 2009, October 1. Anti-Pebble gold movement grows among US jewelry manufacturers. *Mineweb*. Retrieved September 25, 2012, from http://www
.mineweb.com/mineweb/content/en/mineweb-gold-news?oid=90071&sn=Detail.

Kowalski, M. 2004a. *Tiffany & Co: A Case Study in Diamonds and Social Responsibility*. Wharton Business School, University of Pennsylvania, Philadelphia, PA, USA. Retrieved September 23, 2012, from http://knowledge.wharton
.upenn.edu/article.cfm?articleid=1074.

Kowalski, M. 2004b, November 11. And, now, a few words from Tiffany & Co. Interviewed by D. Kosich for *Mineweb.com*. Retrieved September 23, 2012, from http://www.mineweb.com/mineweb/view/mineweb/en/page39?oid=3232&sn
=Detail.

Lake, D. A., and M. D. McCubbins. 2006. The logic of delegation to international organizations. In *Delegation and Agency in International Organizations*, ed. D. G. Hawkins, D. Lake, D. L. Nielson and M. J. Tierney, 341–368. Cambridge: Cambridge University Press.

Lapin, D. 2012, June 20. How intangible corporate culture creates tangible profits. *Fast Company*. Retrieved September 23, 2012, from http://www.fastcompany. com/1840650/how-intangible-corporate-culture-creates-tangible-profits.

Larana, E., H. Johnston, and J. R. Gusfield. 1994. *New Social Movements: From Ideology to Identity*. Philadelphia, PA: Temple University Press.

Larmer, B. 2009. The real price of gold. *National Geographic* 215 (1): 34–61.

Le Billon, P. 2008. Diamond wars? Conflict diamonds and geographies of resource wars. *Annals of the Association of American Geographers* 98 (2): 345–372.

LBMA. 2012. *London Bullion Market Association*. Retrieved September 23, 2012, from http://www.lbma.org.uk/pages/index.cfm.

Leca, B., J. Battilana, and E. Boxenbaum. 2006. Taking stock on institutional entrepreneurship: What do we know? Where do we go? *Academy of Management Meetings*, 1–43.

Leca, B., J. Battilana, and E. Boxenbaum. 2008. *Agency and Institutions: A Review of Institutional Entrepreneurship*. Cambridge, MA: Harvard Business School.

Lee, J. 2012, March 12. Utah's Kennecott mines silver, gold for Tiffany & Co. *Deseret News*. Retrieved January 23, 2016, from http://www.deseretnews.com/ article/865552033/Utahs-Kennecott-mines-silver-gold-for-Tiffany--Co.html?pg
=all.

Levinson, M. 2009. *Guide to Financial Markets*. New York: John Wiley & Sons.

Levy, D. L. 2008. Political contestation in global production networks. *Academy of Management Review* 33 (4): 943–963.

Levy, D. L., and D. Egan. 2003. A Neo-Gramscian approach to corporate political strategy: Conflict and accommodation in the climate change negotiations. *Journal of Management Studies* 40 (4): 803–829.

Levy, D. L., and P. J. Newell. 2005a. *The Business of Global Environmental Governance*. Cambridge, MA: MIT Press.

Levy, D. L., and P. J. Newell. 2005b. A Neo-Gramscian approach to business in international environmental politics: An interdisciplinary, multilevel framework. In *The Business of Global Environmental Governance*, eds. D. L. Levy and P. J. Newell, 47–69. Cambridge, MA: MIT Press.

Levy, D. L., and M. Scully. 2007. The institutional entrepreneur as modern prince: The strategic face of power in contested fields. *Organization Studies* 28 (7): 971–991.

Levy, D. L., and A. Kolk. 2002. Strategic Responses to Global Climate Change: Conflicting Pressures on Multinationals in the Oil Industry. *Business and Politics* 4 (3): 275.

Lindblom, C. E. 1977. *Politics and Markets: The World's Political Economic Systems*. New York: Basic Books.

Lindblom, C. E. 1982. The market as prison. *Journal of Politics* 44 (2): 324–336.

Lipschutz, R. D. 1992. Reconstructing world politics: The emergence of global civil society. *Millennium* 21:389–420.

Lipschutz, R. D., and J. K. Rowe. 2005. *Regulation for the Rest of Us? Globalization, Governmentality, and Global Politics*. London: Routledge.

Lipset, S. M. 1959. Some social requisites of democracy: Economic development and political legitimacy. *American Political Science Review* 53 (1): 69–105.

Lipsky, M. 1980. *Street-Level Bureaucracy: Dilemmas of the Individual in Public Services*. New York: Russell Sage Foundation.

Locke, R., M. Amengual, and A. Mangla. 2009. Virtue out of necessity? Compliance, commitment, and the improvement of labor conditions in global supply chains. *Politics & Society* 37 (3): 319–351. doi:10.1177/0032329209338922.

Locke, R. M. 2013. *The Promise and Limits of Private Power: Promoting Labor Standards in a Global Economy*. Cambridge: Cambridge University Press.

Lukes, S. 1974. *Power: A Radical View*. New York: Palgrave Macmillan.

Lukes, S. 2005a. Power and the battle for hearts and minds. *Millennium* 33 (3): 477–493. doi:10.1177/03058298050330031201.

Lukes, S. 2005b. *Power: A Radical View*. 2nd ed. London: Palgrave Macmillan.

Lyon, T., and J. Maxwell. 2008. Corporate social responsibility and the environment: A theoretical perspective. *Review of Environmental Economics and Policy* 2 (2): 240–260.

MacDonald, K. 2007. Globalising justice within coffee supply chains? Fair trade, Starbucks and the transformation of supply chain governance. *Third World Quarterly* 28 (4): 793–812.

Madison Dialogue Ethical Jewelry Summit. 2007. Minutes from the Madison Dialogue, World Bank Headquarters, New York. Retrieved September 23, 2012, from http://www.madisondialogue.org/Madison_Dialogue_Agenda.pdf.

Maguire, S., C. Hardy, and T. Lawrence. 2004. Institutional entrepreneurship in emerging fields: HIV/AIDS treatment advocacy in Canada. *Academy of Management Journal* 47 (5): 657–679.

March, J. G., and J. P. Olsen. 1996. Institutional perspectives on political institutions. *Governance: An International Journal of Policy, Administration and Institutions* 9:47–264.

Market Watch. 2008, July 14. Wal-Mart joins WWF's Global Forest & Trade Network. *Market Watch*. Retrieved September 23, 2012, from http://www.illegal -logging.info/item_single.php?it_id=2795&it=news&printer=1

Marsh, D. 1983. Interest group activity and structural power: Lindblom's politics and markets. *West European Politics* 6 (2): 3–13. doi:10.1080/01402388308424411.

Martin, R. 2008, September 20. Wal-Mart's eco-gold tarnished, say enviros. *New West Development*. Retrieved September 23, 2012, from http://www.newwest .net/topic/article/wal_marts_eco_gold_tarnished_say_enviros/C35/L35.

Marx, A. 2008. Limits to non-state market regulation: A qualitative comparative analysis of the international sport footwear industry and the Fair Labor Association. *Regulation & Governance* 2 (2): 253–273. doi:10.1111/j.1748-5991 .2008.00037.x.

Marx, A. 2014. Legitimacy, Institutional Design, and Dispute Settlement: The Case of Eco-Certification Systems. *Globalizations* 11 (3): 401–416. doi:10.1080/ 14747731.2014.899245.

Marx, A., and J. Wouters. 2015 (Accepted for publication). Redesigning enforcement in private labor regulation. Will it work? *International Labour Review*. doi:10.1111/j.1564-913X.2015.00040.x.

Mason, M., and J. O'Mahony. 2008. Post-traditional corporate governance. *Journal of Corporate Citizenship* (31): 1–14.

Mattli, W., and N. Woods. 2009. In whose benefit? Explaining regulatory change in global politics. In *The Politics of Global Regulation*, ed. W. Mattli and N. Woods, 1–43. Princeton, NJ: Princeton University Press.

May, C. 2006. *Global Corporate Power*. Boulder, CO: Lynne Rienner.

McAdam, D. 1996. Conceptual origins, current problems, future directions. In *Comparative Perspectives on Social Movements: Political Opportunities, Mobilizing Structures, and Cultural Framings*, eds. D. McAdam, J. D. McCarthy, and M. N. Zald, 23–40. Cambridge: Cambridge University Press.

McAdam, D., J. D. McCarthy, and M. N. Zald. 1996. *Comparative Perspectives on Social Movements: Political Opportunities, Mobilizing Structures, and Cultural Framings*. Cambridge: Cambridge University Press.

McAdam, D., S. Tarrow, and C. Tilly. 2001. *Dynamics of Contention*. Cambridge: Cambridge University Press.

McCarthy, J. D., and M. N. Zald. 1977a. The trend of social movements in America: Professionalization and resource mobilisation. *CRSO Working Paper, 164*. Retrieved September 23, 2012, from http://deepblue.lib.umich.edu/handle/ 2027.42/50939.

McCarthy, J. D., and M. N. Zald. 1977b. Resource mobilisation and social movements: A partial theory. *American Journal of Sociology* 82 (6): 1212–1241.

McWilliams, A., and D. Siegel. 2000. Corporate social responsibility and financial performance: Correlation or misspecification? *Strategic Management Journal* 21 (5): 603–609.

McWilliams, A., and D. Siegel. 2001. Corporate social responsibility: A theory of the firm perspective. *Academy of Management Review* 26 (1): 117–127.

McWilliams, A., D. Siegel, and P. Wright. 2006. Corporate social responsibility: Strategic implications. *Journal of Management Studies* 43 (1): 1–18.

Meckling, J. 2009. *The Global Rise of Carbon Trading: Transnational Business Networks in Global Environmental Politics* (doctoral dissertation), London School of Economics and Political Science, London, UK.

Meckling, J. 2011a. *Carbon Coalitions: Business, Climate Politics, and the Rise of Emissions Trading.* Cambridge, MA: MIT Press.

Meckling, J. 2011b. The globalization of carbon trading: Transnational business coalitions in climate politics. *Global Environmental Politics* 11 (2): 26–50.

Meckling, J. 2015. Oppose, Support, or Hedge? Distributional Effects, Regulatory Pressure, and Business Strategy in Environmental Politics. *Global Environmental Politics* 15 (2): 19–37. doi:10.1162/GLEP_a_00296.

Mercier, L. 2011. Bordering on equality: Women miners in North America. In *Gendering the Field: Towards Sustainable Livelihoods for Mining Communities*, ed. K. Lahiri-Dutt, 33–48. Canberra: ANU Press.

Meyer, D. S. 2003. Political opportunity and nested institutions. *Social Movement Studies* 2 (1): 17–35. doi:10.1080/1474283032000062549.

Meyer, D. S. 2004. Protest and political opportunities. *Annual Review of Sociology* 30 (1): 125–145. doi:10.1146/annurev.soc.30.012703.110545.

Meyer, D. S., and D. C. Minkoff. 2004. Conceptualizing political opportunity. *Social Forces* 82 (4): 1457–1492.

Meyer, D. S., and B. Rowan. 1977. Institutionalized organizations: Formal structure as myth and ceremony. *American Journal of Sociology* 83 (2): 340–363.

Meyer, D. S., and S. Staggenborg. 1996. Movements, countermovements, and the structure of political opportunity. *American Journal of Sociology* 101 (6): 1628–1660.

Meznar, M. B., and D. Nigh. 1995. Buffer or bridge? Environmental and organizational determinants of public affairs activities in American firms. *Academy of Management Journal* 38 (4): 975–996.

Miliband, R. 1969. *The State in Capitalist Society.* New York: Basic Books.

Mills, C. W. 1956. *The Power Elite.* Oxford: Oxford University Press.

Milner, H. 1988a. *Resisting Protectionism: Global Industries and the Politics of International Trade.* Princeton, NJ: Princeton University Press.

Milner, H. 1988b. Trading places: Industries for free trade. *World Politics* 40 (3): 350–376.

Miranda, M., D. Chambers, and C. Coumans. 2005. Framework for responsible mining: A guide to evolving standards. *Center for Science in Public Participation (CSP2) and the World Resources Institute (WRI), 19.* Bozeman, MT. Retrieved September 23, 2012, from http://www.kuskokwimcouncil.org/documents/3.%20 Mining/Framework%20for%20Responsible%20Mining.pdf.

Mittal, S. 2014. UPDATE: World top 10 gold producers—countries and miners. Retrieved from http://www.mineweb.com/regions/europe-and-middle-east/ update-world-top-10-gold-producers-countries-miners.

Mizruchi, M. 1996. What do interlocks do? An analysis, critique, and assessment of research on interlocking directorates. *Annual Review of Sociology* 22:271–298.

Mong, S. 2010. *Mainstreaming Gender in the Extractive Industries: Lessons for Cambodia.* Phnom Penh: UNDP Cambodia. Retrieved September 23, 2012, from http://www.un.org.kh/undp/media/files/Mainstreaming_Gender_in_Extractive _Industries_Lessons_for_Cambodia.pdf.

Mügge, D. 2008. Keeping competitors out: Industry structure and transnational private governance in global finance. In *Transnational Private Governance and Its Limits.* vol. 51. Eds. J. C. Graz and A. Nölke, 29–43. Oxford: Psychology Press.

Mui, Y. 2007, November 24. Wal-Mart extends its influence to Washington. *Washington Post.* Retrieved September 25, 2012, from http://www .washingtonpost.com/wp-dyn/content/article/2007/11/23/AR2007112301927 .html.

Muradian, R., and W. Pelupessy. 2005. Governing the coffee chain: The role of voluntary regulatory systems. *World Development* 33 (12): 2029–2044.

National Jeweler. (2016). National Jeweler: Majors. Retrieved January 23, 2016, from www.nationaljeweler.com/majors.

NDG. (n.d.). *No Dirty Gold.* Retrieved September 23, 2012, from http://www .nodirtygold.org/jewelrygold.cfm.

Nedelmann, B. 1987. Individuals and parties: Changes in processes of political mobilisation. *European Sociological Review* 3 (3): 181–202.

Nest, M. 2011. *Coltan.* London: Polity Press.

Newell, P. 2000. Environmental NGOs and globalization: The governance of TNCs. In *Global Social Movements,* ed. R. Cohen and S. Rai, 117–133. London: Continuum International Publishing Group.

Newell, P. 2001. Managing multinationals: The governance of investment for the environment. *Journal of International Development* 13 (7): 907–919.

Newell, P. 2006. *Climate for Change: Non-State Actors and the Global Politics of the Greenhouse.* Cambridge: Cambridge University Press.

Newell, P. 2008. Civil society, corporate accountability and the politics of climate change. *Global Environmental Politics* 8 (3): 122–153.

Newell, P., and D. L. Levy. 2006. The political economy of the firm in global environmental governance. In *Global Corporate Power,* ed. C. May. Boulder,

CO: Lynne Rienner. Retrieved September 23, 2012, from http://www.faculty.umb
.edu/david_levy/MAY2005IPE.doc.

Newell, P., and M. Paterson. 1998. A climate for business: Global warming, the
state and capital. *Review of International Political Economy* 5 (4): 679–703.

Newell, P., and M. Paterson. 2010. *Climate Capitalism: Global Warming and the
Transformation of the Global Economy*. Cambridge: Cambridge University Press.

Newman, J. 2006. Icons & innovations: Tiffany & Co.: The Tiffany standard.
Robb Report. Retrieved June 11, 2012, from http://robbreport.com/Icons
--Innovations-Tiffany--Co-The-Tiffany-Standard.aspx.

Northwest Mining Association. 2004. Tiffany & Co. attacks the Rock Creek Project in Washington Post ad. Retrieved September 23, 2012, from http://www
.nwma.org/pdf/04aprbul.pdf.

Novellino, T. 2009, October 19. Tiffany leads industry in boycotting Pebble Mine.
National Jeweler.

Nowell, G. P. 1996. International relations theories: Approaches to business and
the state. In *Business and the State in International Relations*, ed. R. W. Cox,
181–197. Boulder, CO: Westview Press.

Olden, P. 2010. Gold and the Jewellery Supply Chain: A Context. Unpublished
presentation. London: Responsible Jewellery Council, May 18. Available at
Responsible Jewellery Council, http://www.responsiblejewellery.com/files/RJC
_18_May_Philip_Olden.pdf.

Oro Verde. n.d. Green Gold—Oro Verde: The Most Loved Gold in the World.
Oro Verde. Retrieved September 25, 2012, from http://www.greengold-oroverde
.org/loved_gold.

Overdevest, C. 2010. Comparing forest certification schemes: The case of ratchet-
ing standards in the forest sector. *Socio-economic Review* 8 (1): 47–76.

Overdevest, C., and J. Zeitlin. 2014. Assembling an experimentalist regime: Transnational governance interactions in the forest sector. *Regulation & Governance*
8 (1): 22–48. doi:10.1111/j.1748-5991.2012.01133.x.

Pattberg, P. 2005a. What role for private rule-making in global environmental
governance? Analysing the Forest Stewardship Council (FSC). *International
Environmental Agreement: Politics, Law and Economics* 5 (2): 175–189.

Pattberg, P. 2005b. The institutionalization of private governance: How business
and nonprofit organizations agree on transnational rules. *Governance: An International Journal of Policy, Administration and Institutions* 18 (4): 589–610.

Pattberg, P. 2005c. The Forest Stewardship Council: Risk and potential of private
forest governance. *Journal of Environment & Development* 14 (3): 356–374.

Pattberg, P. 2006. The influence of global business regulation: Beyond good
corporate conduct. *Business and Society Review* 111 (3): 241–268.

Pattberg, P., and J. Stripple. 2008. Beyond the public and private divide:
Remapping transnational climate governance in the 21st century. *International
Environmental Agreement: Politics, Law and Economics* 8 (4): 367–388.

Patterson, K. 2006, February 12. Pure gold? Precious metal a potent symbol in the battle over corporate social responsibility. *The Ottawa Citizen.*

Paul, C. J. M., and D. Siegel. 2006. Corporate social responsibility and economic performance. *Journal of Productivity Analysis* 26 (3): 207–211.

Pierson, P. 1995. *The Scope and Nature of Business Power: Employers and the American Welfare State, 1900–1935.* Bremen: Zentrum für Sozialpolitik.

Plambeck, E., and L. Denend. (2008). The greening of Wal-Mart. *Stanford Social Innovation Review.* Retrieved September 25, 2012, from http://www.ssireview. org/articles/entry/the_greening_of_wal_mart.

Polsky, A. 2000. When business speaks: Political entrepreneurship, discourse and mobilisation in American partisan regimes. *Journal of Theoretical Politics* 12 (4): 455–476. doi:10.1177/0951692800012004006.

Ponte, S. 2008. Greener than thou: The political economy of fish ecolabeling and its local manifestations in South Africa. *World Development* 36 (1): 159–175.

Porter, M. 2002. What is strategy? In *Strategy for Business: A Reader*, ed. M. Mazzucato, 10–31. Beverley Hills, CA: Sage Publications. (Original work published 1996).

Porter, M., and C. van der Linde. 1995a. Toward a new conception of the environment-competitiveness relationship. *Journal of Economic Perspectives* 9 (4): 97–118.

Porter, M., and C. van der Linde. 1995b. Green and competitive: Ending the stalemate. *Harvard Business Review* 73 (5): 120–133.

Porter, M., and M. Kramer. 2002. The competitive advantage of corporate philanthropy. *Harvard Business Review* 80 (12): 56–68.

Porter, M., and M. Kramer. 2006. The link between competitive advantage and corporate social responsibility. *Harvard Business Review* 84 (12): 78–92.

Porter, M. E. 1996, November 1. What is strategy? *Harvard Business Review.* Retrieved July 8, 2016, from https://hbr.org/1996/11/what-is-strategy.

Porter, T., and K. Ronit. 2010. *The Challenges of Global Business Authority: Democratic Renewal, Stalemate, or Decay?* Albany, NY: SUNY Press.

Portney, P. R. 2008. The (not so) new corporate social responsibility: An empirical perspective. *Review of Environmental Economics and Policy* 2 (2): 261–275.

Powell, W., and P. DiMaggio. 1991. *The New Institutionalism in Organizational Analysis.* Chicago: University of Chicago Press.

Prakash, A. 2000a. *Greening the Firm: The Politics of Corporate Environmentalism.* Cambridge: Cambridge University Press.

Prakash, A. 2000b. Responsible care: An assessment. *Business & Society* 39 (2): 183–209.

Price, R. 2003. Transnational civil society and advocacy in world politics. *World Politics* 55 (4): 579–606.

Princen, T. 1997. The shading and distancing of commerce: When internalization is not enough. *Ecological Economics* 20 (3): 235–253.

Princen, T. 2002. Distancing: Consumption and the severing of feedback. In *Confronting Consumption*, ed. T. Princen, M. Maniates and K. Conca, 103–131. Cambridge, MA: MIT Press.

Princen, T., M. F. Maniates, and K. Conca. 2002. *Confronting Consumption*. Cambridge, MA: MIT Press.

Pulver, S. 2002. Organising business. *Greener Management International, 2002* (39), 55–67.

Pulver, S. 2007. Making sense of corporate environmentalism. *Organization & Environment* 20 (1): 44–83.

Rae, M. 2009. Greg Valerio Interviews Michael Rae, CEO of the Responsible Jewellery Council for Fair Jewelry Action. Retrieved September 23, 2012, from http://www.fairjewelry.org/greg-valerio-interviews-michael-rae-ceo-of-the -responsible-jewellery-council.

Ravenhill, J. 2008. *Global Political Economy*. Oxford: Oxford University Press.

Raynolds, L. T., D. Murray, and A. Heller. 2007. Regulating sustainability in the coffee sector: A comparative analysis of third-party environmental and social certification initiatives. *Agriculture and Human Values* 24 (2): 147–163. doi:10.1007/s10460-006-9047-8.

Reinhardt, F., R. Stavins, and R. Vietor. 2008. Corporate social responsibility through an economic lens. *Review of Environmental Economics and Policy* 2 (2): 219–239.

Renckens, S. 2013. The Basel Convention, US politics, and the emergence of non-state e-waste recycling certification. *International Environmental Agreements: Politics, Law and Economics* 15 (2), 141–158. http://doi.org/ 10.1007/s10784-013-9220-7.

Risse, T., A. Jetschke, and H. P. Schmitz. 2002. *Die Macht der Menschenrechte: Internationale Normen, kommunikatives Handeln und politischer Wandel in den Ländern des Südens*. New York: Nomos.

Rittberger, V., and P. Mayer. 1995. *Regime Theory and International Relations*. Oxford: Oxford University Press.

RJC. 2016. *2016 Annual Progress Report*. London: Responsible Jewellery Council.

Rodriguez, P., D. Siegel, A. Hillman, and L. Eden. 2006. Three lenses on the multinational enterprise: Politics, corruption, and corporate social responsibility. *Journal of International Business Studies* 37 (6): 733–746.

Rogowski, R. 1987. Political cleavages and changing exposure to trade. *American Political Science Review* 81 (4): 1121–1137.

Ronit, K. 2007. *Global Public Policy: Business and the Countervailing Powers of Civil Society*. London: Routledge.

Rosenau, J. N., and E. O. Czempiel. 1992. *Governance without Government: Order and Change in World Politics*. Cambridge: Cambridge University Press.

Rowe, J. 2005. Corporate social responsibility as business strategy. Retrieved September 23, 2012, from http://escholarship.org/uc/item/5dq43315.pdf.

Ruben, A. 2006, December 7. *Promoting Environmental Sustainability.* Talk given at Stanford Graduate School of Business, Centre for Social Innovation, Stanford, CA. Retrieved September 23, 2012, from http://sic .conversationsnetwork.org/shows/detail3199.html.

Rubin, A., and A. Barnea. 2005. Corporate social responsibility as a conflict between shareholders. Retrieved September 23, 2012, from http://apps.olin.wustl .edu/jfi/pdf/csr.conflict.pdf.

Ruggie, J. G. 2002. The theory and practice of learning networks: Corporate social responsibility and the Global Compact. *Journal of Corporate Citizenship* 5:27–36.

Ruggie, J. G. 2004. Reconstituting the global public domain: Issues, actors, and practices. *European Journal of International Relations* 10 (4): 499–531.

Ruggie, J. G. 2013. *Just Business: Multinational Corporations and Human Rights (Norton Global Ethics Series).* London: W. W. Norton & Company.

Sachs, J. D., and A. M. Warner. (1995). Natural resource abundance and economic growth. *National Bureau of Economic Research, 5398.* Retrieved September 23, 2012, from http://www.nber.org/papers/w5398

Sachs, J. D., and A. M. Warner. 1999. The big push, natural resource booms and growth. *Journal of Development Economics* 59 (1): 43–76. doi:10.1016/ S0304-3878(99)00005-X.

Sachs, J. D., and A. M. Warner. 2001. The curse of natural resources. *European Economic Review* 45 (4–6): 827–838. doi:10.1016/S0014-2921(01)00125-8.

Sage, A., and J. Stempel. 2010, April 27. U.S. court strikes blow to Wal-Mart in sex bias suit. *Reuters.* Retrieved September 23, 2012, from http://in.reuters.com/ article/2010/04/26/idINIndia-48016720100426

Salamon, L. M., and J. J. Siegfried. 1977. Economic power and political influence: The impact of industry structure on public policy. *American Political Science Review* 71 (3): 1026–1043.

Salent, J., and L. O'Leary. 2009, August 14. Six lobbyists per lawmaker work on health overhaul. *Bloomberg.* Retrieved September 23, 2012, from www .bloomberg.com

Sapsford, D., and W. Morgan. 1994. *The Economics of Primary Commodities: Models, Analysis and Policy.* London: Edward Elgar.

Sarkar, D. 2008, January 4. No discount on Wal-Mart's lobbying efforts. Associated Press.

Sasser, E. N. 2003. Gaining leverage: NGO influence on certification institutions in the forest products sector. In *Forest Policy for Private Forestry: Global and Regional Challenges,* ed. L. Teeter, B. Cashore and D. Zhang, 229–244. Wallingford: CABI.

Sasser, E. N., A. Prakash, B. Cashore, and G. Auld. 2006. Direct targeting as an NGO political strategy: Examining private authority regimes in the forestry sector. *Business and Politics* 8 (3): 1–32.

Scharpf, F. W. 1997. Economic integration, democracy and the welfare state. *Journal of European Public Policy* 4 (1): 18–36.

Scharpf, F. W. 1999. *Governing in Europe: Effective and Democratic?* Oxford: Oxford University Press.

Schein, E. H. 2010. *Organizational Culture and Leadership.* New York: John Wiley & Sons.

Schirm, S. A. 2004. *New Rules for Global Markets: Public and Private Governance in the World Economy.* London: Palgrave Macmillan.

Schleifer, P. 2010. Only strategic action? Private governance in the global sportswear industry. *Working Paper Series. Papers on International Political Economy.* Freie Universität Berlin.

Schleifer, P. 2015. Private governance undermined: India and the Roundtable on Sustainable Palm Oil. *Global Environmental Politics* 16 (1): 38–58. doi:10.1162/GLEP_a_00335.

Scholte, J. A. 2000. *Globalization: A Critical Introduction.* London: Palgrave Macmillan.

Schuler, D. A., and K. Rehbein. 1997. The filtering role of the firm in corporate political involvement. *Business & Society* 36 (2): 116–139.

Schurman, R. 2004. Fighting 'Frankenfoods': Industry opportunity structures and the efficacy of the anti-biotech movement in Western Europe. *Social Problems* 51 (2): 243–268.

Scott, L. 2005, October 24. Wal-Mart: Twenty-first century leadership. Wal-Mart. Retrieved September 23, 2012, from www.walmartstores.com.

Scott, W. R. 1991. Unpacking institutional argument. In *The New Institutionalism in Organizational Analysis,* eds. P. DiMaggio and W. Powell. Chicago: University of Chicago Press, 164–182.

Sell, S. K. 1999. Multinational corporations as agents of change: The globalization of intellectual property rights. In *Private Authority and International Affairs,* ed. A. C. Cutler, V. Haufler and T. Porter, 169–197. Albany, NY: SUNY Press.

Sell, S. K., and A. Prakash. 2004. Using ideas strategically: The contest between business and NGO networks in intellectual property rights. *International Studies Quarterly* 48 (1): 143–175.

Selznick, P. 1949. *TVA and the Grass Roots: A Study in the Sociology of Formal Organization.* Berkeley: University of California Press.

Selznick, P. 1957. *Leadership in Administration: A Sociological Interpretation.* Berkeley: University of California Press.

Selznick, P. 1996. Institutionalism "old" and "new." *Administrative Science Quarterly* 41 (2): 270–277.

Seth, A., and H. Thomas. 1994. Theories of the firm: Implications for strategy research. *Journal of Management Studies* 31 (2): 165–192. doi:10.1111/j.1467-6486 .1994.tb00770.x.

Shadlen, K. C. 2007. The political economy of AIDS treatment: Intellectual property and the transformation of generic supply. *International Studies Quarterly* 51 (3): 559–581.

Shaffer, B., and A. J. Hillman. 2000. The development of business-government strategies by diversified firms. *Strategic Management Journal* 21 (2): 175–190.

Shah, K. U. 2011. Corporate environmentalism in a small emerging economy: Stakeholder perceptions and the influence of firm characteristics. *Corporate Social Responsibility and Environmental Management* 18 (2): 80–90. doi:10.1002/ csr.242.

Shapiro, D., B. I. Russel, and L. F. Pitt. 2007. Strategic heterogeneity in the global mining industry. *Transnational Corporations* 16 (3): 1–35.

Shaw, R. 1999. *Reclaiming America: Nike, Clean Air, and the New National Activism*. Berkeley: University of California Press.

Sherwell, P. 2007, May 13. Obama called hypocrite for wife's Wal-Mart link. *Telegraph*.

Shin, A., Y. Mui, and N. Tajos. 2008, July 17. The checkout. *Washington Post*.

Siegel, D., and D. Vitaliano. 2006. An empirical analysis of the strategic use of corporate social responsibility. *Rensselaer Working Papers in Economics 0602*. Rensselaer Polytechnic Institute, Department of Economics.

Sikkink, K. 2002. Transnational advocacy networks and the social construction of legal rules. In *Global Prescriptions: The Production, Exportation, and Importation of a New Legal Orthodoxy*, edited by Dezalay, Y., & Garth, B. G. Ann Arbor, MI: Michigan University Press, 37–64.

Simon, B. 2011, March 21. With sales flabby, Wal-Mart turns to its core. Interviewed by Bustillo, M. for the *Wall Street Journal*. Retrieved September 23, 2012, from http://online.wsj.com/article/SB100014240527487033284045762071616 9 2001774.html.

Sinclair, T. J. 2004. *Global Governance: Critical Concepts in Political Science*. London: Routledge.

Skidmore, D. 1995. The business of international politics. *Mershon International Studies Review* 39 (2): 246–254.

Skidmore-Hess, D. 1996. Business conflict and theories of the state. In *Business and the State in International Relations*, eds. R. W. Cox, , 199–216. Boulder, CO: Westview Press.

Skjærseth, J. B., and T. Skodvin. 2001. Climate change and the oil industry: Common problems, different strategies. *Global Environmental Politics* 1 (4): 43–64. doi:10.1162/152638001317146363.

Skogstad, G. 2001. The WTO and food safety regulatory policy innovation in the European Union. *Journal of Common Market Studies* 39 (3): 485–505.

Skogstad, G. 2003. Legitimacy and/or policy effectiveness?: Network governance and GMO regulation in the European Union. *Journal of European Public Policy* 10 (3): 321–338.

Smillie, I. 2014. *Diamonds*. Cambridge: Polity Press.

Smillie, I., L. Gberie, and R. Hazleton. 2001. *The Heart of the Matter: Sierra Leone, Diamonds and Human Security.* Ottawa: DIANE Publishing.

Smith, J. 2003. *Public Summary of Report: International NGO Training and Strategy Seminer on the OECD Guidelines for Multinationals.* Amsterdam: Friends of the Earth. Retrieved September 23, 2012, from http://www.irene -network.nl/download/NCP-OECD.pdf.

Smith, C., and R. Crawford. 2012. Walmart: Love, Earth. *INSEAD Case Study.* Retrieved September 23, 2012, from http://research.insead.edu/2012/06/smith-n .html.

Solomon, F., and G. Nicholls. 2010. Chain-of-custody in the diamond and gold jewellery supply chain: issues and options. Unpublished Discussion Paper. Melbourne: Responsible Jewellery Council.

Soule, S. A. 2012. Social movements and markets, industries, and firms. *Organization Studies* 33 (12): 1715–1733. doi:10.1177/0170840612464610.

Spar, D. L., and L. T. La Mure. 2003. The power of activism: Assessing the impact of NGOs on global business. *California Management Review* 45 (3): 78–101.

State of the Majors. 2009, July 25. *National Jeweler.*

Statista. 2015. Gold consumer demand by major countries 2014. *Statista.* Retrieved 20 December 2015, from http://www.statista.com/statistics/299638/ gold-consumer-demand-by-top-consuming-country/.

Stavins, R., F. L. Reinhardt, and R. H. K. Vietor. 2008. *Corporate Social Responsibility through an Economic Lens.* Fondazione Eni Enrico Mattei. Retrieved September 23, 2012, from http://papers.ssrn.com/sol3/papers.cfm?abstract_id =1123264.

Stevis, D., and V. J. Assetto. 2001. *The International Political Economy of the Environment: Critical Perspectives.* Boulder, CO: Lynne Rienner Publishers.

Strange, S. 1988. *States and Markets.* London: Continuum International Publishing Group.

Sturgeon, T., J. Van Biesebroeck, and G. Gereffi. 2008. Value chains, networks and clusters: Reframing the global automotive industry. *Journal of Economic Geography* 8 (3): 297–321.

Swidler, A. 1979. *Organization without Authority: Dilemmas of Social Control of Free Schools.* Cambridge, MA: Harvard University Press.

Swidler, A. 1986. Culture in action: Symbols and strategies. *American Sociological Review* 51 (2): 273–286.

Tansey, O. 2009. Process tracing and elite interviewing: A case for non-probability sampling. *PS, Political Science & Politics* 40 (4): 765–772.

Tarnished Gold? Assessing the jewelry industry's progress on ethical sourcing of metals. 2010. *No Dirty Gold*. Retrieved September 23, 2012, from www .nodirtygold.org/pubs/TarnishedGoldFinal2010MAR.pdf.

Tarrow, S. 1994. *Power in Movement: Collective Action, Social Movements and Politics*. Cambridge: Cambridge University Press.

Tarrow, S. 1996. States and opportunities: The political structuring of social movements. In *Comparative Perspectives on Social Movements: Political Opportunities, Mobilizing Structures, and Cultural Framings*, eds. D. McAdam, J. D. McCarthy, and M. N. Zald. Cambridge: Cambridge University Press, 41–61.

Tarrow, S. 1998. *Power in Movement: Social Movements and Contentious Politics*. Cambridge: Cambridge University Press.

Tarrow, S. 2005. *The New Transnational Activism*. Cambridge: Cambridge University Press.

Taylor, P. L. 2005. In the market but not of it: Fair trade coffee and Forest Stewardship Council certification as market-based social change. *World Development* 33 (1): 129–147.

Teeter, L., B. Cashore, and D. Zhang. 2003. *Forest Policy for Private Forestry: Global and Regional Challenges*. Wallingford, UK: CABI Publishing.

Tiffany. (n.d.). Corporate social responsibility committee. Tiffany & Co. Retrieved September 23, 2012, from http://files.shareholder.com/downloads/TIF/ 2086755375x0x515010/51d2444d-0bb3-4817-bbc5-786a967a05e4/TIF _WebDoc_5558.pdf

Tiffany. 2012. Corporate responsibility. Retrieved June 11, 2012, from http://www.tiffany.com/csr/

Tiffany & Co. Stock quote and company profile. (n.d.). *Businessweek*. Retrieved September 23, 2012, from http://investing.businessweek.com/research/stocks/ snapshot/snapshot.asp?ticker=TIF:US.

UNEP. (2002). Geo-2000. United Nations Environment Program. Retrieved September 23, 2012, from www.unep.org/geo2000/english/0083.htm.

United States Environmental Protection Agency. 2015. *US EPA Toxics Release Inventory (TRI)*. Retrieved December 21, 2015, from http://www.epa.gov/ toxics-release-inventory-tri-program.

USA Today . 2010, September 2. Group makes deal to buy land near Hollywood sign. *USA Today*.

Useem, M. 1986. *The Inner Circle: Large Corporations and the Rise of Business Political Activity in the U.S. and U.K.* Oxford: Oxford University Press.

Utilities open war on power program of administration: Edison Institute threatens court attack on Roosevelt projects as illegal. 1934, November 26, p. 1. *New York Times*.

Utting, P. 2005. Corporate responsibility and the movement of business. *Development in Practice* 15 (3–4): 375–388.

VandeHei, J. 2000, January 13. Don't discount Wal-Mart's influence after Lott's prodding, retail giant decides to expand lobbying shop. *Roll Call.*

Vernon, R. 1998. *In the Hurricane's Eye: The Troubled Prospects of Multinational Enterprises.* Cambridge, MA: Harvard University Press.

Vogel, D. 1983. The power of business in America: A re-appraisal. *British Journal of Political Science* 13 (01): 19–43.

Vogel, D. 1990. *Fluctuating Fortunes: The Political Power of Business in America.* New York: Basic Books.

Vogel, D. 1996. *Kindred Strangers: The Uneasy Relationship between Politics and Business in America.* Cambridge: Cambridge University Press.

Vogel, D. 1997. *Trading Up: Consumer and Environmental Regulation in a Global Economy.* Cambridge, MA: Harvard University Press.

Vogel, D. 2005. *The Market for Virtue: The Potential and Limits of Corporate Social Responsibility.* Washington, DC: Brookings Institution Press.

Vogel, D. 2008. Private global business regulation. *Annual Review of Political Science* 11:261–282.

Waldman, D., M. Sully de Luque, N. Washburn, and R. House. 2006. Cultural and leadership predictors of corporate social responsibility values of top management: A GLOBE study of 15 countries. *Journal of International Business Studies* 37:823–837.

Walker, E. T., and C. M. Rea. 2014. The Political Mobilization of Firms and Industries. *Annual Review of Sociology* 40 (1): 281–304. doi:10.1146/annurev-soc-071913-043215.

Walmart. n.d. Jewelry: Love, Earth. Walmart.com. Retrieved September 23, 2012, from http://www.walmart.com/cp/Love-Earth/1008379.

Walmart. 2008. Sustainability progress to date 2007–2008: Climate. Walmart. Retrieved September 23, 2012, from http://walmartfacts.com/reports/2006/sustainability/environmentFootprintClimate.html.

Walmart. 2010. Sustainability Progress Report. Wal-Mart Stores, Inc. Retrieved August 1, 2016, from http://cdn.corporate.walmart.com/83/bf/a7d76e7c43a59b3c9d2b655ac6e0/2010-global-sustainability-report.pdf.

Walmart. 2010, February 25. Walmart announces goal to eliminate 20 million metric tons of greenhouse gas emissions from global supply chain. Walmart Corporate. Retrieved September 23, 2012, from http://news.walmart.com/news-archive/2010/02/25/walmart-announces-goal-to-eliminate-20-million -metric-tons-of-greenhouse-gas-emissions-from-global-supply-chain.

Walmart Annual Report. 2012. Annual report—5 year financial. Walmart. Retrieved September 23, 2012, from http://www.walmartstores.com/sites/annual-report/2012/financials.aspx.

Wapner, P. 1995. Politics beyond the state environmental activism and world civic politics. *World Politics* 47 (3): 311–340.

Wapner, P. 1996. *Environmental Activism and World Civic Politics*. Albany, NY: SUNY Press.

Wapner, P. 1997. Governance in global civil society. In *Global Governance: Drawing Insights from the Environmental Experience*, ed. O. R. Young, 65–84. Cambridge, MA: MIT Press.

Ward, H. 1987. Structural power: A contradiction in terms? *Political Studies* 35 (4): 593–610. doi:10.1111/j.1467-9248.1987.tb00207.x.

Washington Post. 2011, June 20. Rundown: Wal-Mart sex discrimination suit goes to Supreme Court. *Washington Post*. Retrieved September 23, 2012, from http://www.washingtonpost.com/blogs/political-economy/post/rundown-wal-mart-sex-discrimination-suit-goes-to-supreme-court/2011/03/25/AFrOw0nB_blog.html.

WDC. n.d. World Diamond Council history. *World Diamond Council*. Retrieved September 23, 2012, from http://www.worlddiamondcouncil.com.

Webb, M. C. 1995. *The Political Economy of Policy Coordination: International Adjustment Since 1945*. Ithaca, NY: Cornell University Press.

Webb, M. C. 2008. Transnational actors and global social welfare policy: The limits of private authority, with the assistance of Emily Sinclair. In *Global Ordering: Institutions and Autonomy in a Changing World*, eds. L. W. Pauly and W. D. Coleman, 166–190. Vancouver: UBC Press.

WGC. n.d. Interactive gold price chart and downloads. Retrieved July 23, 2012, from http://www.gold.org/investment/statistics/gold_price_chart.

WGC. 2011. *Gold: A Commodity Like No Other*. London: World Gold Council.

WGC. 2012a. *World Gold Council Conflict-Free Gold Standard: An Introduction*. London: World Gold Council.

WGC. 2012b. *Conflict-Free Gold Standard: Exposure Draft*. London: World Gold Council.

WGC. 2012c. *Gold Demand Trends: First Quarter 2012*. London: World Gold Council.

WGC. 2012d. *The Economic Contribution of Large-Scale Gold Mining in Peru*. 2nd ed. London: World Gold Council.

WGC. 2015. *Gold Demand Trends: Full Year 2014*. London: World Gold Council.

Williamson, K. 2006, July 28. Beth Gerstein: Searching for the sparkle in a shadowy industry. *SF Examiner*. San Francisco. Retrieved September 25, 2012, from http://www.brilliantearth.com/media/download/sf_examiner_business_20060728.pdf.

Wilson, J. 2003, December. Internationalization and the conservation of Canada's boreal ecosystems. *Canadian American Public Policy* 56.

Woods, N. 2006. *The Globalizers: The IMF, the World Bank, and Their Borrowers*. Ithaca, NY: Cornell University Press.

WWF. 2008, July 14. Wal-Mart joins WWF's global forest and trade network. Press Releases, *WWF*. Retrieved September 23, 2012, from http://worldwildlife .org/press_releases/wal-mart-joins-wwf-s-global-forest-and-trade-network.

Yandle, B. 1983. Bootleggers and baptists: The education of a regulatory economist. *Regulation* 7 (3): 12–16.

Yee, T. 2007. *What Really Matters!: Interview with Brilliant Earth Founders and CEOs Eric Grossberg and Beth Gerstein*. Retrieved September 23, 2012, from http://www.youtube.com/watch?v=qIz7CUWN5lM&feature=youtube_gdata _player.

Index